Kitchen Quickies

Great, Satisfying Meals in Minutes

Marie Caratozzolo
Joanne Abrams

SQUAREONE
PUBLISHERS

Cover Design: Phaedra Mastrocola
Cover Photograph: Jim Arbogast/SuperStock
Text Illustrator: John Wincek
Interior Color Photographs: Victor Giordano
Photo Food Stylist: BC Giordano
Typesetter: Gary A. Rosenberg

Square One Publishers
115 Herricks Road
Garden City Park, NY 11040
516-535-2010
www.squareonepublishers.com

Library of Congress Cataloging-in-Publication Data

Caratozzolo, Marie.
    Kitchen quickies / great, satisfying meals in minutes / Marie
Caratozzolo and Joanne Abrams.
        p. cm.
Includes index.
    ISBN 0-7570-0085-1 (Paperback)
    1. Quick and easy cookery. I. Abrams, Joanne. II. Title.
    TX833.5 .C365 2003
    641.5′55—dc21

                                                    2002011474

Printed in the United States of America

10   9   8   7   6   5   4   3   2   1

Contents

First and foremost, this book is dedicated to my parents,
Roslyn and Max Abrams.
Their love has made everything possible.

This book is also dedicated to Allan McConnach,
whose love, good humor, and joyful approach to life
have made everything wonderful.

JA

To my parents, Elle and Shan D'Amico,
my neverending source of unconditional love and support;
To my children, Jason and Jessica, the joys of my life;
and
To my husband and dearest friend, Jimmy,
the wind beneath my wings.

MC

Acknowledgments

We are both fortunate to have worked with the talented people of Square One Publishers. We would like to thank everyone at Square One for their invaluable assistance, which was provided in the form of encouragement, practical advice, and guidance. We are especially grateful for the generous support of the following co-workers and good friends: Phaedra Mastrocola, Anthony Pomes, Robert Love, Elaine Kennedy, Gary Rosenberg, Ken Kaiman, Shana Shapiro, and Harlan Krawitz. We couldn't have produced this book without you.

In preparing the recipes for this book, we benefited from the assistance of two expert nutritionists. We thank Sandra Woodruff, R.D., for her encouragement and for her practical help. Through her books, Sandi set an example that truly served as an inspiration to us both. We are also most grateful to Andrea Farmer, R.D., for her accurate and conscientious analysis of all of our recipes. We knew that our dishes were fast to make and delicious. Andrea helped us prove that they were also healthful.

As book editors, we appreciate the many elements that go into making a book attractive and lively—a joy to read. For many years, we have considered ourselves lucky to work with three highly dedicated professionals: artist John Wincek, food stylist B.C. Giordano, and photographer Victor Giordano. We were thrilled that they were able to lend their creative talents to this project, and we thank them all for their superlative work.

Joanne would like to thank the friends and family who graciously shared their recipes, their advice, their ideas, their encouragement, and, in some cases, their kitchens during the preparation of this book. Heartfelt thanks go to Monika Abrams, Roslyn Abrams, Jayne Alexander, Catherine Thomas Lo Presti, and Jane Stein. Very special mention is due to Allan McConnach, Meg Abrams, and Gaby Abrams, who showed loving patience and support through hours of cooking, tasting, reformulating, writing, and proofing.

For their generous contributions made to

this project, Marie would like to extend heart-felt appreciation to Connie LaRosa, Rosemarie DeVito, Karen Minutoli, Jen Minutoli, Annette Barbera, and Chuck Cali. She would also like to thank her sister, Deb Wilson, not only for sharing recipe ideas, but also for lending an experienced hand with the kitchen testing. Special acknowledgment goes to her mom, Elle D'Amico, for all of her helpful ideas, recipe suggestions, and moral support. Her kids, Jason and Jessica, must be recognized for their willingness to be honest (sometimes painfully so)

food critics. And finally, Marie extends special recognition to her husband, Jimmy, for providing love and encouragement throughout this project, and for being a constant source of strength and inspiration.

Finally, we are both enormously grateful to our publisher, Rudy Shur. Rudy has served as our compass throughout the writing of this book. We thank him for his guidance, for his confidence in our abilities, and for his invaluable cooking advice. It is no exaggeration to say that without him, this book would not exist.

Preface

Over the years, the two of us have examined, reviewed, and edited many manuscripts. Included among these have been a number of cookbooks. Often, we were amazed by the problems we found in these books. Many authors assumed too much information on the part of the reader. They took it for granted that every reader who picked up the book was an experienced cook with a vast body of knowledge concerning every aspect of cooking and baking. In other cases, it was obvious that many of the recipes simply would not work out well. Perhaps the liquid included was insufficient, or the cooking temperature too high, or the ingredient amounts inadequate for the number of listed servings. Most often, though, we found that the recipes failed to provide some of the most basic information needed to produce the desired product. Cake recipes did not specify pan size. Cooking times were omitted. Or perhaps the reader was given no indication of how he or she might determine when the dish was done.

As we began working on this book, we committed ourselves to avoiding these pitfalls and to providing you, the reader, with clear, simple, *complete* instructions. In addition, because of the emphasis on speed—every recipe can be prepared in forty-five minutes or less—we decided to limit ourselves to five main ingredients plus staples per recipe. (Staples include dried seasonings, broths, and other basics that you are likely to have on hand.) To give you a realistic idea of the time needed to complete the recipe, the stated cooking time includes preparation time—the time needed to cut up the chicken, slice and dice the vegetables, and otherwise ready the ingredients for the actual cooking of the dish. Finally, most recipes contain less than 5 grams of fat.

As we selected the dishes we wished to create for our book, we aimed at presenting foods for a wide range of tastes. We also aimed at creating recipes that anyone with the most basic cooking skills could follow with ease. Thus, we avoided recipes that were technically difficult—

those with tricky sauces, for instance—as well as recipes made intimidating (and often time-consuming) by numerous steps. Sometimes, although a dish turned out well, it was not included because we simply could not complete it in the maximum cooking time, or because we could not prepare it to our satisfaction using the maximum number of ingredients. In many other cases, though, we were able to devise ways of reducing ingredient numbers or cooking time without compromising taste. For instance, initially, Garlic and Rosemary Roasted Pork Tenderloin took far too much time to cook because we used the traditional roasting temperature of 350°F. Through experimentation, we found that by increasing the temperature to 475°F, we could sharply reduce cooking time and still produce a tender, flavorful roast.

One of the greatest challenges we faced was the need to create recipes that were quick to fix, and yet lower in sodium than the recipes found in most fast-and-easy cookbooks. Although canned foods and other processed ingredients help reduce cooking time, they often add too much salt. While fresh ingredients like tomatoes, onions, and the like help keep salt and fat down, they increase the time needed to prepare the recipe by adding time for cleaning, chopping, and slicing. Our solution was to blend high-quality processed foods with fresh foods.

In some recipes, we specify the use of low-sodium or no-salt-added canned products to further reduce sodium. In a few, we specify the use of organic canned beans, which have far less sodium than most commercial canned beans. We also make good use of high-quality frozen vegetables. While not all of our dishes are ultra-low in sodium, most are considerably lower in salt than their counterparts in other cookbooks.

To make our cookbook as easy to use as possible, we begin, in Chapter 1, with basic information on the ingredients and equipment that can help you reduce preparation time, speed cooking time, and keep fat and sodium to a minimum. Included is a complete list of the ingredients that we consider to be staples. After this initial chapter, each chapter focuses on a specific type of dish. Included are chapters on soups, sandwiches, salads, pasta, poultry, beef and pork, seafood, vegetarian entrées, vegetables, and desserts. You will also find insets that provide additional ideas for speeding food preparation.

It is our hope that this cookbook presents simple, easy-to-follow, foolproof recipes for dishes that are quick to prepare, healthful, and truly delicious. If we convince you that real food can be prepared in the real world—in other words, using a few basic ingredients, and in a reasonable period of time—we have met our goal.

INTRODUCTION

Have you ever left work after a long, hard day feeling totally exhausted, yet knowing that the second you arrive home, another job awaits—you have to make a meal, *fast*? What did you do? Pick up a pie at the local pizzeria? Load your family into the car and then drive to the nearest fast food place? Decide to pop yet another frozen dinner into the microwave? Pray that your cats spent *their* day watching the food channel and mastering the secrets of a good stir-fry?

If this scenario sounds all too familiar, we have a lot in common. As book editors with full-time jobs, we know what it's like to get home at six, seven, even eight o'clock, and to face the task of getting dinner on the table—preferably before midnight. And over the years, we have found what most working men and women have also discovered: after a long day's work, cooking a meal isn't the joyful experience it's cracked up to be. Many of the traditional dishes we grew up loving, such as pot roast and lasagna, require long cooking times—too much

time for a busy weeknight. And many supposedly quick-cooking dishes, like stir-fries, often require lengthy periods of preparation. Ironically, although we spend many hours editing cookbooks, after several years of working, we realized that cooking had become a frustrating, frenzied activity for each of us, with our repertoires limited by time and energy. All too often, we simply opted for takeout. Fast? Sure. Healthy? Not really.

At some point, we realized that we needed help if we were to get a healthy, satisfying dinner on the table, and still have time for something other than work and cooking! Having edited books for so long, it was natural for us to first turn to the many "fast-and-easy" cookbooks available at our local libraries and bookstores. While some recipes were great, many more, we found, left a great deal to be desired. Many of the recipes were far from healthy. In fact, they were full of high-fat ingredients. Some, although supposedly kitchen tested, turned out poorly. Most amazing, many recipes

1

took far longer to prepare than the books indicated. Some didn't take into account the prep work—all that cleaning, chopping, and slicing that must be done before the cook can even begin cooking. (We wondered if these people all had assistants—or magic wands.) Some recipes had so many ingredients that the grocery shopping alone took half the evening. Our favorite was the recipe that claimed to take only twenty minutes from beginning to end. A more careful reading, though, revealed that the cooking time alone was twenty-five minutes!

There we were—a couple of tired, hungry, annoyed editors, who couldn't find a simple book that provided simple recipes, recipes that worked well, were quick to prepare, and tasted good. On our own, we had each developed some recipes that met these criteria. They were fast. They were healthy. And they tasted great! "Maybe we should write a cookbook of our own," one of us suggested. We looked at each other. Just when would we have time to write a book like this? "Well, there goes weekends," the other said.

And so we wrote *Kitchen Quickies*. Through over 170 tempting recipes and a wealth of tips, we guide you in preparing dishes that are fast and easy to make, remarkably low in fat, and truly delicious. But what makes this book so different from all the other fast-and-easy cookbooks out there? Read on!

OUR GOALS

As we created and tested the recipes for *Kitchen Quickies*, we constantly kept you, the harried cook living in the real world, in mind. Whether you have a demanding job out of the home or spend your day taking care of a house and driving your kids from school to baseball practice to music lessons, we know that you are tired and hungry by day's end. For this reason, we save

you time at every step of the way—in the food store, during "prep" time, and during actual cooking time. Plus, we believe that since you picked up this book to begin with, you are interested in cooking healthy meals for your family. But you don't want to sacrifice taste for nutrition. A tall order? Sure. That's why every recipe meets the following guidelines.

❐ Virtually every recipe uses no more than five main ingredients—ingredients other than staples. These ingredients are labeled as such in the recipe so that you can spend less time making up your shopping list, and, of course, less time in the grocery store.

❐ Every recipe uses only easy-to-find ingredients and high-quality convenience products. No exotic must-be-ordered-from-London chutneys. No mysterious spice mixtures.

❐ Every recipe can be prepared in forty-five minutes or less. The time listed in the recipe includes not just cooking time, but preparation time, too. (We know that onions don't magically slice themselves on your cutting board.)

❐ Many dishes are complete meals, and are labeled as such. You may want to add a packaged salad or a loaf of crusty bread, but you won't have to cook additional dishes to make a meal that is satisfying and well balanced.

❐ Every dish is low in fat, with most containing less than 5 grams per serving.

❐ Every recipe works. We tested. We tinkered. We forced our friends, our family, and even our co-workers to sample the results. No recipe went into this book until all of us were satisfied.

WHAT'S IN THIS BOOK?

Once we developed the guidelines for our recipes, we decided to make our book as easy to use as possible. How? To put it simply, we begin at the beginning. In Chapter 1, we start by discussing the basics of fast-and-easy cooking. You'll learn about the staples you'll want to have on hand to speed meal preparation, as well as many other ingredients—some of which you can keep in your pantry along with your staples, and some of which must be bought fresh—that can shorten your time in the kitchen. You'll also learn how to choose kitchen equipment that can reduce not only prep and cooking time, but cleanup time, too. And you'll learn that by marrying the right blend of ingredients with the right cookware, your meals can be not only fast to make, but also low in fat and salt, and high in nutrients!

Following this important information, each chapter focuses on a specific type of dish. If you think that the only fast soup is a canned soup, turn to Chapter 2, "Soup Sensations." Sensational? Yes. Time-consuming? No. From colorful Harvest Pumpkin Soup to savory Tomato Beef Barley Soup, these are soups that are truly terrific, yet can be made in less than forty-five minutes. Want to pair your bowl of soup with a great sandwich? We've got more than a dozen of them! And from Broiled Portabella Cheeseburgers to Smoked Turkey Wraps, every one's a winner. Still other chapters will show you how to make refreshing salads like Black Bean Salad with Corn and Peppers; fabulous pasta dishes like Linguine with Spicy Red Pepper Sauce; tempting chicken and turkey dishes like Twenty-Minute Salsa Chicken and Rice; hearty

beef and pork dishes like Garlic and Rosemary Roasted Pork Tenderloin; sizzling seafood dishes like crisp Savory Crab Cakes; meatless delights like White Bean and Salsa Quesadillas; and tempting vegetables and grains like delectable Green Beans with Caramelized Onions. And if you feel that even a kitchen quickies cook should be able to end the meal with a satisfying dessert, you'll be delighted to find that there's a whole world of quick-to-fix desserts that don't come from the cookie aisle of your local supermarket, and aren't loaded with fat. This doesn't mean, though, that you can't make cookies in no time flat! Crisp and temptingly sweet, our Cinnamon Tortilla Crisps take only twenty minutes to make. Or try a dramatic dessert like Classic Cherries Jubilee (only fifteen minutes), or perhaps a down-home delight such as Homestyle Baked Apples (thirty-five minutes). Throughout the book, we've highlighted tips and tricks that can make your time in the kitchen a little bit easier and a lot more fun.

No, we can't claim that any of the above chapters contains a recipe for a fifteen-minute pot roast. But we do believe that *Kitchen Quickies* presents a wealth of recipes that will allow you to work a full day; cook a delicious, healthful meal; and still have time to read that magazine article, watch that movie from Blockbuster, or simply spend more time with family and friends. And if you prefer to follow dinner with kitchen quickies of a more romantic nature, you have our blessings—and some free time, as well.

1. THE BASICS

No special skills, techniques, ingredients, or equipment is needed to successfully follow the recipes in this book. That's the beauty of *Kitchen Quickies!* Each and every recipe can be prepared quickly and easily with very basic skills, with cookware and utensils that you probably already own, and with ingredients that can be easily found in your local supermarket. But while creating the recipes for this book—and while preparing meals for family and friends—we have found that some cookware and other kitchen tools can speed preparation and cooking, as well as make cleanup faster and easier. Similarly, we've found that certain ingredients are a wonderful boon to the kitchen-quickies cook.

This chapter is designed to acquaint you with our discoveries, some of which may already be old favorites of yours, and some of which may become highly valued companions in all your cooking adventures. And because our dishes are not just fast and easy to make, but also healthy, this chapter will also take a brief look at the whys and wherefores of low-fat eating.

THE BENEFITS OF HEALTHY EATING

These days, very few people need to ask the question, "Why should I eat a low-fat diet?" Study after study has shown that a high-fat diet not only leads to weight gain, but also increases the risk of diabetes, high blood pressure and other cardiovascular disorders, inflammatory diseases, and even cancer. On the other hand, a diet that's low in fat reduces the risk of these disorders and helps keep your weight under control. Just how low in fat should your diet be? Experts recommend that no more than 30 percent of your total daily calorie intake come from fat.

The recipes in this book are designed to fit into a low-fat diet. The use of nonfat and low-fat ingredients and simple fat-saving cooking techniques will help you create delicious, healthful fare quickly and easily. Remember, though, that you don't have to cook fat-free to be healthy. As in so many other things, balance is important in cooking. That's why in these recipes, we've used a balance of no-fat and low-fat ingredients, plus an occasional *small* amount of flavorful, high-fat ingredients—a touch of extra virgin olive oil or some sliced ripe olives, for instance. We know that as important as it is for dishes to be healthful, they also must be delicious, or your family simply will not eat them. Always keep the big picture in mind when choosing dishes for your table. It is your overall diet—not every individual side dish or entrée—that should derive no more than 30 percent of its calories from fat.

When creating these recipes, we were also well aware that for a dish to be healthy, it must be more than just low in fat. It also must be high in nutrients. Just as important, sodium counts should be kept under control. By using plenty of fresh and frozen produce, legumes, and lean proteins like white meat chicken and fish, we found it easy to make dishes that are high in nutrients. Controlling sodium was a little trickier, though. As you probably know, one of the cornerstones of fast-and-easy cooking is the use of certain convenience foods, like canned tomatoes and jarred salsa. But while these ingredients reduce prep and cooking time, they add sodium—sometimes a *lot* of sodium! The solution? A blend of fresh ingredients and processed foods designed to speed cooking time while retaining a fresh taste and keeping the sodium count down to a reasonable level. We have also made use of the increasing availability of reduced-sodium, low-sodium, and no-salt-added products. Did we *always* opt for a lower-sodium ingredient? No. Here, again, balance was the key. To optimize taste, we used a combination of regular and reduced-sodium foods. Naturally, if a health condition makes it important for you to watch your sodium intake,

you will want to use low- and no-sodium products whenever they're available. You will also want to keep an eye on the Nutritional Facts that appear at the end of each recipe. These facts—which list calories, carbohydrates, cholesterol, fat, fiber, protein, and sodium per serving—will help you select dishes that meet your nutritional needs.

THE INGREDIENTS

Shopping for kitchen-quickie dishes is no different from shopping for regular dishes—except that it's faster! Why? Because these dishes use no more than five ingredients other than staples. And what do we consider staples? On page 7, you'll find a complete list of the basic ingredients that you'll want to keep on hand to speed both grocery shopping and cooking times. Below, we'll take a look at a number of other ingredients that will help you cut cooking time, reduce fat, and optimize both flavor and nutrients. (For more shopping tips, see the inset on page 11.)

Bagged salad mixes and precut, prewashed vegetables. Remember the days when serving a fresh salad meant time spent washing and drying greens? Fortunately, those days are gone. Now a wide variety of washed salad mixes—including mesclun (a mixture of tender, baby greens), cole slaw mix, Caesar salad mix, and the greatest time-saver of them all, washed spinach—allows you to serve a salad in minutes. Along with these handy mixes, you'll find bags of precut fresh vegetables like broccoli and carrots. Use all of these convenient products as we do, not only to make quick salads, but to speed the preparation of side dishes, too.

Beef, pork, and poultry. Meat and poultry can add significant amounts of fat to your diet—

Staples

A well-stocked pantry is a cook's best friend. With the following ingredients on hand, you'll need only a few fresh items—no more than five!—to cook virtually any dish in this book. You'll probably want to add other ingredients to this list, such as your favorite jarred salsa, a few boxes of pasta, and canned tomatoes. By keeping your pantry stocked with these and other basics, you'll find that both shopping and cooking become easier and more enjoyable.

Basics

All-purpose unbleached flour

Brown sugar

Cornstarch

Honey

Lemon juice

Reduced-fat or low-fat milk

Reduced-sodium chicken, beef, and vegetable broths

Sugar

Oils

Canola oil

Olive oil

Sesame oil

Vegetable-oil cooking spray

Dried Seasonings

Allspice

Basil

Bay leaves

Black pepper

Cajun spice blend

Caraway seeds

Cayenne pepper

Chili powder

Cinnamon, ground

Crushed red pepper

Cumin, ground

Curry powder

Dill

Garlic powder

Ginger, ground

Italian seasoning blend

Mrs. Dash seasoning blend

Mustard, dry

Nutmeg, ground

Old Bay Seasoning or other seafood blend

Onion powder

Oregano

Paprika

Parsley

Rosemary

Sage, ground

Salt

Tarragon

Thyme

Turmeric

Dry Goods

Bread crumbs, plain and flavored

Low-sodium chicken, beef, and vegetable bouillon cubes or granules

Produce

Garlic

Onions

Condiments

Light (lower-sodium) ketchup

Light (low-fat or fat-free) mayonnaise

Light (lower-sodium) soy sauce

Mustard, Dijon-style

Tabasco or other hot pepper sauce

Worcestershire sauce

Vinegars

Balsamic vinegar

Red wine vinegar

Rice vinegar

White wine vinegar

Wines

Marsala

Dry sherry

Dry white wine

unless you choose lean cuts, remove all visible fat, and limit portions to a reasonable size. Then these valuable foods will add high-quality protein to your meals without boosting fat and calories to unhealthy levels.

In our recipes, we use skinless chicken and turkey breast, 93-percent lean ground beef, lean Canadian bacon, pork tenderloin, London broil, and other lean meats. To reduce cooking time, we've often cut beef and poultry into bite-sized pieces, or pounded it thin. There are some exceptions. We've found, for instance, that an elegant pork tenderloin roast can be made quickly by raising the oven temperature to 475°F. In the following pages, you'll find many more ways to make meat and poultry a delicious part of your diet without compromising your health *or* spending all night in the kitchen.

Broths and bouillons. Canned chicken, beef, and vegetable broths, as well as bouillon granules and cubes, are wonderfully handy ingredients for the busy cook. These products provide an ever-ready base for soups and sauces; make a flavorful substitute for water when preparing rice, couscous, and other grains; and add richness to meat and poultry dishes. Do be aware, though, that most commercial broths and bouillons will add a good deal of sodium to your dish, with some containing more than 1,000 milligrams per one-cup serving! Some will add several grams of fat, too. That's why we've used products like Swanson's Natural Goodness Chicken Broth to prepare our recipes. Fat-free, and with a third less sodium than regular broth, this is a far better choice than most commercial products. Of course, when a recipe calls for only a small amount of broth, you won't want to open a can. That's why you'll want to keep a supply of reduced- or low-sodium bouillon granules on hand. These granules can be quickly stirred into hot water to make broth for dressings, sauces, and many other dishes.

Brown rice. Nutritious and flavorful, brown rice is a favorite of ours and is used in a wide variety of the dishes in this book, from spicy black beans and rice, to cold salads, to warming soups. Regular brown rice does take a good deal of time to cook, though—about twice as long as white rice. Fortunately, a number of excellent quick-cooking brown rices are now on the market. Because it cooks so quickly and is so readily available, we used Uncle Ben's quick brown rice when creating many of the recipes for this book. The results that we achieved with this brand were excellent. However, we do admit that this rice does not have the exact texture of regular brown rice. If it is important for you to duplicate the consistency of regular rice, you might want to try Arrowhead Mills quick brown rice. Available in health food stores and some grocery stores, this product is nearly identical to regular brown rice in flavor and texture. Just be aware that it will add about ten minutes to your cooking time.

Canned goods. Canned chopped tomatoes, tomato sauce, canned corn, canned beans—the list of canned goods that can quickly add flavor and nutrition to your dishes is endless. We have made good use of a number of these handy products in our recipes. Of course, when using these ingredients, you should keep in mind that they will add sodium to your dish. Fortunately, low-sodium and no-salt-added products are becoming increasingly available. We've used these products in many of our recipes, especially in those that include more than one canned product. And if sodium is a concern to you, you'll want to choose these healthful products as often as possible.

Canned beans deserve a special mention.

These products save you literally hours of soaking and cooking time, enabling you to make delicious chilis, salads, stews, and much more. But, of course, they also tend to be high in sodium. That's why all of our recipes instruct you to *rinse* all canned beans before you use them. This washes away up to 20 percent of the beans' sodium. Want to save even more salt? Stock up on a variety of organic canned beans, which you'll find in most health food stores. Organic canned beans have just a fraction of the salt of regular brands. Some, in fact, contain almost no sodium at all.

Chopped jarred garlic. Garlic adds zest to many dishes, and is an absolute necessity in a variety of cuisines. Both of us grew up adding liberal amounts of garlic to many vegetables, to stews, to soups—to nearly everything except chocolate mousse! Now jarred chopped garlic makes it easier than ever to add flavor to your favorite dishes. To keep fat to a minimum, look for garlic packed in water, not oil. But do keep in mind that although this is a time-saving product, once the jar has been opened, it will last for only a week or two in the refrigerator. So if you don't think you'll use it up quickly, you might want to opt for fresh garlic, which has a much longer shelf life. If you *do* choose to use jarred garlic, simply substitute $\frac{1}{2}$ teaspoon for each chopped clove of garlic specified in a recipe. You'll be delighted to find that this product saves time without compromising taste.

Condiments. A variety of condiments—from mayonnaise to soy sauce to ketchup to Tabasco sauce—allow you to quickly enhance the flavor of a stir-fry, moisten a sandwich, or dress a salad. But some of these condiments, such as mayonnaise, can also add a good deal of fat to your dish, while others, such as soy sauce, can be very high in sodium. In this book, we used only light and reduced-fat mayonnaise, and light (reduced-sodium) soy sauce and ketchup. These ingredients, which can be found in the condiments section of your supermarket, will enable you to add great taste without compromising nutrition.

Couscous. Growing up, neither one of us even heard of couscous, much less tasted it. Now we couldn't plan meals without it! Actually a pasta that has been shaped into small grains, couscous cooks superfast—in just five minutes. We use it in salads, in side dishes, as a bed for stews and stir-fries—anywhere we'd ordinarily use rice. And if you've ever had trouble turning out light, fluffy rice, you'll *love* couscous. This product always turns out perfectly. Look for it in the rice aisle of your supermarket.

Egg substitute. Want to enjoy great omelets and frittatas without overloading on fat and cholesterol? Instead of using whole eggs, use egg substitutes. This healthful alternative, which is available in handy cartons in the refrigerated section of your supermarket, has the taste, the texture, even the appearance of whole eggs, but adds no fat or cholesterol to your dish. *Plus* it's quick and easy to use. (No need to break eggs.) Just be sure that the product you choose is marked "fat-free," as some substitutes are made with vegetable oil.

Frozen vegetables. We all know that fresh vegetables are good for us. Unfortunately, all the washing, chopping, peeling, and seeding required to prepare them is so time-consuming! For this reason, we often make use of the many high-quality frozen vegetables now available in the freezer case. You will find that frozen bagged mixed vegetables can speed the preparation of stir-fries, that chopped spinach makes a savory bed for a spicy shrimp dish, and that frozen carrots make a quick and delicious side dish when blanketed in an easy-to-make glaze. Just as important, you'll be delighted to know that frozen vegetables are high in nutrients—much more so than canned vegetables. In fact, some experts believe that vegetables frozen in their prime can be far healthier than "fresh" vegetables that have passed their prime.

While you are perusing your local supermarket's selection of frozen vegetables, be sure to look for some great time-saving products that you might never have noticed before. Chopped onions and bell peppers can both be found frozen in bags, ready for use in a variety of dishes. What a boon for the kitchen-quickies cook! Be aware, though, that frozen onions and peppers tend to be very coarsely chopped, so if your recipe calls for *minced* onion, you'll probably have to chop it yourself. In addition, these products cook up softer than the fresh versions—a feature that you may or may not like. Try them out. If you like them, they will save you a good deal of time and energy. If you do decide to use these products, keep in mind the following equivalents:

1 small onion = ¾ cup coarsely chopped onion

1 medium onion = 2 cups coarsely chopped onion

1 large onion = 3 cups coarsely chopped onion

1 medium bell pepper = 1 cup coarsely chopped bell pepper

One final word is in order about frozen vegetables. Some recipes call for the frozen veggies to be thawed before use. If you don't have time to thaw them in the fridge, you have one of two options. First, you can place them in a covered microwave-safe container, and microwave them on high power for a minute at a time until thawed. Or, if you prefer, place the frozen veggies in a bowl or colander, and run warm water over them until they are fully thawed.

Low-fat and no-fat cheeses. For many years, anyone seeking to limit fat and calories had to reduce their consumption of cheese. Not anymore! Now the dairy case is full of low-fat and nonfat cheeses that can add wonderful flavor to your dishes without sending fat and calorie counts sky high. In our recipes, we've used no- and low-fat versions of Cheddar, mozzarella, and feta cheese, all with great results. When choosing a cheese for your own cooking, keep in mind that if the dish is not cooked—when making cold salads, for instance—you can use either fat-free or low-fat cheeses, whichever you prefer. But when making a cooked dish such as pizza, you should always choose a low-fat cheese, as it melts far better.

Salsa. What did we ever do before salsa came along? This product really defines the word versatile. Everyone knows that it makes a great fat-free dip. But salsa can fill so *many* roles in cooking. In our recipes, we use it to make a fast sauce for black beans and rice, as a topping for tortilla pizzas, as a filling ingredient in quesadillas, and for so much more. Unfortunately, like many prepared foods, salsa can add a lot of sodium to your dish. To help keep sodium in check—especially in recipes that use several processed foods—look for a reduced-sodium brand such as Green Mountain Gringo salsa. For even less sodium, try Enrico's no-salt-added salsa. These products will add great flavor and color without all that unnecessary salt.

Wines and liqueurs. Want to make a delicious sauce for vegetables or meats, to add an intriguing flavor to fresh fruits, or to make vanilla

Supermarket Savvy

If you're responsible for meal preparation in your home, you know that it begins way before you walk into the kitchen. Food shopping can take up a good deal of your valuable time and energy. Fortunately, there are simple ways to make your trips to the store both shorter and more productive. Here are just a few ideas:

❏ Always write out a shopping list before you leave home or work. This will help you speed through the supermarket aisles, as you'll know exactly what you're looking for. Just as important, a complete list will prevent you from forgetting any important items.

❏ If possible, shop for several days' worth of groceries at a time. Although this takes more initial planning, it will save you time by reducing the number of individual shopping trips.

❏ Stock up on items such as canned foods, dried pasta, and other nonperishables. Frozen foods—bagged stir-fry vegetables and chicken breasts, for instance—are also good to buy in quantity. With a supply of these basics on hand, you'll always have the makings of a fast meal. Just as important, you'll be able to avoid many "emergency" trips to the supermarket.

❏ Get to know your local supermarkets, as well as any specialty stores in your area. Some are likely to have especially good selections of bagged prewashed salads, precut vegetables, and fresh herbs. Some may have a deli section that offers cooked chicken breasts, grilled vegetables, and other time-saving items. Still others will have especially good selections of no- and low-fat cheeses or lean meats. By knowing where you can find the ingredients you need, you'll avoid driving from store to store in search of the desired items.

❏ Make friends with your butcher. An accommodating butcher will gladly flatten chicken breasts, slice meats for stir-fries, and perform other tasks that you would otherwise have to take care of yourself when you get home. He may also grind extra-lean beef for that low-fat chili recipe—or simply stock the leanest ground beef available.

❏ Always keep your eyes open for new products. Only in the last few years have bagged salads, jarred chopped garlic, and precut vegetables become widely available. By making yourself familiar with new products as they come out, you'll constantly learn new ways to speed prep and cooking time.

yogurt taste like a gourmet dessert? Stir in your favorite wine or liqueur! These products add flavor quickly and easily *without fat*. In our recipes we have used dry white wine, sherry, Marsala, and a variety of liqueurs, including apricot liqueur, Grand Marnier, kirsch, and crème de cacao. You can use whichever wine or liqueur you prefer.

When choosing a wine for cooking, keep in mind that an inexpensive brand is fine. Just be sure to avoid cooking sherry, as this product contains added salt. Depending on the brand, liqueurs can be relatively expensive. But since you generally need very little liqueur to flavor a dish, you can buy it in those tiny "airline-size" bottles, which cost only a few dollars each. One of your local liquor stores is sure to have a good selection.

KITCHEN EQUIPMENT

It's amazing what the proper kitchen equipment can do. It can reduce prep time; it can reduce the need for cooking fat; it can cut cleanup time; and it can give you more consistent results. You may already own some of the following kitchen tools. In other cases, you may wish to add the suggested equipment to your collection. We hope you'll find these items as helpful and easy to use as we have.

Garlic press. Everyone knows that crushed garlic adds a distinctive flavor and aroma to a variety of dishes, from soups to sauces to herbed breads. What you may not know is that crushed garlic is a great, easy-to-make substitute for *minced* garlic—as long as you own a good garlic press that will enable you to make this invaluable ingredient quickly and easily. Fortunately, there are many presses on the market that do a fine job. Our personal favorite, though, is the Susi press by Zyliss. A nice size, able to accommodate several cloves at once, this efficient press comes with a handy plastic device that quickly cleans the crushed garlic out of the tiny holes. Now even cleanup is a snap!

Kitchen scale. When we began creating the recipes for this book, we each bought a cooking scale at our local supermarket. Why? We wanted to make sure that the ingredient amounts we listed were accurate—that we actually used just 2 ounces of cheese or 12 ounces of potatoes, for instance. What we found was these scales are great even if you're *not* writing a cookbook. Inexpensive, easy to use, and easy to store, they allow you to measure quickly and accurately, ensuring consistent results.

Knives. Anyone who has ever tried to slice an onion with a knife that was too dull or too small, knows the importance of using the right knife for the job—and of keeping that knife sharp. Although a small paring knife is good for some jobs—for removing the peel from an apple, for instance—for most jobs, a good-sized chef's knife is far better. These knives are great for slicing and chopping vegetables, for slicing raw meat, and for so much more. Are any other knives useful for food preparation? Well, a long serrated bread knife is a must for slicing bread for sandwiches. For nearly everything else, though, a chef's knife is our tool of choice!

As mentioned above, your kitchen knives must be kept sharp. This will not only make your work go more quickly, but will also allow you to make neater, more precise cuts. It will also make you less likely to cut yourself, as you won't have to use undue pressure to get the job done. Many of the newer serrated knives never need sharpening. A straight-edged chef's knife, however, must be sharpened well and often.

Measuring cups and spoons. These truly are a *must*. Without a standard set of measuring cups —both the see-through variety designed to measure liquid ingredients and those designed to measure dry ingredients—you will not be able to follow most recipes with success. Measuring spoons, too, are a necessity. Fortunately, all of these items are relatively inexpensive and available in most supermarkets.

Nonstick skillets. These skillets are such a pleasure to use! They allow you to cook foods with only a light coating of cooking spray. They also allow cleanup in no time flat, as any bits of food remaining in the pan can be removed with just a short soaking. In our recipes, we usually use either a 10- or 12-inch skillet. Both sizes are easily found in kitchen stores, and in most supermarkets, as well. An 8-inch skillet also comes in handy for some small jobs. And we've learned that you don't have to spend a lot of money to get a decent skillet. The moderately priced ones give results equal to those achieved with higher-priced cookware.

Although many recipes require that you cover the skillet for a portion of the cooking time, for some reason, most nonstick skillets do not come with covers. Fortunately, well-stocked kitchen stores often have a good selection of these items, so that you can buy a cover in whatever size you need. You can even buy what is called a universal cover—a cover cleverly made with concentric grooves so that it fits a variety of pot and skillet sizes.

Nonstick woks. If you don't own a wok, we humbly suggest that you're missing a truly wonderful kitchen tool—one that can save you both cooking time and cleanup time. What makes woks so special? Well, a good-sized wok is so deep that you can quickly and easily toss even large amounts of ingredients—from stir-fried beef, to sautéed potatoes, to spinach—without fear of tossing the ingredients out of the pot. And because the food stays in the wok, you will spend less time cleaning the stove! Moreover, because the bottom of the wok is fairly narrow, you can also easily cook small amounts of food, and still enjoy good results. What a perfect piece of cookware!

We are specifically recommending a wok with a nonstick finish, as this will allow you to cook with only a light coating of cooking spray, and will speed cleanup time. We also recommend that you choose a wok with a flat bottom that sits directly on the burner—not one that sits on a ring. The flat-bottomed woks are much more stable and much easier to use. Like your skillets, your wok should have a cover. If it doesn't come with one, and if none of your skillet covers fits your wok, you'll be able to find an inexpensive cover at a well-stocked kitchen supply store.

Saucepans and pots. No special saucepans or pots are needed to successfully follow the recipes in this book. But you may want to make sure that you have one each of the most convenient and versatile sizes: a 1-quart saucepan, a 2-quart saucepan, and a 4-quart saucepan. By the way, liquids, including large pots of water, will heat up faster in a thinner pot. Over the years, you may have heard that thicker pots are better—and this is true when slow-simmering a sauce or cooking a pot roast. But when time in the kitchen is limited, a thinner pot is the wiser choice.

ABOUT THE NUTRITIONAL ANALYSIS

The Food Processor II (ESHA Research) computer nutrition analysis system, along with product information from manufacturers, was used to calculate the nutritional data—calorie, carbohydrate, cholesterol, fat, fiber, protein, and sodium counts—for the recipes in this book. Nutrients are always listed per serving—not for the entire recipe. These counts were designed to guide you in fitting each recipe into a healthy meal plan.

In this chapter, we've discussed many aspects of cooking, including ingredients, kitchen tools, and much more. But there is one aspect that we did *not* touch on: the incalculable benefits of cooking a meal for your family, and then having your loved ones sit down together to share both good food and one another's company. While eating out can be fun, and eating takeout meals can be fuss-free, nothing compares to the warmth and closeness created by a home-cooked meal enjoyed in your own kitchen. We hope that the recipes found in the following pages will allow you to more often make such meals a part of your life.

2. SOUP SENSATIONS

Soup. Ah, the very word conjures images of warmth and comfort, of a cozy kitchen on a rainy day. Yet for most people, it also conjures another image—one of hours spent watching over a slow-simmering pot; of an entire morning devoted to the preparation of a single dish.

Back when we began creating the recipes for this book, we, too, believed that all soups take hours to make. What we were delighted to find is that this simply isn't the case. Many soups can be made in well under an hour, with little fuss and with great results!

How can you prepare delicious soups in under forty-five minutes? Most of our soups begin with a base of reduced-sodium chicken, beef, or vegetable broth, so that there's no need to simmer for hours to develop a long-simmered flavor. We then add a variety of fast-cooking ingredients, from canned beans and corn, to packaged cheese-filled tortellini, to quick-cooking barley, to lean chicken. Fresh

garlic and onion, herbs and spices, a splash of wine, and savory ingredients like Canadian bacon and Parmesan cheese impart irresistible flavor. The result? Soups so sensational that no one will ever guess they took just minutes to make!

The following pages present a wide range of dishes—soups for every taste and occasion. Looking for a soup that sticks to your ribs? Try Savory Bean and Pasta, a dish so hearty that it's a meal in itself. Company coming? Colorful Harvest Pumpkin Soup is as festive as it is foolproof. Only twenty minutes till dinnertime? You have plenty of time to make Escarole-Rice Soup. Still other choices include Hearty Black Bean Soup, Creamy Potato Soup, and Garlicky Garbanzo and Spinach Soup.

So take out your soup pot, and set aside a few—a *very* few—minutes. That's all you'll need to make a steaming bowl of soup. Comfort never tasted so good!

CLASSIC CORN CHOWDER

TIME: 40 minutes   **YIELD:** 4 servings

MAIN INGREDIENTS

2 cans (15.25 ounces each)
   no-salt-added whole kernel
   corn, drained, divided

½ cup chopped celery

1 cup diced peeled potato

⅔ cup diced Canadian bacon

Shredded low-fat Cheddar
   cheese (optional)

STAPLES

1 tablespoon canola oil

½ cup chopped onion

2 cups reduced-sodium,
   fat-free chicken broth

1 cup 2% reduced-fat milk

1 tablespoon all-purpose flour

¼ teaspoon freshly ground
   black pepper

Bits of Canadian bacon add smoky flavor to this classic chowder.

1. Place half of the corn in a blender, and purée until smooth. Set aside.

2. Place the oil in a 4-quart pot, and preheat over medium heat. Add the onion and celery, and sauté, stirring occasionally, for about 5 minutes, or until soft.

3. Add the broth, potato, puréed corn, and remaining corn kernels to the pot. Increase the heat to high, and bring the ingredients to a boil. Reduce the heat to low and simmer for 20 minutes, stirring occasionally.

4. Place the milk in a small bowl, and add the flour. Stir until smooth.

5. Stir the milk mixture into the pot along with the black pepper and Canadian bacon. Simmer uncovered for another 5 to 7 minutes, or until the potato is tender.

6. Serve immediately, as is or topped with a sprinkling of shredded low-fat Cheddar cheese.

NUTRITIONAL FACTS (PER SERVING)

Calories: 245 Carbohydrates: 30 g Cholesterol: 20 mg Fat: 8 g Fiber: 6 g Protein: 15 g Sodium: 376 mg

CREAMY POTATO SOUP

TIME: 45 minutes   YIELD: 4 servings

Silky smooth and absolutely delicious, this soup tastes great piping hot, as well as chilled. When preparing the ingredients, keep in mind that the smaller you cut the potatoes and celery, the quicker their cooking time.

1. Place the potatoes, scallions, celery, and milk in a 4-quart pot over high heat. Just as the ingredients begin to boil, reduce the heat to low and simmer covered, stirring occasionally to prevent sticking, for 20 minutes, or until the potatoes are soft.

2. Transfer the mixture to a blender or food processor along with the parsley, tarragon, and salt. Purée until smooth.

3. Serve immediately or refrigerate and enjoy chilled. Garnish with chopped scallion or chives, if desired.

MAIN INGREDIENTS

6 medium red or brown new potatoes (about 1½ pounds), peeled and cut into small cubes

4 medium scallions, thinly sliced

2 small celery stalks, thinly sliced

Chopped scallion or chives (optional)

STAPLES

3½ cups 2% reduced-fat milk

2 teaspoons dried parsley

2 teaspoons dried tarragon

½ teaspoon salt

NUTRITIONAL FACTS (PER SERVING)

Calories: 222 Carbohydrates: 33 g Cholesterol: 16 mg Fat: 4.5 g Fiber: 3.5 g Protein: 11.5 g Sodium: 417 mg

EASY TURKEY-CARROT SOUP

TIME: 30 minutes   **YIELD:** 4 servings

MAIN INGREDIENTS

8 ounces 99% lean ground
  turkey

2 medium carrots, peeled and
  thinly sliced

½ cup small shell pasta

STAPLES

6 cups reduced-sodium,
  fat-free chicken broth

1 teaspoon dried parsley

½ teaspoon dried thyme

¼ teaspoon freshly ground
  black pepper

Feel free to use cubed precooked turkey or chicken instead of ground for this hearty soup.

1. Coat a 4-quart pot with cooking spray, and preheat over medium heat. Add the turkey and cook, stirring to crumble, for 4 minutes, or until no pink remains.

2. Add the broth, carrots, parsley, thyme, and black pepper to the pot. Bring to a boil, then reduce the heat to low and simmer for 10 minutes, stirring occasionally.

3. Bring the ingredients to a second boil and add the pasta. Reduce the heat to low, cover, and simmer for 10 to 12 minutes, or until the pasta is cooked. Serve immediately.

NUTRITIONAL FACTS (PER SERVING)

Calories: 161 Carbohydrates: 11.5 g Cholesterol: 28 mg Fat: 1 g Fiber: 1.5 g Protein: 26 g Sodium: 306 mg

Soups in a Snap

The recipes in this chapter demonstrate that a very few ingredients are all that is needed to make a savory pot of soup. In fact, many of these soups are simply ready-made broths made flavorful and filling with the addition of various fast-cooking ingredients. But please don't limit yourself to the recipes in this chapter. Instead, be adventurous and concoct soups of your own. Start with a pot of simmering ready-made chicken, beef, or vegetable broth. Then stir in the ingredients of your choosing. For instance, you might toss in cooked chicken, leftover rice, and some fresh spinach. Another tasty combination is cooked shrimp, sliced scallions, sliced mushrooms, and water chestnuts. When the ingredients are already cooked, such as steamed vegetables and cooked rice, simply heat through. When adding uncooked pasta or rice, follow package directions and cook in the broth until done. Finally, season to taste with spices, herbs, and perhaps a splash of wine or lemon juice, and serve.

The following are just a few suggested on-the-run soup ingredients. You're sure to think of more.

❒ Chopped or sliced large spinach leaves, or whole baby spinach leaves

❒ Chopped escarole leaves

❒ Sliced fresh scallions

❒ Canned sliced water chestnuts

❒ Sliced fresh mushrooms

❒ Leftover steamed vegetables

❒ Frozen vegetables

❒ Canned corn

❒ Canned crab meat (rinse well and drain)

❒ Cubed or shredded cooked chicken, turkey, beef, pork, or ham

❒ Cooked shrimp

❒ Packaged fresh tortellini or ravioli

❒ Fine noodles, pastina, or other small pasta

❒ Instant or cooked rice

❒ Cooked or canned beans (rinse well and drain)

❒ Chopped or snipped fresh herbs, such as parsley, chives, dill, and thyme

ESCAROLE-RICE SOUP

TIME: 20 minutes   **YIELD:** 4 servings

MAIN INGREDIENTS

8 cups (loosely packed) fresh
escarole, torn into bite-sized
pieces

1 cup instant brown or white
rice

STAPLES

6 cups reduced-sodium,
fat-free chicken broth

2 teaspoons dried parsley

¼ teaspoon freshly ground
black pepper

*Twenty minutes is all you need to prepare this simple,
heart-warming soup.*

1. Place the broth in a 4-quart pot, and bring to a boil over
high heat. Add the escarole, and bring to a second boil.

2. Stir in the rice, reduce the heat to low, and cover. Simmer for 10 minutes, or until the rice and escarole are tender.

3. Add the parsley and black pepper to the pot, and simmer for another minute. Serve immediately.

NUTRITIONAL FACTS (PER SERVING)

Calories: 153 Carbohydrates: 23.5 g Cholesterol: 0 mg Fat: 0 g Fiber: 3.5 g Protein: 13.5 g Sodium: 279 mg

GARLICKY GARBANZO AND SPINACH SOUP

TIME: 30 minutes

YIELD: 4 servings

Brimming with fresh spinach, this soup is thick, creamy, and garlicky good.

1. Place all of the ingredients, except for the spinach, in a 4-quart pot, and bring to a boil over high heat. Reduce the heat to low and simmer for about 10 minutes, while stirring occasionally.

2. Transfer the ingredients to a blender, and purée until smooth.

3. Return the purée to the pot and stir in the spinach. Cover, and cook over medium-low heat for 5 to 7 minutes, or until the spinach is tender. Serve immediately.

MAIN INGREDIENTS

29-ounce can chickpeas, rinsed and drained

2 cups (packed) packaged, prewashed baby spinach*

STAPLES

3 cups reduced-sodium, fat-free chicken broth

8 large cloves garlic

1½ teaspoons dried oregano

¼ teaspoon dried rosemary

* If packaged baby spinach is unavailable, use thinly sliced regular spinach leaves.

NUTRITIONAL FACTS (PER SERVING)

Calories: 226 Carbohydrates: 34.5 g Cholesterol: 0 mg Fat: 4 g Fiber: 12 g Protein: 14 g Sodium: 583 mg

HARVEST PUMPKIN SOUP

TIME: 35 minutes   **YIELD:** 4 servings

MAIN INGREDIENTS

½ cup finely chopped red bell pepper

½ cup frozen hash brown potatoes, thawed

⅔ cup canned whole kernel corn, drained

1¼ cups canned solid pack pumpkin

STAPLES

½ cup chopped onion

2½ cups reduced-sodium, fat-free chicken broth

¼ teaspoon freshly ground black pepper

¼ teaspoon ground cumin

⅛ teaspoon salt (optional)

With its rich colors of orange, gold, and red, this hearty soup is the perfect first course for your next Thanksgiving meal. It's so easy to make, though, that you'll want to serve it all year round. For tips on quick thawing, see page 10.

1. Coat a 3-quart pot with cooking spray, and preheat over medium-high heat. Add the onion and red pepper and cook, stirring frequently, for 4 to 5 minutes, or just until the onion is soft.

2. Add the broth, potatoes, and corn to the pot, and bring to a boil. Reduce the heat to medium-low, cover, and simmer for 5 minutes, or until the red pepper is soft.

3. Add the pumpkin, black pepper, cumin, and salt, if desired, to the broth mixture, and stir to mix well. Heat through and serve immediately.

NUTRITIONAL FACTS (PER SERVING)

Calories: 102 Carbohydrates: 19 g Cholesterol: 0 mg Fat: < 1 g Fiber: 4 g Protein: 7 g Sodium: 176 mg

HEARTY BLACK BEAN SOUP

TIME: 25 minutes   YIELD: 4 servings

There's nothing better than this thick, hearty black bean soup on a crisp autumn or cold winter's day. Canadian bacon gives it a wonderfully smoky flavor with very little added fat.

1. Coat a 4-quart pot with cooking spray, and preheat over medium-low heat. Add the Canadian bacon and half of the onion, and sauté, stirring frequently, for 3 to 4 minutes, or until the onion begins to soften.

2. Place two-thirds of the black beans in a large bowl, and coarsely mash with a fork. Add the mashed beans to the pot along with the remaining whole black beans, broth, cumin, Tabasco sauce, oregano, and black pepper. Increase the heat to medium-high, and simmer for about 10 minutes, or until hot.

3. Serve immediately, garnishing each bowl with some of the remaining onion and a teaspoon of sour cream.

MAIN INGREDIENTS

½ cup diced Canadian bacon

2 cans (19 ounces each) organic black beans, undrained

4 teaspoons fat-free sour cream

STAPLES

½ cup finely chopped onion, divided

1 cup reduced-sodium, fat-free vegetable or chicken broth

½ teaspoon ground cumin

½ teaspoon Tabasco sauce

½ teaspoon dried oregano

¼ teaspoon freshly ground black pepper

NUTRITIONAL FACTS (PER SERVING)

Calories: 226 Carbohydrates: 38 g Cholesterol: 25 mg Fat: 3.5 g Fiber: 13 g Protein: 26 g Sodium: 466 mg

MANHATTAN CLAM CHOWDER

TIME: 35 minutes

YIELD: 4 servings

MAIN INGREDIENTS

2½ cups crushed tomatoes in purée

1 cup low-sodium tomato sauce

2 cups clam juice

2 cans (6.5 ounces each) chopped clams, undrained

1 cup potato, peeled and cut into ½-inch cubes

STAPLES

1 teaspoon dried oregano

½ teaspoon onion powder

½ teaspoon garlic powder

½ teaspoon paprika

¼ teaspoon freshly ground black pepper

Each spoonful of this hearty clam chowder is filled with chunks of potato and juicy clams.

1. Place all of the ingredients in a 4-quart pot, and bring to a boil over high heat.

2. Reduce the heat to low, cover, and simmer, stirring occasionally, for 15 to 20 minutes, or until the potato is tender. Serve immediately.

NUTRITIONAL FACTS (PER SERVING)

Calories: 140 Carbohydrates: 22.5 g Cholesterol: 17 mg Fat: 0.5 g Fiber: 6 g Protein: 11 g Sodium: 1,603 mg

MEXICALI SOUP

TIME: 35 minutes   YIELD: 4 servings

This tasty, Mexican-inspired soup is a heart-warming potpourri of colors and flavors.

1. Poach the chicken by placing it in a 4-quart pot with just enough water to cover. Bring to a boil over high heat. Then immediately reduce the heat to low, cover, and simmer for 7 to 10 minutes, or until no longer pink inside when cut with a knife. Transfer the chicken to a plate and allow it to cool a bit.

2. Discard the poaching water from the pot, then add the broth and tomatoes. Bring to a boil over high heat. Stir in the corn, black beans, and cilantro, and reduce the heat to low.

3. Using a fork, shred the chicken and add it to the pot. Stir the soup, cover, and simmer for about 15 minutes, stirring occasionally.

4. Serve immediately, garnishing each bowlful with a tablespoon of shredded cheese.

MAIN INGREDIENTS

8 ounces boneless, skinless chicken breasts

1 cup canned diced tomatoes, undrained

1 cup canned Mexican-style corn (Mexicorn), drained

1 cup canned black beans, rinsed and drained

2 teaspoons chopped fresh cilantro

4 tablespoons shredded light Mexican cheese blend*

STAPLES

3 cups reduced-sodium, fat-free chicken broth

* Sargento brand Light 4 Cheese Mexican Recipe Blend is a good choice.

NUTRITIONAL FACTS (PER SERVING)

Calories: 218 Carbohydrates: 22 g Cholesterol: 35.5 mg Fat: 2.5 g Fiber: 5.5 g Protein: 26 g Sodium: 845 mg

TOMATO BEEF BARLEY SOUP

TIME: 40 minutes   **YIELD:** 4 servings

MAIN INGREDIENTS

8 ounces 93% lean ground beef

14-ounce can (about 2 cups) peeled, chopped tomatoes

½ cup quick-cooking barley*

STAPLES

2 teaspoons canola oil

½ cup chopped onion

4 cups reduced-sodium, fat-free beef broth

½ teaspoon garlic powder

¼ teaspoon paprika

¼ teaspoon dried oregano

* Quaker brand Quick-Cooking Barley is a good choice.

Each satisfying spoonful of this savory soup is thick with beef and barley in a stewlike broth.

1. Place the oil in a 4-quart pot, and preheat over medium heat. Add the onion and sauté for 3 to 4 minutes, or until soft and beginning to brown. Add the beef, and cook, stirring to crumble, until no longer pink.

2. Add the tomatoes, broth, garlic powder, paprika, and oregano, and bring to a boil over high heat. Reduce the heat to low and simmer, partially covered, for 5 minutes.

3. Increase the heat to high and return to a second boil. Stir in the barley and reduce the heat to medium. Simmer uncovered for 15 to 20 minutes, or until the barley is tender. Serve immediately.

NUTRITIONAL FACTS (PER SERVING)

Calories: 270 Carbohydrates: 25.5 g Cholesterol: 35.5 mg Fat: 10.5 g Fiber: 4.5 g Protein: 19.5 g Sodium: 397 mg

SAVORY BEAN AND PASTA SOUP

TIME: 35 minutes

YIELD: 4 servings

Want a quick, satisfying meal? Simply serve this hearty soup with some crusty whole grain bread and a fresh mixed green salad.

1. Place the broth, beans, onion, and celery in a 4-quart pot, and bring to a boil over high heat. Reduce the heat to low, and stir in the garlic, parsley, and black pepper. Cover and simmer for 15 minutes, stirring occasionally.

2. Increase the heat to high, and bring the ingredients to a boil. Add the pasta, stir, and reduce the heat to medium. Cook uncovered for 10 minutes, or until the pasta is tender.

3. Serve immediately, as is or topped with a sprinkling of Parmesan cheese.

MAIN INGREDIENTS

2 cups canned cannellini beans (white kidney beans), rinsed and drained

½ cup thinly sliced celery

½ cup small shell pasta

Grated Parmesan cheese (optional)

STAPLES

4 cups reduced-sodium, fat-free beef broth

1 medium onion, coarsely chopped

2 cloves garlic, minced

1 tablespoon dried parsley

¼ teaspoon freshly ground black pepper

NUTRITIONAL FACTS (PER SERVING)

Calories: 193 Carbohydrates: 30 g Cholesterol: 0 mg Fat: 2 g Fiber: 6 g Protein: 12 g Sodium: 358 mg

ONION SOUP

TIME: 35 minutes   YIELD: 4 servings

MAIN INGREDIENTS

2 teaspoons cognac

1 teaspoon Gravy Master*

Grated Parmesan cheese
(optional)

STAPLES

3 medium onions (about 1½
 pounds), halved lengthwise
 and thinly sliced crosswise

1 tablespoon all-purpose flour

1 teaspoon sugar

4 cups reduced-sodium,
 fat-free beef broth

¼ teaspoon freshly ground
 black pepper

* Gravy Master is a browning and
 seasoning sauce.

*Rich in color and flavor, this is one onion soup that does not
need gobs of cheese to be satisfying and delicious.*

1. Spray a 4-quart pot with cooking spray, and preheat
over medium-high heat. Add the onions and cook, stirring
often, for about 10 minutes, or until soft.

2. Sprinkle the flour and sugar over the onions, and stir
while cooking for 1 minute.

3. Stir the broth into the onion mixture, and cook for
about 3 minutes, or until hot. Add the cognac, Gravy Master, and black pepper, and cook for an additional minute
or 2.

4. Serve immediately, as is or topped with a sprinkling of
Parmesan cheese.

NUTRITIONAL FACTS (PER SERVING)

Calories: 124 Carbohydrates: 19 g Cholesterol: 0 mg Fat: 1.5 g Fiber: 3 g Protein: 7 g Sodium: 80 mg

TOMATO SOUP WITH RICE

TIME: 20 minutes

YIELD: 4 servings

Did you know that you can make a great soup in your microwave oven? This soup—bright with tomatoes and aromatic with garlic—will make a believer out of you.

1. Place the water in a 1-quart saucepan, and bring to a boil over high heat. Stir in the rice, cover, and reduce the heat to medium-low. Simmer for 10 minutes, or until all of the water has been absorbed.

2. While the rice is cooking, use a knife to coarsely cut up the tomatoes in the can. Place the tomatoes and their liquid in a 3-quart microwave-safe bowl. Add all of the remaining ingredients except for the cheese. Cover the bowl tightly with plastic wrap, and microwave on high power for 7 minutes.

3. Carefully remove the plastic wrap and stir the cooked rice into the soup. Serve immediately, as is or topped with a sprinkling of grated Parmesan cheese.

MAIN INGREDIENTS

⅔ cup instant brown rice

2 cans (14 ounces each) no-salt-added peeled tomatoes

Grated Parmesan cheese (optional)

STAPLES

⅔ cup water

2 cups reduced-sodium, fat-free chicken broth

2 large cloves garlic, crushed

¼ teaspoon freshly ground black pepper

NUTRITIONAL FACTS (PER SERVING)

Calories: 112 Carbohydrates: 20.5 g Cholesterol: 0 mg Fat: < 1 g Fiber: 2.5 g Protein: 7 g Sodium: 109 mg

TORTELLINI EN BRODO WITH SPINACH

TIME: 20 minutes   **YIELD:** 4 servings

MAIN INGREDIENTS

2 cups refrigerated tortellini*

2 cups (packed) packaged, prewashed baby spinach**

STAPLES

6 cups reduced-sodium, fat-free chicken broth

¼ teaspoon freshly ground black pepper

* Buitoni Three Cheese Tortellini is a good choice.

** If packaged baby spinach is unavailable, use thinly sliced regular spinach leaves.

This soup is as delicious and satisfying as it is fast and easy to make.

1. Place the broth in a 4-quart pot, and bring to a boil over high heat. Stir in the tortellini, lower the heat to the point of a simmer, and cook uncovered for about 8 minutes, or until the pasta is done.

2. Add the spinach and black pepper to the pot, and stir to mix. Cook for an additional minute, or just until the spinach is wilted. Serve immediately.

NUTRITIONAL FACTS (PER SERVING)

Calories: 189 Carbohydrates: 23.5 g Cholesterol: 17.5 mg Fat: 2.5 g Fiber: 2 g Protein: 18.5 g Sodium: 467 mg

TURKEY MUSHROOM BARLEY SOUP

TIME: 40 minutes   YIELD: 4 servings

You can substitute canned mushrooms for the fresh in this delicious soup.

1. Place the oil in a 4-quart pot, and preheat over medium heat. Add the onion, and cook, stirring frequently, for 3 or 4 minutes, or until soft and beginning to brown. Add the turkey, and cook, stirring to crumble, for 4 minutes or until no longer pink.

2. Add the mushrooms, broth, and seasoning blend, and bring to a boil over high heat. Reduce the heat to low and simmer, partially covered, for 5 minutes.

3. Increase the heat to high and return to a second boil. Stir in the barley, and reduce the heat to medium. Simmer uncovered for 15 to 20 minutes, or until the barley is tender. Serve immediately.

MAIN INGREDIENTS

12 ounces 99% lean ground turkey

1 cup packaged, presliced mushrooms

½ cup quick-cooking barley*

STAPLES

2 teaspoons canola oil

½ cup chopped onion

6 cups reduced-sodium, fat-free chicken broth

2 teaspoons Mrs. Dash original seasoning blend

* Quaker brand Quick-Cooking Barley is a good choice.

NUTRITIONAL FACTS (PER SERVING)

Calories: 233 Carbohydrates: 17.5 g Cholesterol: 42 mg Fat: 4 g Fiber: 2.5 g Protein: 33.5 g Sodium: 313 mg

3. SATISFYING SANDWICHES

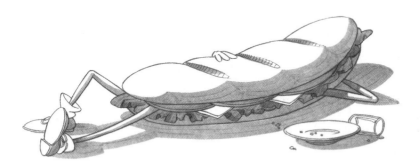

When the Earl of Sandwich requested that meat be placed between two slices of bread so that he could eat without leaving the gaming table, he unknowingly invented the first fast food. And we've been enjoying a love affair with the sandwich ever since.

Without a doubt, the sandwich is the fastest of fast foods—quick and easy to make, and just as quick and fuss-free to eat. Its versatility is also well known. A light bread spread with an equally light filling can make a great snack, while a heartier filling enclosed in a more substantial bread can be a meal in itself. Take our Crab Louis on Light White, for instance. Filled with canned crab tossed in a spicy but low-fat dressing, this sandwich makes a great light lunch. Another dish that won't weigh you down is the Hummus-Veggie Pitawich, a vegetarian delight filled with a variety of healthy veggies plus a dollop of store-bought hummus. But if you're looking for heartier fare, you'll find a wide selection of choices here, too. Open-Face Steak Sandwiches with Mushrooms and Onions are satisfying,

indeed, with their savory topping of herbed filet mignon, onions, and mushrooms. Or try our Mushroom Turkey Burgers with Horseradish Sauce. If you've ever found turkey burgers dry and tasteless, you'll be delighted to find how a blend of sautéed vegetables adds moistness and flavor to this super-lean meat. A creamy sauce adds further moistness, as well as the irresistible tang of horseradish. And for those days when you're in the mood for hearty vegetarian fare, treat yourself to Broiled Portabella Cheeseburgers. Juicy and flavorful, these are a snap to make and are so good! Other great choices include Smoked Turkey Wraps, Grilled Eggplant with Mozzarella and Arugula Heroes, and Roasted Pepper Pitas.

So whether you're looking for a quick bite to tame those late-night hunger pangs or a filling feast capable of satisfying the heartiest of appetites, you need look no further. Easy to make and a pleasure to serve and eat, these are satisfying sandwiches indeed. We think the Earl would approve.

BLACK RUSSIANS

TIME: 20 minutes

YIELD: 4 sandwiches

MAIN INGREDIENTS

6 slices fat-free turkey bacon

¼ cup sliced almonds

8 slices black bread or
  pumpernickel

8 ounces thinly sliced smoked
  turkey breast*

Leaf lettuce

STAPLES

½ cup low-fat mayonnaise

2 tablespoons plus 2 teaspoons
  lower-sodium ketchup

* Boar's Head Hickory Smoked
  Black Forest Turkey Breast is
  a good choice.

This sandwich unites a medley of ingredients with delicious results! You will especially enjoy the sprinkling of almonds, which adds both a toasted flavor and a delightful crunch.

1. Preheat the oven to 350°F.

2. Cook the bacon according to package directions until crisp. Set aside.

3. Spread the almonds on a baking sheet, and place in the oven for 5 minutes, or until lightly toasted. Watch carefully to prevent burning. Set aside.

4. To make the dressing, place the mayonnaise in a small dish. Add the ketchup, and stir until well blended. Set aside.

5. Spread one side of each slice of bread with a rounded tablespoon of the dressing. Set aside half of the slices. On each of the remaining slices, layer 1 tablespoon of the toasted almonds followed by 2 ounces of turkey, 1½ slices of bacon, and some lettuce. Crown with a reserved slice of bread, cut in half, and serve.

NUTRITIONAL FACTS (PER SANDWICH)

Calories: 331 Carbohydrates: 38.5 g Cholesterol: 48 mg Fat: 9 g Fiber: 4.5 g Protein: 23 g Sodium: 1,173 mg

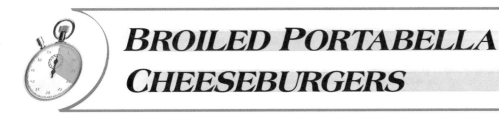

BROILED PORTABELLA CHEESEBURGERS

TIME: 20 minutes   YIELD: 4 burgers

If you have never had a broiled Portabella mushroom, you'll be delighted to find how meaty, juicy, and flavorful they are. These double burgers are a real treat!

1. Preheat the oven broiler to 500°F.

2. Place the oregano, garlic powder, and black pepper in a small dish, and stir to mix well. Set aside.

3. Spray a shallow baking pan with cooking spray. Arrange the mushrooms, top side up, on the pan, and spray with cooking spray. Sprinkle each with the seasoning mixture and spray once more.

4. Place the mushrooms under the broiler, about 5 inches below the heat source. Broil without turning for 4 to 5 minutes, or just until the mushrooms are tender when pierced with a fork and the juices begin to run.

5. Transfer half of the mushroom caps to a plate and cover to keep warm. (Do not place them on the buns yet, or the bread may become soggy.) Top each remaining mushroom cap with ½ ounce of the cheese and a piece of red pepper. Return to the broiler for about 1 minute, or just until the cheese melts.

6. Place a plain mushroom cap on the bottom half of each bun. Top the plain cap with a cheese-covered cap and, if desired, 3 basil leaves. Crown with a bun top and serve immediately.

MAIN INGREDIENTS

8 Portabella mushroom caps (each about 3½ inches in diameter)*

2 ounces light mozzarella cheese, very thinly sliced

4 pieces jarred roasted red peppers, drained and blotted dry (each about 3 inches square)

4 hamburger buns

12 fresh basil leaves (optional)

STAPLES

½ teaspoon dried oregano

½ teaspoon garlic powder

¼ teaspoon freshly ground black pepper

Olive-oil cooking spray

* Portabella mushrooms that come 3 to 4 in a package are perfect for this recipe.

NUTRITIONAL FACTS (PER BURGER)

Calories: 162 Carbohydrates: 26.5 g Cholesterol: 7 mg Fat: 4 g Fiber: 6 g Protein: 10.5 g Sodium: 289 mg

CRAB LOUIS ON LIGHT WHITE

TIME: 20 minutes   YIELD: 4 sandwiches

MAIN INGREDIENTS

2 cans (6 ounces each) crab
  meat

¼ cup finely chopped scallion

¼ cup finely chopped green
  bell pepper

8 slices light white bread

Leaf lettuce

STAPLES

¼ cup plus 2 tablespoons
  low-fat mayonnaise

2 tablespoons lower-sodium
  ketchup

2 teaspoons lemon juice

1 teaspoon Old Bay Seasoning
  or other seafood seasoning

4 dashes Tabasco sauce

2 dashes Worcestershire sauce

*The creamy Crab Louis filling is slightly spicy and simply
delicious. Serve this light treat to the seafood lovers in
your house.*

1. Place the crab meat in a wire mesh strainer and rinse
under cool running water. Pick over the crab, removing any
cartilage. Carefully press out all of the water. Pat dry with
paper towels, and transfer to a medium-sized bowl. Set
aside.

2. Place the mayonnaise and ketchup in a small dish, and
stir until smooth and well mixed. Add the mayonnaise mixture and all of the remaining ingredients, except for the
bread and lettuce, to the crab meat, and stir well until
mixed.

3. Set aside half of the bread slices. Spread each of the
remaining slices with about ⅓ cup of the crab filling and
top with some lettuce. Crown with a reserved slice of bread,
cut in half, and serve.

NUTRITIONAL FACTS (PER SANDWICH)

Calories: 208 Carbohydrates: 31 g Cholesterol: 44 g Fat: 2.5 g Fiber: 5 g Protein: 18 g Sodium: 1,054 mg

ENGLISH MUFFIN CHICKEN REUBENS

TIME: 20 minutes

YIELD: 4 sandwiches

This unlikely ingredient combination makes a surprisingly delicious sandwich.

1. Preheat an outdoor barbecue grill or oven broiler.

2. Lightly coat both sides of the chicken cutlets with cooking spray, and sprinkle with Mrs. Dash seasoning. Place on a preheated outdoor barbecue grill, or under a broiler, about 5 inches from the heat source, and cook about 3 to 4 minutes on each side, or until the chicken is no longer pink inside when cut with a knife. Set aside.

3. Place the sauerkraut in a medium-sized bowl. Add the sour cream, and stir to mix well. Set aside.

4. Place a cooked cutlet on the bottom half of each muffin. Top each with $\frac{1}{2}$ cup of the sauerkraut mixture and 2 tablespoons of cheese.

5. Place the topped muffins under the broiler or top brown in a toaster oven for about 1 minute, or just until the cheese melts. Crown with a muffin top and serve immediately.

MAIN INGREDIENTS

4 thinly sliced chicken cutlets (about 4 ounces each)

1-pound can sauerkraut, well drained (about 2 cups loosely packed)

$\frac{1}{2}$ cup nonfat sour cream

4 sandwich-size English muffins, toasted*

$\frac{1}{2}$ cup shredded reduced-fat Swiss cheese**

STAPLES

Cooking spray

2 tablespoons Mrs. Dash original seasoning blend

* If sandwich-size muffins are unavailable, use 8 regular-size English muffins.

** Alpine Lace brand is a good choice.

NUTRITIONAL FACTS (PER SANDWICH)

Calories: 417 Carbohydrates: 48 g Cholesterol: 72.5 mg Fat: 8.5 g Fiber: 6 g Protein: 35 g Sodium: 1,148 mg

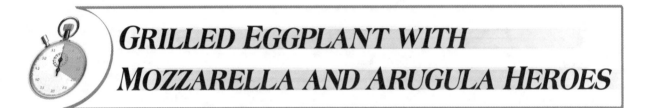

GRILLED EGGPLANT WITH MOZZARELLA AND ARUGULA HEROES

TIME: 20 minutes   YIELD: 4 heroes

MAIN INGREDIENTS

4 cups (packed) fresh arugula

½ cup plus 2 tablespoons fat-free Italian salad dressing, divided

1 medium eggplant (about 1 pound), unpeeled and cut into ½-inch-thick slices

4 Italian bread sandwich rolls, halved

1½ cups shredded fat-free mozzarella cheese

STAPLES

Olive-oil cooking spray

The woodsy, slightly bitter arugula makes an interesting crown for this hearty eggplant hero.

1. Preheat an outdoor barbecue grill or oven broiler.

2. Place the arugula in a large bowl. Add ½ cup of the salad dressing, and toss to coat. Set aside.

3. Lightly spray both sides of each eggplant slice with cooking spray, and place on the heated grill or under the broiler, about 5 inches from the heat source. Cook for 3 to 4 minutes on each side, or until browned and soft.

4. Brush the cut sides of the rolls with the remaining salad dressing, and place on the grill or under the broiler. Toast for about 1 minute, or until lightly browned. (Be careful not to burn.)

5. Place a fourth of the eggplant slices on the bottom half of each roll. Top with one-quarter of the cheese and 1 cup of the arugula, and crown with a roll top. Serve immediately.

NUTRITIONAL FACTS (PER HERO)

Calories: 293 Carbohydrates: 55 g Cholesterol: 7.5 mg Fat: 2 g Fiber: 4 g Protein: 18 g Sodium: 1,014 mg

HAM, CHEDDAR, AND PINEAPPLE ON SEVEN-GRAIN

TIME: 10 minutes

YIELD: 4 sandwiches

Creamy Cheddar spread and pineapple give a refreshing twist to the ever-popular ham and cheese sandwich.

1. Set aside half of the bread slices. Spread each of the remaining slices with 1 tablespoon of the cheese spread. Over the cheese, layer 2 ounces of ham, 2 slices of pineapple, and some lettuce.

2. Crown each sandwich with a reserved slice of bread. Cut in half and serve.

MAIN INGREDIENTS

8 slices low-fat seven-grain bread*

¼ cup light Cheddar cheese spread**

8 ounces thinly sliced lean ham

8 slices canned pineapple in juice, drained

Leaf lettuce

* Pepperidge Farm Light Style 7 Grain is a good choice.

** Try WisPride Lite Sharp Cheddar.

NUTRITIONAL FACTS (PER SANDWICH)

Calories: 259 Carbohydrates: 36 g Cholesterol: 34 mg Fat: 5.5 g Fiber: 4 g Protein: 18 g Sodium: 1,113 mg

HUMMUS-VEGGIE PITAWICHES

TIME: 15 minutes   YIELD: 4 sandwiches

MAIN INGREDIENTS

4 whole wheat pita pockets
   (6-inch rounds)

1 cup prepared low-fat
   hummus*

2 vine-ripe tomatoes, thinly
   sliced (about 16 slices)

16 thin slices cucumber

2 cups alfalfa sprouts

STAPLES

8 thin slices sweet red onion,
   separated into rings

* Wakim's Foods Old Fashioned
   Hummus is a good choice.

Prepared hummus makes a creamy, flavorful spread in this veggie-packed sandwich. For the lowest fat count possible, look for a hummus made without tahini (sesame seed paste).

1. Cut a thin slice off the top of each pita round, and carefully open the round without separating the halves. Spread $1/4$ cup of hummus inside each pocket, spreading half over each side.

2. Arrange several tomato slices, 4 cucumber slices, and some onion rings in each pocket. Top with $1/2$ cup of sprouts, and serve immediately.

NUTRITIONAL FACTS (PER SANDWICH)

Calories: 280 Carbohydrates: 53 g Cholesterol: 0 mg Fat: 5 g Fiber: 8.5 g Protein: 10 g Sodium: 488 mg

LIGHT TUNA MELT

TIME: 20 minutes   YIELD: 4 sandwiches

This slimmed-down version of a lunchtime favorite is delightfully piquant with the tang of fresh lemon juice.

1. Preheat the oven broiler.

2. Place the tuna in a medium-sized bowl, and flake with a fork. Add all of the remaining ingredients, except the bread and cheese, and stir to mix well.

3. Arrange the bread slices on a baking pan, and spread about 1/2 cup of the tuna mixture over each slice. Top with 1/4 cup of the cheese.

4. Place the sandwiches under the broiler, about 4 inches below the heat source. Broil for 1 to 2 minutes, or just until the cheese melts. Serve immediately.

MAIN INGREDIENTS

2 cans (6.5 ounces each) solid white water-packed tuna, well drained

3 tablespoons plain nonfat yogurt

4 slices low-fat 7 grain bread, toasted*

1 cup shredded reduced-fat Cheddar cheese

STAPLES

1/4 cup low-fat mayonnaise

1/4 cup lemon juice

1/4 cup finely chopped red onion

1/2 teaspoon Worcestershire sauce

1/4 teaspoon freshly ground black pepper

* Pepperidge Farm Light Style 7 Grain is a good choice.

NUTRITIONAL FACTS (PER SANDWICH)

Calories: 263 Carbohydrates: 16 g Cholesterol: 45 mg Fat: 7 g Fiber: 2 g Protein: 33 g Sodium: 764 mg

OPEN-FACE STEAK SANDWICHES WITH MUSHROOMS AND ONIONS

TIME: 35 minutes

YIELD: 4 sandwiches

MAIN INGREDIENTS

4 filet mignon steaks (about 4 ounces each)

1 pound packaged, presliced white button mushrooms (about 5 cups)

4 Italian bread sandwich rolls, halved

To give this hearty sandwich added flavor, try grilling the ingredients on an outdoor barbecue.

1. Preheat the oven broiler.

2. Prepare a basting sauce by combining the broth, olive oil, garlic powder, oregano, and thyme in a small bowl. Set aside.

3. Trim away any excess fat from the steaks, and sprinkle both sides with black pepper and salt, if desired. Place under the broiler, 5 to 6 inches below the heat source, and cook for 3 to 5 minutes on each side, depending on the thickness of the steaks and the desired degree of doneness. Transfer the cooked steaks to a warm plate, cover, and set aside.

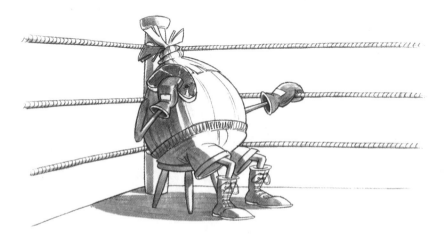

4. Place the onion slices and mushrooms in a shallow baking pan, and brush with some of the basting sauce. Place under the broiler, about 5 inches below the heat source. Cook, turning and basting occasionally, for about 10 minutes, or until the mushrooms are tender and the onions are soft and browned.

5. While the mushrooms and onions are cooking, brush the inside of each roll half with some of the basting sauce and lightly toast under the broiler. Be sure the bread doesn't burn. Place the halves cut side up on individual plates.

6. Thinly slice each steak and arrange the slices over the roll halves.

7. Toss the mushrooms and onions with the remaining basting sauce. Spoon over the steak, letting any excess fall over the sides onto the plate. Serve immediately.

STAPLES

½ cup reduced-sodium, fat-free beef broth

2 teaspoons olive oil

1 tablespoon garlic powder

1 teaspoon dried oregano

½ teaspoon dried thyme

¼ teaspoon freshly ground black pepper

¼ teaspoon salt (optional)

1 large Vidalia or other sweet onion, cut into ½ inch slices

NUTRITIONAL FACTS (PER SANDWICH)

Calories: 414 Carbohydrates: 46 g Cholesterol: 70.5 mg Fat: 13 g Fiber: 3 g Protein: 33.5 g Sodium: 288 mg

ROASTED PEPPER PITAS

TIME: 20 minutes   YIELD: 4 sandwiches

MAIN INGREDIENTS

6 large red and/or green bell
   peppers

½ cup fat-free Italian salad
   dressing

4 whole wheat pita pockets
   (6-inch rounds)

8 cups (packed) packaged,
   precut mixed salad greens

4 cups alfalfa sprouts

In this stuffed pita sandwich, roasted bell peppers are bathed in flavorful Italian dressing.

1. Preheat the oven broiler.

2. Cut the peppers in half lengthwise, remove the seeds, and place cut side down under the broiler, about 5 inches from the heat source. Broil for 5 to 7 minutes, or until the skins are black and bubbled. Immediately place the peppers in a plastic bag, seal, and let steam for about 10 minutes to loosen the skin.

3. Peel the skin from the peppers with your fingers, and discard the skin. Cut the peppers into wide strips and place in a bowl. Add the salad dressing, and toss to coat.

4. Cut a thin slice off the top of each pita round, and carefully open the round without separating the halves. Line the pita pockets with salad greens, stuff with some of the roasted pepper strips and sprouts, and serve.

NUTRITIONAL FACTS (PER SANDWICH)

Calories: 259 Carbohydrates: 54 g Cholesterol: 0 mg Fat: 2.5 g Fiber: 9 g Protein: 10.5 g Sodium: 732 mg

Roasting Peppers

Although there is nothing quicker than buying jarred roasted bell peppers, keep in mind that you can prepare your own in under 30 minutes. Roasting gives peppers an incomparable mellow, smoky flavor and velvety texture, while freeing them of their skins. You can, of course, roast standard green peppers. But red, yellow, orange, or purple peppers make a dish appealing visually and give you a wonderful, sweet flavor that green peppers don't have. That's because red peppers, and their colorful cousins, are vine-ripened versions of green peppers. Be aware, though, that ripe peppers are both more expensive and more perishable than the immature green variety.

You can roast peppers in an oven broiler, on a barbecue grill, or over the open flame of a gas burner. When using a broiler or grill, cut the peppers in half or quarters, and remove the stems and seeds before placing them 4 to 5 inches from the heat source. Roast for 5 to 7 minutes, or until the peppers are soft and the skin is blistered and blackened.

When using a gas burner, roast the pepper whole. Just be sure to make a small cut near the stem to allow the steam to escape. Using tongs, hold the pepper over a medium flame (or place it right on the burner), frequently turning until the skin is blackened and blistered.

Whether you've grilled, broiled, or roasted your peppers over an open flame, immediately place the hot cooked peppers in a plastic bag. Seal the bag and allow the peppers to steam for about 10 minutes. When they are cool enough to handle, peel off the skin.

You can use your peppers immediately or store them in a tightly sealed container in the refrigerator for up to a week. To add extra tang, marinate peppers in flavored vinegar, such as balsamic or wine vinegar, or fresh lemon juice during storage. Roasted peppers also freeze beautifully.

MUSHROOM TURKEY BURGERS WITH HORSERADISH SAUCE

TIME: 45 minutes

YIELD: 4 burgers

MAIN INGREDIENTS

½ cup nonfat sour cream

2 tablespoons prepared horseradish, well drained

3-ounce can sliced mushrooms, drained

1 pound 99% lean ground turkey

4 sesame seed-topped hamburger buns

STAPLES

⅛ teaspoon freshly ground black pepper

1 medium onion, coarsely chopped

1 teaspoon Worcestershire sauce

¼ teaspoon Tabasco sauce

Sautéed onions and mushrooms make these burgers moist and flavorful. A creamy horseradish sauce makes them absolutely irresistible.

1. Place the sour cream in a small bowl, and stir in the horseradish and black pepper. Cover and chill until ready to serve.

2. Coat a 12-inch nonstick skillet with cooking spray, and preheat over medium-high heat. Add the onion, and cook, stirring constantly, for about 3 minutes, or until slightly soft. Add the mushrooms, and cook for another minute.

3. Place the ground turkey in a large bowl, and add the onion mixture, Worcestershire sauce, and Tabasco sauce. Mix well with your hands or a large fork. Form the mixture into 4 burgers, each about 1 inch thick.

4. Spray the same skillet with cooking spray and preheat over medium heat. Add the burgers, cover, and cook for about 5 minutes, or until browned on the bottom. Turn the burgers over, cover, and cook for 5 additional minutes, or until no longer pink in the center when cut with a knife.

5. Spread 1 tablespoon of the chilled horseradish sauce on the bottom half of each bun. Top with a burger, crown with a bun top, and serve immediately.

NUTRITIONAL FACTS (PER BURGER)

Calories: 295 Carbohydrates: 31.5 g Cholesterol: 55.5 mg Fat: 4 g Fiber: 2.5 g Protein: 33.5 g Sodium: 453 mg

SMOKED TURKEY AND ROASTED PEPPER SUBS

TIME: 15 minutes

YIELD: 4 sandwiches

You'll love the combination of smoked turkey, roasted peppers, mozzarella cheese, and honey-Dijon dressing. The slight bitterness of the arugula beautifully complements the sweetness of the dressing.

1. Cut each bread loaf in half crosswise. Then cut each piece in half lengthwise. Spread the cut side of each piece with 1 tablespoon of dressing.

2. On each bottom bread half, arrange 2 peppers, cutting them as necessary so that they'll lie flat. Follow with 2 ounces of turkey, 1 ounce of cheese, and a layer of arugula.

3. Crown with the top halves of the bread, and serve. Garnish with additional arugula, if desired.

MAIN INGREDIENTS

Two Italian bread loaves (8 ounces each)

½ cup fat-free honey-Dijon salad dressing

8 jarred roasted sweet red peppers, drained and blotted dry

8 ounces thinly sliced, reduced-sodium, low-fat smoked turkey breast*

4 ounces fat-free mozzarella cheese, thinly sliced

4 small handfuls arugula or other bitter greens

* Boar's Head Hickory Smoked Black Forest Turkey Breast is a good choice.

NUTRITIONAL FACTS (PER SANDWICH)

Calories: 490 Carbohydrates: 76 g Cholesterol: 30.5 mg Fat: 6 g Fiber: 3 g Protein: 29.5 g Sodium: 1,500 mg

TOMATO AND MOZZARELLA BRUSCHETTA

TIME: 45 minutes   **YIELD:** 4 servings (3 bruschetta each)

MAIN INGREDIENTS

6 tomatoes (about 2 pounds), seeded and chopped

3 large scallions, chopped (about ¼ cup)

¼ cup chopped fresh basil

6 ounces fat-free mozzarella cheese, finely diced

12 slices Italian bread, each ½-inch thick

STAPLES

2 cloves garlic, chopped

3 tablespoons balsamic vinegar

1 tablespoon plus 1 teaspoon olive oil

¼ teaspoon freshly ground black pepper

These savory open-face sandwiches are best when made with juicy vine-ripe tomatoes. Hot-house tomatoes simply don't yield the same results.

1. Preheat the oven to 400°F.

2. Place the tomatoes, scallions, basil, cheese, and garlic in a large bowl, and stir to mix.

3. Place the vinegar and oil in a small bowl and mix well. Add the vinegar mixture and the black pepper to the tomato mixture and stir well. Cover and allow to sit at room temperature until ready to serve.

4. Arrange the bread slices in a single layer on a baking sheet, and place in the oven for 3 to 5 minutes, or until the bottoms are golden brown. Turn the slices over and bake for another 3 minutes, or until the second side is golden brown.

5. Place 3 of the toasted slices on each individual serving plate. Spoon even amounts of the tomato mixture over each slice, and serve immediately. Eat with a knife and fork.

NUTRITIONAL FACTS (PER SERVING)

Calories: 389 Carbohydrates: 58.5 g Cholesterol: 7.5 mg Fat: 8.5 g Fiber: 4.5 g Protein: 20.5 g Sodium: 875 mg

SMOKED TURKEY WRAPS

TIME: 15 minutes

YIELD: 4 sandwich wraps

The fiery spark of jalapeño pepper coupled with the sweet zing of sweetened dried cranberries complement the smoked turkey perfectly in this convenient sandwich wrap. Feel free to build on the ingredients presented in this recipe. Sprouts, lettuce, chopped bell pepper, and low-fat Swiss cheese are all good choices.

1. Place the jalapeño pepper and mayonnaise in a small bowl, and stir to blend. Spread even amounts of the mixture on each tortilla.

2. Top the mayonnaise with a portion of the turkey and the tomatoes. Sprinkle with the cranberries.

3. Roll up the tortillas as shown on page 53. Cut in half and serve.

MAIN INGREDIENTS

1 medium jalapeño pepper,*
  finely chopped

4 flour tortillas (10-inch rounds)

12 ounces thinly sliced
  reduced-sodium, low-fat
  smoked turkey breast**

2 small plum tomatoes,
  chopped

¼ cup sweetened dried
  cranberries***

STAPLES

¼ cup fat-free mayonnaise

  * Be sure to wear plastic gloves
    when handling the peppers.

 ** Boar's Head Hickory Smoked
    Black Forest Turkey Breast is
    a good choice.

*** Ocean Spray Craisins are
    available in most major
    grocery stores.

NUTRITIONAL FACTS (PER WRAP)

Calories: 262 Carbohydrates: 35 g Cholesterol: 38 mg Fat: 8 g Fiber: 1.5 g Protein: 21.5 g Sodium: 965 mg

VEGGIE CRUNCH WRAPS

TIME: 15 minutes   YIELD: 4 sandwich wraps

MAIN INGREDIENTS

3 cups packaged cole slaw mix*

1 cup chopped tomato

¾ cup chopped red and/or
green bell pepper

½ cup fat-free ranch salad
dressing, or the flavor of
your choice

4 large romaine lettuce
leaves

4 flour tortillas (10-inch
rounds)

STAPLES

½ cup chopped red onion

* Cole slaw brands like Dole contain
both shredded green cabbage and
carrots.

These simple-to-assemble sandwich wraps are stuffed with crisp, crunchy vegetables. They make a terrific lunchtime meal.

1. Place the cole slaw, tomato, bell pepper, and onion in a medium-sized bowl. Add the dressing and stir to mix well. Set aside.

2. Place a lettuce leaf on the center of each tortilla. Top with equal amounts of the vegetable mixture. Roll up the tortillas as shown on page 53. Cut in half and serve.

NUTRITIONAL FACTS (PER WRAP)

Calories: 184 Carbohydrates: 39.5 g Cholesterol: 0 mg Fat: 5 g Fiber: 4 g Protein: 5 g Sodium: 625 mg

SANDWICH WRAPS ITALIANO

TIME: 30 minutes   YIELD: 4 sandwich wraps

Sautéed onion and bell peppers are combined with cannellini beans and melted mozzarella cheese in these spicy Tuscan-style sandwich wraps.

1. Preheat the oven to 350°F.

2. Coat a 12-inch nonstick skillet with cooking spray, and preheat over medium-low heat. Add the onion and bell pepper, and sauté, stirring occasionally.

3. While the vegetables are sautéing, place the beans in a bowl, and slightly crush with the back of a fork. Add the beans to the skillet, mix well, and continue to cook, stirring occasionally, for 5 to 7 minutes, or until the onion is brown and the pepper is soft.

4. Add the oregano, garlic powder, crushed red pepper, salt, if desired, and black pepper to the bean mixture. Mix well and remove from the heat.

5. Divide the filling mixture among the tortillas, and top each with ¼ cup mozzarella and 1 teaspoon Parmesan, if desired. Roll up the tortillas as shown on page 53, then wrap each in aluminum foil.

6. Place the wraps in the oven and heat for 5 to 10 minutes, or until the cheese is melted. Remove the foil wrapper, cut in half, and serve immediately.

MAIN INGREDIENTS

1 cup chopped red and/or green bell pepper

14-ounce can cannellini beans (white kidney beans), rinsed and drained

4 flour tortillas (10-inch rounds)

1 cup shredded light mozzarella cheese

4 teaspoons grated Parmesan cheese (optional)

STAPLES

1½ cups chopped onion

1 teaspoon dried oregano

1 teaspoon garlic powder

½ teaspoon crushed red pepper

½ teaspoon salt (optional)

¼ teaspoon freshly ground black pepper

NUTRITIONAL FACTS (PER WRAP)

Calories: 372 Carbohydrates: 43.5 g Cholesterol: 33 mg Fat: 12 g Fiber: 3 g Protein: 23 g Sodium: 778 mg

It's a Wrap!

Take a standard flour tortilla, pile it with your favorite assortment of sandwich fillings, then roll it up into a neatly sealed package. Voila! You have just created a sandwich wrap.

Perfect for today's fast-paced lifestyle, sandwich wraps are quickly becoming the nation's latest craze. They are showing up on menus everywhere—from cafés and fast-food chains to "wrap" restaurants that specialize in this new tortilla cuisine. Launched in California during the early nineties, the sandwich wrap—also known as a wrapper or twister—is basically a spin-off of the burrito. But unlike burritos, which are traditionally stuffed with a standard meat and/or bean combination, sandwich wraps are characterized by their "sky's-the-limit" fillings.

Not only are wraps fast and fun to make, but they are also easy to handle. You can prepare a wrap in the morning, cover it tightly with plastic wrap or aluminum foil, and refrigerate it until you are ready to enjoy it later that day. Simply peel away a little of the wrapping from one end of the sandwich, and enjoy. Continue to remove the wrapping as you work your way down to the bottom.

While your basic flour tortilla makes a fine wrapper, be aware that there is a wide variety of flavored tortillas available in most gourmet shops and major grocery stores. You can find spinach, sundried tomato, garlic, basil, cilantro, whole wheat, chorizo, black bean, and spicy Cajun-flavored tortillas, to name just a few. There are even dessert tortillas in chocolate, strawberry, pumpkin, wild berry, and apple-cinnamon flavors.

There are a few basic rolling methods for forming sandwich wraps. We recommend any one of the methods shown on the facing page.

If a tortilla isn't fresh enough, it may tend to crack during the rolling. Simply warm the tortilla in a microwave oven for 15 seconds or so before adding the filling. This will allow you to roll up the tortilla easily, "crack-free."

No matter how you roll them, wraps are a snap and fun to make. Use the wraps in this chapter as springboards to develop your own creations. And don't forget—wraps with ingredients like cheese are great heated. Here are a few suggested filling combinations to help you get started:

❒ Diced cooked chicken, arugula, chopped cucumber, and fat-free ranch dressing.

❒ Diced cooked turkey, shredded Swiss cheese, chopped bell pepper, shredded cabbage, and low-fat Russian dressing.

❒ Cooked baby shrimp, rice, green peas, and sautéed onion and red bell pepper.

❒ Shredded lettuce, crumbled turkey bacon, chopped plum tomatoes, crumbled blue cheese, and fat-free mayonnaise.

❒ Tuna salad, shredded lettuce, and chopped walnuts.

❒ Belgian endive, radicchio, diced tomatoes, goat cheese, pine nuts, chopped fresh basil, and fat-free mayonnaise.

❒ Sliced ham, shredded mozzarella, capers, and Dijon-style mustard.

❒ Black beans, shredded Cheddar cheese, diced onions, chopped cilantro, and salsa.

❒ Chickpeas, cooked couscous, raisins or chopped fresh mango, and almonds.

❒ Strips of Canadian bacon, shredded romaine lettuce, and Cheddar cheese spread.

Method One: Fold the right and left sides of the tortilla over the filling. Then, starting at the bottom, roll up the tortilla into a neat package that is sealed at both ends (it will resemble an overstuffed egg roll).

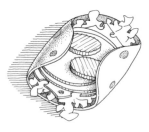

1. Fold the right and left sides of the tortilla over the filling.

2. Roll the tortilla from the bottom up.

Method Two: Fold one side of the tortilla over the filling before rolling it up. This will result in a wrap that is sealed at one end and open at the other.

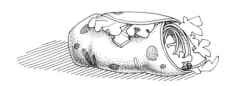

1. Fold one side of the tortilla over the filling.

2. Roll the tortilla from the bottom up.

Method Three: No folding necessary. Simply roll up the tortilla. (Be aware that both ends of the wrap will be open with this method. To help prevent the filling from falling out, a "tight" roll is suggested.)

1. Simply roll up the tortilla over the filling.

2. The completed wrap, open at both ends.

SCRAMBLED BREAKFAST WRAPS

TIME: 25 minutes

YIELD: 4 sandwich wraps

MAIN INGREDIENTS

¾ cup chopped red and/or
  green bell pepper

2½ ounces Canadian bacon, cut
  into small pieces

2 cups fat-free egg substitute

4 fat-free flour tortillas
  (10-inch rounds)

STAPLES

2 teaspoons olive oil

¾ cup chopped onion

½ teaspoon salt (optional)

½ teaspoon freshly ground
  black pepper

Here comes breakfast in a neatly wrapped package.

1. Coat a 12-inch nonstick skillet with cooking spray, add the oil, and preheat over medium-low heat. Add the onion and bell pepper, and sauté, stirring occasionally, for 5 to 7 minutes, or until the onion is brown and the pepper is soft.

2. Add the Canadian bacon to the skillet. Mix well, and continue to cook, stirring occasionally, for 2 minutes.

3. Pour the egg substitute over the sautéed vegetables, sprinkle with the salt, if desired, and the black pepper, and cook, stirring to scramble, until done to taste.

4. Warm the tortillas according to package directions.

5. Divide the filling mixture among the warm tortillas, and roll the tortillas as shown on page 53. Cut in half and serve.

NUTRITIONAL FACTS (PER WRAP)

Calories: 234 Carbohydrates: 30.5 g Cholesterol: 10.5 mg Fat: 3.5 g Fiber: 2 g Protein: 21.5 g Sodium: 721 mg

4. SAVORY SALADS

Salads are now enjoying greater popularity than ever, and for good reason. When made properly, salads fit beautifully into a light and healthy lifestyle. They're also a natural for fast and easy cooking—a true delight for the kitchen-quickies cook. And salads are the most versatile of foods, as they can serve as a first course, a side dish, or even an entrée.

This chapter reflects the salad's versatility—as well as the fun we had creating these recipes. If you're looking for a snappy side dish, you'll find a range of choices, from flavorful Black Bean Salad with Corn and Peppers, to piquant Chili-Lime Tabbouleh, to classic Creamy Caraway Cole Slaw. Need a sweet starter for your next meal? Try Fresh Citrus Salad, an unexpected blend of juicy citrus fruits, vegetables, and herbs. Want something more substantial? You'll be delighted to find that a number of our salads are complete meals. Southwest Rice and Smoked Turkey Salad, for instance, blends savory smoked turkey, golden corn, and a south-of-the-border dressing for a truly satisfying dish. Or try Lemony Scallop Salad—lemon-kissed scallops served over a bed of tender greens. All you need add is a crusty loaf of bread.

Of course, all of these salads are a snap to prepare, as they make use of packaged cole slaw mix and other prewashed greens; of deli-bought turkey and chicken; of quick-cooking couscous and rice; and of many other time- and effort-saving foods. How do we keep them low in fat? By using products such as lemon juice, light sour cream, light mayonnaise, a variety of flavorful vinegars, and an occasional touch of high-quality olive oil—as well as crushed garlic and a sprinkling of herbs and spices—we've found that we can add spark to salads while keeping them light and healthy.

So if you've always enjoyed salads, or if you're planning to add more of them to your diet, this chapter is for you. Fast, easy, and bursting with flavor, these fuss-free delights are sure to please every member of your family.

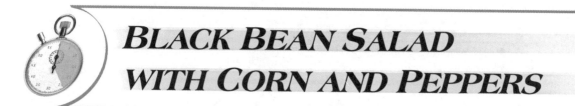

BLACK BEAN SALAD WITH CORN AND PEPPERS

TIME: 25 minutes

YIELD: 4 servings

MAIN INGREDIENTS

2 cans (1 pound each) black
  beans, rinsed and drained

9-ounce can whole kernel corn,
  drained

½ cup chopped green bell
  pepper

½ cup chopped red bell pepper

STAPLES

½ cup chopped sweet red
  onion

½ teaspoon freshly ground
  black pepper

¼ cup balsamic vinegar

1 tablespoon olive oil

1 teaspoon brown sugar

1 large clove garlic, minced

¼ teaspoon ground cumin

*Colorful and full of flavor, this is a great accompaniment to
sandwiches, and roasted or grilled poultry and meats.*

1. Place the beans, corn, onion, and bell peppers in a large
bowl. Sprinkle with black pepper and toss to mix well.

2. To make the dressing, measure the vinegar into a 1-cup
measuring cup. Add the oil, brown sugar, garlic, and
cumin, and stir until the sugar is dissolved.

3. Pour the dressing over the bean mixture, and toss to
mix well. Serve immediately, or cover and chill until ready
to serve.

NUTRITIONAL FACTS (PER SERVING)

Calories: 294 Carbohydrates: 50.5 g Cholesterol: 0 mg Fat: 6 g Fiber: 14.5 g Protein: 14.5 g Sodium: 561 mg

BREAD SALAD

TIME: 35 minutes

YIELD: 4 servings

In this savory Italian salad, a low-fat vinaigrette plus the juice of ripe tomatoes soften day-old bread. If you are using fresh bread, toast the cubes lightly under the broiler (about 30 seconds on each side) before adding them to the salad.

1. Place the bread, tomatoes, onion, cucumber, basil, and garlic in a large bowl, and toss to mix well.

2. To make the dressing, place all of the remaining ingredients in a small bowl, and stir to mix.

3. Pour the dressing over the salad, and toss to mix. Allow to stand for 10 minutes at room temperature before serving.

MAIN INGREDIENTS

2½ cups day-old Italian bread, cut into 1-inch cubes

2 medium-large tomatoes, seeded and coarsely chopped (about 2 cups)

½ medium cucumber, peeled and cut into chunks

¼ cup coarsely chopped fresh basil

STAPLES

½ medium red onion, cut into thin wedges and separated

2 medium cloves garlic, minced

2 tablespoons red wine vinegar

1 tablespoon olive oil

1 tablespoon reduced-sodium, fat-free chicken broth

⅛ teaspoon freshly ground black pepper

NUTRITIONAL FACTS (PER SERVING)

Calories: 107   Carbohydrates: 15 g   Cholesterol: 0.5 mg   Fat: 4.5 g   Fiber: 2 g   Protein: 3 g   Sodium: 105 mg

CARROT-PINEAPPLE SALAD

TIME: 30 minutes

YIELD: 4 servings

MAIN INGREDIENTS

3 cups shredded carrots
(4 large)

1-pound can crushed
pineapple, drained

½ cup dark raisins

½ cup plain nonfat yogurt

8 cups packaged, precut
mixed salad greens

STAPLES

1 tablespoon sugar

This refreshingly sweet, delicately crunchy salad takes less than 15 minutes to prepare. The rest of the time is needed for chilling.

1. Place all ingredients, except for the salad greens, in a large bowl, and toss to mix. Cover and chill for 15 to 20 minutes.

2. Line 4 individual plates with the greens. Top with the chilled carrot salad and serve.

NUTRITIONAL FACTS (PER SERVING)

Calories: 174 Carbohydrates: 40.5 g Cholesterol: 0.5 mg Fat: 0.5 g Fiber: 6.5 g Protein: 5.5 g Sodium: 86 mg

CHICKEN SALAD BOMBAY

TIME: 20 minutes

YIELD: 4 servings

To make this flavorful, aromatic salad, you can use leftover chicken or cooked chicken from your local grocery store, gourmet shop, or deli.

1. Dice the chicken into bite-sized pieces, and place in a large bowl. Add all of the remaining ingredients, except for the salad greens, and mix well. Cover and chill for 15 minutes.

2. Line 4 individual plates with the salad greens. Top with the chilled chicken salad, and serve.

COMPLETE MEAL

MAIN INGREDIENTS

1 pound cooked boneless, skinless chicken breasts

1 cup canned Mandarin oranges, drained

½ cup dark raisins

2 tablespoons sliced almonds

8 cups packaged, precut mixed salad greens

STAPLES

½ cup fat-free mayonnaise

2 tablespoons light soy sauce

1 tablespoon lemon juice

2 teaspoons curry powder

NUTRITIONAL FACTS (PER SERVING)

Calories: 285 Carbohydrates: 33.5 g Cholesterol: 67 mg Fat: 5 g Fiber: 3.5 g Protein: 28.5 g Sodium: 750 mg

CHILI-LIME TABBOULEH

TIME: 35 minutes

YIELD: 4 servings

MAIN INGREDIENTS

1¼ cups bulgur wheat
(5.25-ounce package)

½ cup thinly sliced scallions

¼ cup chopped fresh parsley

2 fresh medium-hot red chili
peppers, seeded, deveined,
and minced*

¼ cup lime juice (about 3 limes)

STAPLES

1 cup boiling water

1 tablespoon olive oil

* Be sure to wear plastic gloves
when handling the peppers.

This Southwestern twist on the usual tabbouleh salad is delightfully piquant and refreshing. Enjoy it with Savory Crab Cakes (page 151).

1. Place the bulgur wheat in a large heatproof bowl, and stir in the boiling water. Cover and chill for 25 minutes, or until all of the water has been absorbed.

2. Add the scallions, parsley, and chili peppers to the wheat, and toss to mix. Add all of the remaining ingredients, and toss until well mixed.

3. Serve immediately, or cover and chill until ready to serve.

NUTRITIONAL FACTS (PER SERVING)

Calories: 198 Carbohydrates: 38 g Cholesterol: 0 mg Fat: 4 g Fiber: 9 g Protein: 6 g Sodium: 13 mg

Quick and Easy Salad Dressings and Veggie Dips

Although the salads in this book come complete with dressings, sometimes all you really want is a fresh and flavorful topping for a salad of mixed greens—perhaps for a super-convenient bagged salad. Below, you will find a fabulous collection of quick- and easy-to-make dressings for your tossed green salads, as well as dips for those fresh-cut vegetables. A few, like the Creamy Garlic Herb, Green Chili Salsa, and Creamy Horseradish Dressings, are perfect baked potato toppers, too.

CREAMY HORSERADISH DRESSING

YIELD: 1½ cups

1 cup nonfat sour cream

¼ cup fat-free mayonnaise

1 clove garlic, crushed

1 tablespoon prepared horseradish

1 tablespoon white wine vinegar

Pinch freshly ground black pepper

Pinch salt (optional)

1. Place the sour cream and mayonnaise in a small bowl, and stir until well mixed. Add all of the remaining ingredients, and stir well.

2. Use immediately, or cover and chill until ready to serve.

NUTRITIONAL FACTS (PER TABLESPOON)

Calories: 13 Carbohydrates: 2 g Cholesterol: 0 mg Fat: 0 g
Fiber: 0 g Protein: 0.5 g Sodium: 26 mg

LEMON-LIME VINAIGRETTE

YIELD: 2/3 cup

1/4 cup fresh lime juice

1/4 cup fresh lemon juice

2 tablespoons water

1 tablespoon white wine vinegar

1 tablespoon honey

1 tablespoon olive oil

1 tablespoon finely chopped
fresh chives

1/4 teaspoon dried oregano

1/4 teaspoon freshly ground
black pepper

1. Place all of the ingredients in a small bowl, and stir until well mixed.

2. Use immediately, or cover and chill until ready to serve.

NUTRITIONAL FACTS (PER TABLESPOON)

Calories: 21 Carbohydrates: 3 g Cholesterol: 0 mg Fat: 1.5 g
Fiber: 0 g Protein: 0 g Sodium: 0 mg

ORIENTAL DRESSING

YIELD: 1/2 cup

1/3 cup white wine vinegar

1 tablespoon light soy sauce

1 tablespoon dark brown sugar

1 teaspoon sesame oil

1 teaspoon grated fresh ginger,
or 1/2 teaspoon ground ginger

1 teaspoon toasted sesame
seeds

1/4 teaspoon crushed red pepper
(optional)

1. Place the vinegar and soy sauce in a small bowl. Add the brown sugar, and stir to dissolve. Add all of the remaining ingredients, and stir until well mixed. For a fiery spark, add the red pepper.

2. Use immediately, or cover and chill until ready to serve.

NUTRITIONAL FACTS (PER TABLESPOON)

Calories: 17 Carbohydrates: 2.5 g Cholesterol: 0 mg Fat: 0.5 g
Fiber: 0 g Protein: 0 g Sodium: 113 mg

Top: Harvest Pumpkin Soup (page 22)
Bottom Left: Mexicali Soup (page 25)
Bottom Right: Escarole-Rice Soup (page 20)

Top Right: Tomato and Mozzarella Bruschetta (page 48)

Bottom Left: Smoked Turkey and Roasted Pepper Subs (page 47) and Creamy Caraway Cole Slaw (page 66)

Bottom Right: Veggie Crunch Wraps (page 50)

Left: Black Bean Salad with Corn and Peppers (page 56)
Right: Lemony Scallop Salad (page 73)
Bottom: Fresh Mozzarella and Tomato Salad (page 71)

Top Left: Linguine with Fresh Tomato Sauce (page 89)

Top Right: Bow Ties with Artichoke Hearts and Sundried Tomatoes (page 80)

Bottom: Potato Gnocchi with Quick Meat Sauce (page 95)

CREAMY GARLIC HERB DRESSING

1. Place the yogurt and mayonnaise in a small bowl, and stir until well mixed. Add all of the remaining ingredients, and stir well.

2. Use immediately, or cover and chill until ready to serve.

YIELD: 1½ cups

1 cup plain nonfat yogurt

¼ cup fat-free mayonnaise

2 cloves garlic, crushed

1 scallion, finely chopped

1½ teaspoons chopped fresh parsley, or ½ teaspoon dried

½ teaspoon dried dill

¼ teaspoon Worcestershire sauce

Pinch freshly ground black pepper

Pinch salt (optional)

NUTRITIONAL FACTS (PER TABLESPOON)

Calories: 8 Carbohydrates: 1.5 g Cholesterol: 0 mg Fat: 0 g
Fiber: 0 g Protein: 0.5 g Sodium: 26 mg

GREEN CHILI SALSA

1. Place all of the ingredients in a small bowl, and toss well to mix.

2. Use immediately, or cover and chill until ready to serve.

YIELD: 1½ cups

3 large plum tomatoes, diced (about 1¼ cups)

4-ounce can chopped green chilies, drained

¼ cup diced onion

1 tablespoon finely chopped fresh cilantro

1 tablespoon fresh lime juice

¼ teaspoon white wine vinegar

⅛ teaspoon freshly ground black pepper

NUTRITIONAL FACTS (PER ¼ CUP)

Calories: 18 Carbohydrates: 4 g Cholesterol: 0 mg Fat: 0 g
Fiber: 0.5 g Protein: 1 g Sodium: 14 mg

CREAMY DIJON-CAPER DRESSING

YIELD: 1¼ cups

1 cup nonfat sour cream

¼ cup fat-free mayonnaise

1 tablespoon Dijon-style
mustard

1½ teaspoons capers,
drained

⅛ teaspoon freshly ground
black pepper

1. Place the sour cream, mayonnaise, and mustard in a small bowl, and stir until well mixed. Add the capers and black pepper, and stir well.

2. Use immediately, or cover and chill until ready to serve.

NUTRITIONAL FACTS (PER TABLESPOON)

Calories: 15 Carbohydrates: 2.5 g Cholesterol: 0 mg Fat: 0 g
Fiber: 0 g Protein: 1 g Sodium: 57 mg

BASIL-PARMESAN DRESSING

YIELD: ¾ cup

½ cup nonfat sour cream

1 tablespoon olive oil

1 tablespoon white wine
vinegar

½ teaspoon Dijon-style
mustard

¼ cup freshly grated
Parmesan cheese

2 tablespoons minced
fresh basil

1. Place the sour cream, oil, vinegar, and mustard in a small bowl, and stir until well mixed. Add the Parmesan and basil, and stir well.

2. Use immediately, or cover and chill until ready to serve.

NUTRITIONAL FACTS (PER TABLESPOON)

Calories: 31 Carbohydrates: 2 g Cholesterol: 1.5 mg Fat: 2 g
Fiber: 0 g Protein: 1.5 g Sodium: 51 mg

HONEY-MUSTARD DRESSING

1. Place all of the ingredients in a small bowl, and blend well with a whisk.

2. Use immediately, or cover and chill until ready to serve.

YIELD: 1/2 cup

1/4 cup white wine vinegar

2 tablespoons honey

2 teaspoons Dijon-style mustard

1 teaspoon canola oil

Pinch freshly ground black pepper

NUTRITIONAL FACTS (PER TABLESPOON)

Calories: 25 Carbohydrates: 5 g Cholesterol: 0 mg Fat: 0.5 g
Fiber: 0 g Protein: 0 g Sodium: 32 mg

GARLIC-BASIL VINAIGRETTE

1. Place all of the ingredients in a small bowl, and stir until well mixed.

2. Use immediately, or cover and chill until ready to serve.

YIELD: 1/2 cup

1/4 cup red wine vinegar

1/4 cup balsamic vinegar

1/4 cup water

1 large clove garlic, minced

2 tablespoons finely chopped fresh basil

1 tablespoon olive oil

1 teaspoon dried oregano

Pinch freshly ground black pepper

Pinch salt (optional)

NUTRITIONAL FACTS (PER TABLESPOON)

Calories: 16 Carbohydrates: 1.5 g Cholesterol: 0 mg Fat: 1 g
Fiber: 0 g Protein: 0 g Sodium: 2 mg

CREAMY CARAWAY COLE SLAW

TIME: 20 minutes   **YIELD:** 4 servings

MAIN INGREDIENTS

4 cups packaged cole slaw mix*

1/2 cup diced green bell pepper

1/2 cup thinly sliced scallions

1 small apple, peeled and grated

1/4 cup plus 2 tablespoons
   nonfat sour cream

STAPLES

1/4 cup low-fat mayonnaise

1/4 cup lemon juice

2 teaspoons Dijon-style
   mustard

1 teaspoon sugar

1/2–1 teaspoon caraway seeds

1/4 teaspoon freshly ground
   black pepper

* Cole slaw brands like Dole contain
  both shredded green cabbage and
  carrots.

Packaged cole slaw mix makes it a snap to toss together this flavorful version of a summertime favorite.

1. Place all of the vegetables and the apple in a medium-sized bowl, and toss to mix well. Set aside.

2. Place all of the remaining ingredients in a small dish, and stir to mix well.

3. Pour the sour cream mixture over the cabbage mixture, and toss well. Serve immediately, or cover and chill until ready to serve.

NUTRITIONAL FACTS (PER SERVING)

Calories: 101 Carbohydrates: 20.5 g Cholesterol: 0 mg Fat: 1.5 g Fiber: 3.5 g Protein: 3 g Sodium: 235 mg

COLD SESAME NOODLES

TIME: 30 minutes   YIELD: 4 servings

A small amount of sesame oil goes a long way in flavoring these Oriental-style noodles. Enjoy them as a light lunch entrée or a super side dish.

1. Preheat an 8-inch nonstick skillet over medium heat. Add the sesame seeds, and dry-roast, stirring frequently, for 3 to 4 minutes, or until the seeds begin to brown. (Be careful not to burn the seeds, or they will become bitter.) Transfer the seeds to a plate, and set aside to cool.

2. Bring a 4-quart pot of water to a rolling boil. Add the pasta, and cook according to package directions.

3. Drain the pasta; then return it to the pot and cover with ice water. Let set for 5 to 7 minutes to chill. *Drain very well.*

4. Place the pasta in a large bowl. Add the sesame oil and soy sauce, and toss well to coat. Add the toasted sesame seeds, scallions, and red pepper. Mix well and serve.

MAIN INGREDIENTS

2 teaspoons sesame seeds

8 ounces angel hair pasta

2 large scallions, thinly sliced

STAPLES

1 tablespoon plus 1 teaspoon sesame oil

2 tablespoons light soy sauce

¼ teaspoon crushed red pepper

NUTRITIONAL FACTS (PER SERVING)

Calories: 276 Carbohydrates: 45.5 g Cholesterol: 0 mg Fat: 6.5 g Fiber: 5 g Protein: 8 g Sodium: 454 mg

PASTA TABBOULEH

TIME: 25 minutes   **YIELD:** 4 servings

MAIN INGREDIENTS

2 cups tiny shells, orzo, or
 other small pasta

½ cup finely chopped fresh
 mint leaves

1 medium tomato, chopped

2 scallions, finely chopped

8 cups packaged, precut
 mixed salad greens

STAPLES

½ cup lemon juice

½ teaspoon salt

¼ teaspoon freshly ground
 black pepper

*Tiny pasta shells replace the usual bulgur wheat in this
tabbouleh salad variation. It's perfect as a light summer
meal or a flavorful side dish.*

1. Bring a 4-quart pot of water to a rolling boil. Add the
pasta, and cook according to package directions.

2. While the water is heating up, place the mint, tomato,
and scallions in a medium-sized bowl, and toss to mix. Set
aside.

3. Drain the pasta; then return it to the pot and cover with
ice water. Let sit for 5 to 7 minutes to chill. *Drain very well.*

4. Add the pasta, lemon juice, salt, and black pepper to
the tomato mixture, and toss together well.

5. Divide the salad greens among 4 individual plates. Top
with the tabbouleh and serve.

NUTRITIONAL FACTS (PER SERVING)

Calories: 193 Carbohydrates: 39.5 g Cholesterol: 0 mg Fat: 1 g Fiber: 4.5 g Protein: 7.5 g Sodium: 326 mg

CREAMY DILLED CUCUMBER SALAD

TIME: 20 minutes   **YIELD:** 4 servings

A summertime classic, this refreshing salad is wonderful with everything from sandwiches to grilled meats.

1. Place the cucumbers and onion in a large bowl, and toss to mix well. Set aside.

2. Place all of the remaining ingredients in a small bowl, and stir to mix well.

3. Add the sour cream mixture to the cucumbers, and mix well. Serve immediately, or cover and chill until ready to serve.

MAIN INGREDIENTS

4 medium-large cucumbers, peeled and sliced ⅛-inch thick

½ cup plus 2 tablespoons light sour cream

2 tablespoons chopped fresh dill, or 2 teaspoons dried

STAPLES

½ cup thinly slivered onion

¼ teaspoon freshly ground black pepper

⅛ teaspoon salt

NUTRITIONAL FACTS (PER SERVING)

Calories: 75 Carbohydrates: 11 g Cholesterol: 7.5 mg Fat: 2.5 g Fiber: 2.5 g Protein: 4 g Sodium: 97 mg

FRESH CITRUS SALAD

TIME: 15 minutes   **YIELD:** 4 servings

MAIN INGREDIENTS

2 cans (11 ounces each)
  Mandarin oranges, undrained

1 large grapefruit, peeled and
  cut into bite-sized pieces*

1 small cucumber, unpeeled
  and thinly sliced

8 cherry tomatoes, halved

¼ cup fat-free Italian salad
  dressing

2 tablespoons chopped fresh
  parsley

STAPLES

1 small red onion, thinly sliced

1 tablespoon honey

¼ teaspoon freshly ground
  black pepper

* You can also use 2 cups of the
  bottled grapefruit sections found
  in the refrigerated foods section
  of most grocery stores.

A refreshing blend of citrus fruits and fresh vegetables makes this salad the perfect lunch on a hot summer day. As this salad is best served chilled, keep the canned Mandarin oranges and the other ingredients refrigerated before preparing.

1. Drain and reserve the juice from the mandarin oranges. Place the oranges, grapefruit, cucumber, tomatoes, and onion in a large bowl, and toss to mix well. Set aside.

2. To make the dressing, place the reserved orange juice in a small bowl. Add all of the remaining ingredients, and stir to mix well.

3. Pour the dressing over the citrus mixture, and toss well. Serve immediately, or cover and chill until ready to serve.

NUTRITIONAL FACTS (PER SERVING)

Calories: 159 Carbohydrates: 40.5 g Cholesterol: 0 mg Fat: 0.5 g Fiber: 3 g Protein: 2 g Sodium: 160 mg

FRESH MOZZARELLA AND TOMATO SALAD

TIME: 30 minutes   **YIELD:** 4 servings

The longer this salad marinates, the better it tastes. To reduce preparation time even further, you can use your favorite fat-free Italian salad dressing instead of the one given below.

1. Place the mozzarella, tomatoes, scallions, celery, basil, and, if desired, the olives in a medium-sized bowl, and toss to mix well. Set aside.

2. To make the dressing, place all of the remaining ingredients in a small bowl, and stir to mix well.

3. Pour the dressing over the salad, and toss well. Cover and chill for at least 10 minutes before serving.

MAIN INGREDIENTS

1 pound fat-free mozzarella cheese, cut into ½-inch cubes

6 medium plum tomatoes, quartered lengthwise and cut into pieces

2 large scallions, finely chopped

2 medium celery stalks, thinly sliced

½ cup chopped fresh basil

8 pitted black olives, halved (optional)

STAPLES

¼ cup plus 2 tablespoons balsamic or white wine vinegar*

¼ cup water

1 teaspoon garlic powder

1 teaspoon dried oregano

½ teaspoon dried rosemary

¼ teaspoon freshly ground black pepper

¼ teaspoon salt (optional)

* As red balsamic vinegar tends to turn the mozzarella cheese "gray," use white wine vinegar if you wish to keep the cheese white.

NUTRITIONAL FACTS (PER SERVING)

Calories: 195 Carbohydrates: 16 g Cholesterol: 20.5 mg Fat: 0.5g Fiber: 2 g Protein: 30 g Sodium: 925 mg

LEMON-DILL TUNA PLATTER

TIME: 15 minutes   **YIELD:** 4 servings

COMPLETE MEAL

MAIN INGREDIENTS

2 cans (12 ounces each) solid
   white water-packed tuna,
   well drained

2 cans (15 ounces each) sliced
   beets, well drained

2 cups loosely packed Chinese
   snow pea pods

24 fresh baby carrots

2 small lemons, cut into wedges

STAPLES

1 cup fresh lemon juice

1 teaspoon dried dill

¼ teaspoon freshly ground
   black pepper

This lemony fresh tuna salad, surrounded by colorful vegetables, is perfect hot-weather fare. We like the crisp snap of fresh baby carrots and Chinese snow pea pods, but feel free to accompany this tuna with the vegetables of your choice. As this dish is best served chilled, keep the tuna and beets refrigerated before preparing.

1. Place the tuna in a medium-sized bowl, and flake with a fork.

2. Make the dressing by placing the lemon juice, dill, and black pepper in a small bowl, and stir to mix well. Pour the dressing over the tuna, and toss to mix well.

3. On the center of each of 4 serving plates, arrange a fourth of the beet slices in a circle. Mound even amounts of tuna in the middle of each circle. Border with ½ cup of the pea pods and 6 carrots. Garnish with the lemon wedges, and serve.

NUTRITIONAL FACTS (PER SERVING)

Calories: 343 Carbohydrates: 32.5 g Cholesterol: 72 mg Fat: 6 g Fiber: 7.5 g Protein: 44.5 g Sodium: 718 mg

LEMONY SCALLOP SALAD

TIME: 20 minutes

YIELD: 4 servings

This simple yet lovely luncheon entrée is the perfect choice when you're entertaining guests.

1. Preheat the oven broiler.

2. Place the lemon juice, garlic, oregano, and black pepper in a small bowl, and stir to mix. Set aside.

3. Divide the scallops into 4 portions, and thread each portion onto a skewer.* Brush both sides of the scallops with the lemon mixture.

4. Place the scallops under the broiler, about 4 inches below the heat source. Broil, occasionally basting with the remaining lemon mixture, for 3 to 4 minutes; then turn the scallops over, and continue to broil and baste for another 3 to 4 minutes, or until the scallops are no longer translucent.

5. Divide the salad greens among 4 individual salad plates. Arrange the onion rings and tomato wedges over the greens. Top each serving with a skewer of scallops. Serve with lemon wedges.

* If using wooden skewers, be sure to soak them in water for 30 minutes before using.

COMPLETE MEAL

MAIN INGREDIENTS

1½ pounds sea scallops

8 cups packaged, precut mixed salad greens

1 medium tomato, cut into wedges

1 lemon, cut into wedges

STAPLES

1 cup lemon juice

2 cloves garlic, minced

½ teaspoon dried oregano

¼ teaspoon freshly ground black pepper

1 medium red onion, thinly sliced into rings

NUTRITIONAL FACTS (PER SERVING)

Calories: 204 Carbohydrates: 17 g Cholesterol: 56 mg Fat: 1.5 g Fiber: 3 g Protein: 31.5 g Sodium: 306 mg

MEDITERRANEAN COUSCOUS SALAD WITH CHICKPEAS

TIME: 30 minutes   YIELD: 4 servings

COMPLETE MEAL

MAIN INGREDIENTS

1⅓ cups couscous

1½ cups canned chickpeas, rinsed and drained

1 cup chopped green bell pepper

¼ cup sliced black olives

2 ounces reduced-fat feta cheese, crumbled (about ⅔ cup), optional

STAPLES

2 cups water

⅔ cup chopped red onion

¼ cup plus 2 tablespoons fresh lemon juice

1 tablespoon olive oil

½ teaspoon dried oregano

½ teaspoon freshly ground black pepper

This Mediterranean-inspired salad makes a great vegetarian entrée. Or serve it as a hearty side dish.

1. Place the water in a 1-quart saucepan, and bring to a boil over high heat. Stir in the couscous and cover. Remove from the heat, and allow to sit for 5 minutes, or until all of the water has been absorbed.

2. Transfer the couscous to a large bowl, and chill for 5 minutes.

3. Add the chickpeas, green pepper, olives, and onion to the couscous, and toss to mix. Set aside.

4. Place the lemon juice and olive oil in a small dish, and stir to mix well. Add to the couscous mixture along with the oregano, black pepper, and feta cheese, if desired. Toss to mix well.

5. Serve immediately, or cover and chill until ready to serve.

NUTRITIONAL FACTS (PER SERVING)

Calories: 403 Carbohydrates: 67.5 g Cholesterol: 5 mg Fat: 6.5 g Fiber: 10 g Protein: 15 g Sodium: 404 mg

ORZO WITH MUSTARD-THYME DRESSING

TIME: 20 minutes

YIELD: 4 servings

Be sure to save any leftovers of this cold pasta salad to enjoy the next day.

1. Bring a 4-quart pot of water to a rolling boil. Add the orzo, and cook according to package directions.

2. While the water is heating up, make the dressing by placing the broth, vinegar, mustard, and thyme in a medium-sized bowl, and stir with a whisk to mix well. Set aside.

3. Drain the cooked orzo, return it to the pot, and cover with ice water. Let stand for 5 minutes to chill.

4. Drain the chilled pasta well, and add it to the dressing, along with the scallions and red pepper. Toss to coat evenly. Serve as is or over a bed of crisp salad greens.

MAIN INGREDIENTS

2 cups orzo pasta

3 scallions, thinly sliced

½ cup red bell pepper, seeded and cut into small strips

STAPLES

1½ cups reduced-sodium, fat-free chicken broth

2 tablespoons red wine vinegar

2 teaspoons Dijon-style mustard

1 teaspoon dried thyme

NUTRITIONAL FACTS (PER SERVING)

Calories: 338 Carbohydrates: 66 g Cholesterol: 0 mg Fat: 1.5 g Fiber: 3 g Protein: 14 g Sodium: 137 mg

SOUTHWEST RICE AND SMOKED TURKEY SALAD

TIME: 35 minutes   **YIELD:** 4 servings

COMPLETE MEAL

MAIN INGREDIENTS

1½ cups instant brown rice

2 cups cubed reduced-sodium, low-fat smoked turkey breast (about 10 ounces)

1 large tomato, diced

1 cup matchstick-size pieces green bell pepper

1 cup canned whole kernel corn, drained

STAPLES

1½ cups water

½ cup chopped red onion

2 tablespoons plus 2 teaspoons rice vinegar

1 tablespoon olive oil

1 tablespoon Dijon-style mustard

1 teaspoon ground cumin

½ teaspoon freshly ground black pepper

¼ teaspoon cayenne pepper

Pieces of smoked turkey, kernels of golden corn, and a dressing sparked with cumin and cayenne give this spicy salad its southwestern flair.

1. Place the water in a 1-quart saucepan, and bring to a boil over high heat. Stir in the rice and cover. Reduce the heat to medium-low, and cook for 10 minutes, or until all of the water has been absorbed.

2. Transfer the rice to a small bowl, and chill for 10 minutes, or until ready to use.

3. Place the rice, turkey, tomato, green pepper, corn, and onion in a large bowl, and toss to mix well. Set aside.

4. To make the dressing, place all of the remaining ingredients in a small dish, and beat until well mixed. Pour the dressing over the salad, and toss to mix well.

5. Serve immediately, or cover and chill until ready to serve.

NUTRITIONAL FACTS (PER SERVING)

Calories: 314 Carbohydrates: 41.5 g Cholesterol: 31.5 mg Fat: 8 g Fiber: 4 g Protein: 20.5 g Sodium: 627 mg

TUSCAN TUNA SALAD

TIME: 20 minutes   YIELD: 4 servings

Use the sweetest onion, the most aromatic basil, and the best-quality olive oil for this Mediterranean-inspired dish, and you will have a truly memorable meal in minutes.

1. Place the beans and olive oil in a large bowl, and toss until the beans are lightly coated with the oil.

2. Add all of the remaining ingredients to the beans, and gently toss to mix. Avoid breaking up the beans or mashing the tuna.

3. Divide the salad among individual plates and serve at room temperature, topping each portion with an extra squeeze of lemon and grinding of pepper, if desired.

COMPLETE MEAL

MAIN INGREDIENTS

2 cans (1 pound each) cannellini beans (white kidney beans), rinsed and drained

12-ounce can solid white water-packed tuna, well drained

⅓–½ cup thinly sliced fresh basil

Juice of 1 lemon (about 2 tablespoons)

STAPLES

1 tablespoon olive oil

½ medium sweet Vidalia or red onion, halved lengthwise and thinly sliced

½ teaspoon freshly ground black pepper

NUTRITIONAL FACTS (PER SERVING)

Calories: 348 Carbohydrates: 38 g Cholesterol: 36 mg Fat: 6 g Fiber: 10 g Protein: 35 g Sodium: 1,122 mg

5. PASTA POTPOURRI

Pasta. It's fast and easy to make. It's naturally low in fat. And everybody loves it. If ever there was a friend of the kitchen-quickies cook, pasta is it.

This chapter is a celebration of pasta in its many forms and guises. As both of us are long-time pasta lovers—Marie was raised on it!—it certainly came as no surprise to us that so many delicious, healthful pasta dishes could be made in under forty-five minutes. That's why we found it so easy to create dishes designed to suit every taste and fancy. Looking for a dish for the seafood lover in your house? Try Linguine with White Clam Sauce. Redolent with garlic and spiced with crushed red pepper, this is sure to become a favorite. Prefer poultry? In half an hour, your family can enjoy Fusilli with Chicken, a savory blend of white meat chicken, spinach, and other flavorful ingredients served over fusilli pasta. Tired of the same old pasta shapes? Gnocchi—light little potato dumplings that can be easily found in grocery and gourmet stores—make a wonderful change of pace, es-

pecially when topped with a flavorful, fast-to-make meat sauce. And on those hot summer days when you don't feel like cooking even a fast sauce, try Linguine with Fresh Tomato Sauce, a dish made both colorful and flavorful with a garden-fresh no-cook topping. Other possibilities include Linguine with Spicy Red Pepper Sauce, Greek Isle Pasta, and Penne from Heaven. The variations are endless—and delicious!

If we haven't yet convinced you that pasta is the ultimate fast food, consider this: Most of the dishes in this chapter are complete meals. This means that you don't have to spend time making side dishes, because your entrée is already bursting with vegetables, legumes, and, of course, grains. Add just a loaf of good Italian bread, and perhaps a simple green salad topped with a light dressing, and dinner is ready. Fast food, indeed!

So take out your pasta pot, select a few simple ingredients, and get ready for a treat. Pasta; we love it!

BOW TIES WITH ARTICHOKE HEARTS AND SUNDRIED TOMATOES

TIME: 30 minutes   **YIELD:** 4 servings

COMPLETE MEAL

MAIN INGREDIENTS

1 pound bow tie pasta
(farfalle)

⅔ cup thinly sliced sundried
tomatoes

2 cans (14 ounces each)
artichoke hearts, drained

¼ cup chopped fresh parsley

Grated Parmesan cheese
(optional)

STAPLES

2 teaspoons olive oil

6 large cloves garlic, minced

2 cups reduced-sodium, fat-free
chicken broth, divided

¼ teaspoon freshly ground
black pepper

Juicy artichokes and slices of sundried tomatoes are spotlighted in this garlicky pasta dish.

1. Bring a 4-quart pot of water to a rolling boil. Add the pasta, and cook according to package directions.

2. While the water is heating up, coat a deep 12-inch non-stick skillet with cooking spray, add the oil, and preheat over medium heat. Add the garlic, and cook, stirring often, for 1 to 2 minutes, or until soft but not brown.

3. Add the sundried tomatoes, artichoke hearts, and 2 or 3 tablespoons of the broth to the skillet. Toss well to mix, and reduce the heat to low. Simmer the ingredients gently as the pasta cooks.

4. When the pasta is almost cooked, add the remaining broth to the skillet along with the parsley and black pepper. Increase the heat to medium, and continue to heat.

5. Drain the pasta well, and return it to the pot. Add the sauce, and toss well to coat.

6. Spoon the pasta into individual serving dishes and serve immediately, as is or topped with a sprinkling of Parmesan cheese.

NUTRITIONAL FACTS (PER SERVING)

Calories: 576 Carbohydrates: 114.5 g Cholesterol: 0 mg Fat: 5 g Fiber: 17 g Protein: 22 g Sodium: 407 mg

BROCCOLI MACARONI

TIME: 30 minutes

YIELD: 4 servings

It takes just a few minutes to thaw the broccoli for this flavorful pasta dish. For tips on quick thawing, see page 10.

1. Bring a 4-quart pot of water to a rolling boil. Add the pasta, and cook according to package directions.

2. While the water is heating up, coat a deep 12-inch non-stick skillet with cooking spray, add the oil, and preheat over medium-low heat. Add the garlic, and cook, stirring often, for 1 to 2 minutes, or until soft but not brown.

3. Add the broccoli, tomatoes, Parmesan cheese, and black pepper to the skillet. Mix well, increase the heat to medium, and cook for 5 minutes, stirring occasionally.

4. Add the broth to the skillet, and increase the heat to high. Bring to a boil; then reduce the heat to low and simmer for 7 to 10 minutes.

5. Drain the pasta well, and add it to the skillet. Toss to mix well.

6. Spoon the pasta into individual serving dishes, and serve immediately.

COMPLETE MEAL

MAIN INGREDIENTS

1 pound medium shell pasta

10-ounce box frozen broccoli, thawed, well drained, and cut into bite-sized pieces

4 large plum tomatoes, diced

2 tablespoons grated Parmesan cheese

STAPLES

2 teaspoons olive oil

4 large cloves garlic, crushed

¼ teaspoon freshly ground black pepper

2 cups reduced-sodium, fat-free chicken broth

NUTRITIONAL FACTS (PER SERVING)

Calories: 544 Carbohydrates: 99.5 g Cholesterol: 2.5 mg Fat: 6 g Fiber: 7 g Protein: 23 g Sodium: 170 mg

CHICKEN AND MUSHROOM MARINARA

TIME: 45 minutes   YIELD: 4 servings

COMPLETE MEAL

MAIN INGREDIENTS

2 cups packaged, presliced
   mushrooms

28-ounce can crushed tomatoes
   in purée

½ cup coarsely chopped fresh
   basil

1 pound chicken breast cutlets

1 pound angel hair pasta

STAPLES

1 tablespoon olive oil

6 large cloves garlic, chopped

1 cup water

1 tablespoon dried oregano

¼ teaspoon freshly ground
   black pepper

¼ teaspoon salt (optional)

Be sure to save any extra sauce from this dish and use it to dress up baked potatoes, steamed vegetables, or egg white omelets.

1. Coat a deep 12-inch nonstick skillet with cooking spray, add the oil, and preheat over medium heat. Add the garlic, and cook, stirring often, for 1 to 2 minutes, or until soft but not brown. Toss in the mushrooms, and continue to sauté for 2 minutes.

2. Stir the crushed tomatoes, water, basil, oregano, black pepper, and salt, if desired, into the skillet. Increase the heat to high, and bring to a boil. Reduce the heat to low, and simmer uncovered.

3. Slice the chicken breasts into thin strips. Stir the chicken into the sauce, and continue to simmer.

4. While the sauce simmers, bring a 4-quart pot of water to a rolling boil. Add the pasta, and cook according to package directions.

5. Drain the pasta well, and return it to the pot. Top with half the sauce, and toss well. Spoon the pasta into individual dishes, top with additional sauce and chicken, and serve immediately.

NUTRITIONAL FACTS (PER SERVING)

Calories: 750 Carbohydrates: 119.5 g Cholesterol: 66 mg Fat: 7 g Fiber: 16.5 g Protein: 49 g Sodium: 698 mg

DITALINI WITH PEAS

TIME: 30 minutes   YIELD: 4 servings

Sautéed bits of onion add just the right touch of sweetness to this hearty pasta dish. For a tasty variation, try adding some thinly sliced strips of prosciutto or other ham.

1. Bring a 4-quart pot of water to a rolling boil. Add the pasta, and cook according to package directions.

2. While the water is heating up, coat a 12-inch nonstick skillet with cooking spray, add the oil, and preheat over medium-low heat. Add the onion, and cook, stirring occasionally, for 2 to 3 minutes, or until soft.

3. Add the undrained sweet peas, broth, and black pepper to the skillet, and stir well. Reduce the heat to low, and simmer uncovered as the pasta cooks, stirring occasionally.

4. Drain the pasta well, and add it to the skillet. Stir to mix well.

5. Spoon the pasta into individual serving dishes and serve immediately, as is or topped with a sprinkling of Parmesan cheese.

COMPLETE MEAL

MAIN INGREDIENTS

3 cups (12 ounces) ditalini (tubetti) pasta

15-ounce can sweet peas, undrained

Grated Parmesan cheese (optional)

STAPLES

2 teaspoons olive oil

1 cup chopped onion

2 cups reduced-sodium, fat-free chicken broth

¼ teaspoon freshly ground black pepper

NUTRITIONAL FACTS (PER SERVING)

Calories: 382 Carbohydrates: 69.5 g Cholesterol: 0 mg Fat: 3.5 g Fiber: 6 g Protein: 16.5 g Sodium: 424 mg

Pasta Shapes

Part of pasta's universal appeal comes from its endless variety of shapes and sizes. Basically, pasta types fall into one of three main categories: long, short, and fancy shapes. Long pastas include spaghetti and spaghetti-type pastas like linguine, angel hair, and fusilli. Penne, ditalini, and ziti are examples of short pastas, while bow ties and shells fall into the fancy category.

Most pasta is enjoyed tossed with a sauce; however, very small pasta like small shells and orzo, and long, very thin pasta like angel hair are great additions to soups. Other pasta, like large shells, are commonly stuffed with a meat, cheese, or vegetable filling before they are topped with a sauce and served.

We have used the following pasta types in this book:

Angel hair (capellini). Very fine spaghetti-type pasta.

Elbows. Small, slightly curved tubes of pasta, often used in macaroni-and-cheese casseroles.

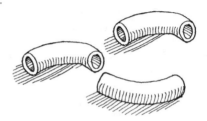

Bow ties (farfalle). Pasta that resembles bow ties. The literal translation is "butterflies."

Fettuccine. Flat, spaghetti-type pasta thicker than linguine.

Ditalini (tubetti). Small, short, tube-shaped pasta.

Fusilli. Gently spiraled, long spaghetti-type pasta.

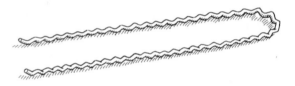

Gnocchi. Tiny dumplings generally made from potatoes or semolina flour.

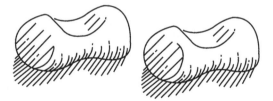

Linguine. Flat spaghetti-type pasta thinner than fettuccine.

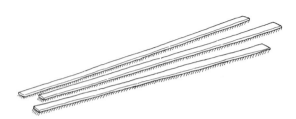

Orzo. Elongated rice-shaped pasta, often used in place of rice. Also popular in soups.

Penne. Tube-shaped pasta, about two inches long with diagonally cut ends. It comes in two varieties: grooved (rigati) and smooth (lisci).

Shells (maruzze). Shell-shaped pasta, which comes in different sizes.

Spaghetti. Long, round lengths of pasta, which come in assorted thicknesses.

Tortellini. Tiny pasta pockets filled with meat, cheese, or vegetables.

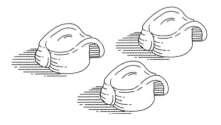

Ziti. Gently curved, smooth tube-shaped pasta, approximately two inches long.

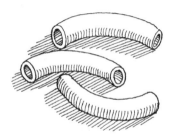

FAST AND HEARTY PASTA WITH LENTILS

TIME: 25 minutes

YIELD: 4 servings

COMPLETE MEAL

MAIN INGREDIENTS

1 pound small shell pasta

19-ounce can lentil soup*

¼ cup grated Parmesan cheese

STAPLES

½ teaspoon garlic powder

¼ teaspoon freshly ground black pepper

* Progresso brand is a good choice.

This dish is as delicious as it is fast and easy to make. Keep these ingredients in the pantry, and you'll be able to pull together a satisfying meal in minutes.

1. Bring a 4-quart pot of water to a rolling boil. Add the pasta, and cook according to package directions.

2. While the water is heating up, place the soup in a 1-quart saucepan and cook over medium heat, stirring occasionally until hot. Stir in the garlic powder and black pepper.

3. Drain the pasta well, and return it to the pot. Pour the soup on top, and toss well.

4. Spoon the pasta into individual dishes. Top each with a tablespoon of Parmesan, and serve immediately.

NUTRITIONAL FACTS (PER SERVING)

Calories: 567 Carbohydrates: 105 g Cholesterol: 5 mg Fat: 5 g Fiber: 8 g Protein: 23.5 g Sodium: 539 mg

FUSILLI WITH CHICKEN

TIME: 30 minutes

YIELD: 4 servings

Garlicky pasta complete with fresh spinach and pieces of juicy chicken makes for a delicious and satisfying meal. Sometimes we add a handful of pignoli (pine) nuts to make this dish really special.

1. Bring a 4-quart pot of water to a rolling boil. Add the pasta, and cook according to package instructions.

2. While the water is heating up, sprinkle the chicken cutlets with the garlic powder and place them in the bottom of a large saucepan. Add just enough water to cover, and bring to a boil over high heat. Then immediately reduce the heat to low, cover, and simmer for 7 to 10 minutes, or until no longer pink inside when cut with a knife. Transfer the chicken to a plate, and cool for about 5 minutes.

3. Discard the poaching water from the pot, and add the chicken broth and chopped garlic. Bring to a boil over high heat; then reduce the heat to low and add the spinach.

4. Cut the chicken into bite-sized pieces, and add it to the pot. Simmer gently until the pasta is ready.

5. Drain the pasta, and return it to the cooking pot. Pour the chicken-spinach mixture on top, and toss.

6. Spoon the pasta into individual serving dishes and serve immediately, as is or topped with a sprinkling of Parmesan cheese.

COMPLETE MEAL

MAIN INGREDIENTS

1 pound fusilli pasta

12 ounces boneless, skinless chicken breasts

4 cups (loosely packed) coarsely chopped packaged, prewashed spinach

Grated Parmesan cheese (optional)

STAPLES

1 teaspoon garlic powder

2 cups reduced-sodium, fat-free chicken broth

4 large cloves garlic, coarsely chopped

NUTRITIONAL FACTS (PER SERVING)

Calories: 566 Carbohydrates: 92 g Cholesterol: 49 mg Fat: 3.5 g Fiber: 9.5 g Protein: 39.5 g Sodium: 168 mg

GREEK ISLE PASTA

TIME: 30 minutes   **YIELD:** 4 servings

COMPLETE MEAL

MAIN INGREDIENTS

1 pound ziti pasta

12 ounces 93% lean ground beef

29-ounce can crushed tomatoes in purée

14.5-ounce can low-sodium tomato sauce

Crumbled feta cheese (optional)

STAPLES

2 teaspoons olive oil

½ cup chopped onion

2 tablespoons minced garlic

½ cup water

2 teaspoons dried oregano

1 teaspoon ground cinnamon

¼ teaspoon allspice

A hint of cinnamon gives this pasta—a variation of classic Greek-style pastitsio—its unusual flavor.

1. Bring a 4-quart pot of water to a rolling boil. Add the pasta, and cook according to package directions.

2. While the water is heating up, coat another 4-quart pot with cooking spray, add the oil, and preheat over medium-low heat. Add the onion and garlic, and cook, stirring often, for 1 to 2 minutes, or until the onion and garlic begin to soften.

3. Increase the heat to medium, and add the ground beef. Cook, stirring to crumble, for about 4 minutes, or until no pink remains.

4. Add the crushed tomatoes, tomato sauce, water, oregano, cinnamon, and allspice to the beef, and stir to mix. Bring to a boil; then reduce the heat to low and simmer uncovered, stirring occasionally, as the pasta cooks.

5. Drain the pasta, and return it to the cooking pot. Top with half the sauce, and toss well. Spoon the pasta into individual serving dishes, top with additional sauce, and serve immediately, as is or topped with crumbled feta cheese.

NUTRITIONAL FACTS (PER SERVING)

Calories: 666 Carbohydrates: 109 g Cholesterol: 53 mg Fat: 7.5 g Fiber: 10 g Protein: 39.5 g Sodium: 375 mg

LINGUINE WITH FRESH TOMATO SAUCE

TIME: 45 minutes

YIELD: 4 servings

This is a great dish to serve in the summertime, when tomatoes are ripe and bursting with fresh flavor.

1. Place the tomatoes, scallions, basil, and garlic in a large bowl, and toss to mix well.

2. Place the vinegar and oil in a small dish, and stir to mix. Add the vinegar mixture and the pepper to the tomato mixture, and toss well to mix. Cover and allow to sit at room temperature for at least 20 minutes, stirring occasionally.

3. While the tomato mixture is marinating, bring a 4-quart pot of water to a rolling boil. Add the pasta, and cook according to package directions.

4. Drain the pasta well, and add it to the tomato mixture. Toss to mix well.

5. Spoon the pasta into individual serving dishes and serve immediately, as is or topped with a sprinkling of Parmesan cheese.

COMPLETE MEAL

MAIN INGREDIENTS

5 medium tomatoes (about 1½ pounds), seeded and chopped

¼ cup chopped scallions

⅓ cup chopped fresh basil

1 pound linguine pasta

Grated Parmesan cheese (optional)

STAPLES

2 large cloves garlic, chopped

2 tablespoons balsamic vinegar

1 tablespoon olive oil

¼ teaspoon freshly ground black pepper

NUTRITIONAL FACTS (PER SERVING)

Calories: 519 Carbohydrates: 99 g Cholesterol: 0 mg Fat: 6 g Fiber: 10.5 g Protein: 17 g Sodium: 20 mg

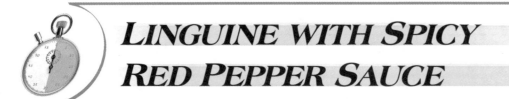

LINGUINE WITH SPICY RED PEPPER SAUCE

TIME: 30 minutes   YIELD: 4 servings

COMPLETE MEAL

MAIN INGREDIENTS

2 tablespoons crushed walnuts

1 pound linguine pasta

2 large red bell peppers, thinly sliced

4 large scallions, sliced

STAPLES

2 cups reduced-sodium, fat-free chicken broth

1 tablespoon plus 1 teaspoon red wine vinegar

1 tablespoon plus 1 teaspoon honey

½ teaspoon cayenne pepper

1 teaspoon salt (optional)

2 teaspoons olive oil

6 large cloves garlic, thinly sliced

For an even spicier version of this dish, add some crushed red pepper flakes.

1. Preheat an 8-inch nonstick skillet over medium heat. Add the walnuts and cook, stirring frequently, for 1 to 2 minutes, or until lightly toasted. Transfer the nuts to a plate to cool.

2. Place the broth, vinegar, honey, cayenne pepper, and salt, if desired, in a small bowl, and stir to mix. Set aside.

3. Bring a 4-quart pot of water to a rolling boil. Add the pasta, and cook according to package directions.

4. While the water is heating up, coat a 12-inch nonstick skillet with cooking spray, add the oil, and preheat over medium heat. Add the garlic and cook, stirring often, for 2 minutes, or until soft but not brown.

5. Increase the heat to high, and add the red bell peppers and half of the broth mixture to the skillet. Bring to a boil; then reduce the heat to low, cover, and simmer for 10 minutes. Stir in the scallions and the remaining broth mixture, and continue to simmer for 2 to 3 minutes, or until the peppers are just soft.

6. Drain the pasta, and add it to the skillet along with the toasted walnuts. Toss to mix well.

7. Spoon the pasta into individual serving dishes, and serve immediately.

NUTRITIONAL FACTS (PER SERVING)

Calories: 563 Carbohydrates: 104.5 g Cholesterol: 0 mg Fat: 7 g Fiber: 11 g Protein: 20.5 g Sodium: 96 mg

LINGUINE WITH WHITE CLAM SAUCE

TIME: 25 minutes

YIELD: 4 servings

This pasta is deliciously garlicky! For a less pungent dish, simply decrease the garlic to suit your taste.

1. Bring a 4-quart pot of water to a rolling boil. Add the pasta, and cook according to package directions.

2. While the water is heating up, coat a 2-quart pot with cooking spray, and preheat over medium heat. Add the garlic and cook, stirring often, for about 3 minutes, or until soft but not brown.

3. Add the clams and their juice to the pot, along with the black pepper, red pepper, oregano, and parsley. Cook, stirring often, for 5 to 10 minutes, or until the sauce is hot and the flavors are well blended.

4. Drain the pasta well, and return it to the cooking pot. Pour the clam sauce on top, and toss well.

5. Spoon the pasta into individual serving dishes, and serve immediately, as is or topped with a sprinkling of Parmesan cheese.

COMPLETE MEAL

MAIN INGREDIENTS

1 pound linguine pasta

2 cans (6.5 ounces each) chopped clams, undrained

2 tablespoons chopped fresh parsley

Grated Parmesan cheese (optional)

STAPLES

8 medium cloves garlic, thinly sliced

¼ teaspoon freshly ground black pepper

Pinch crushed red pepper

Pinch dried oregano

NUTRITIONAL FACTS (PER SERVING)

Calories: 483 Carbohydrates: 93 g Cholesterol: 14 mg Fat: 2 g Fiber: 10 g Protein: 21 g Sodium: 515 mg

PASTA FAGIOLI

TIME: 30 minutes   YIELD: 4 servings

COMPLETE MEAL

MAIN INGREDIENTS

2 cups (8 ounces) ditalini
(tubetti) pasta

2 cans (10.5 ounces each)
cannellini beans (white
kidney beans), rinsed
and drained

2 cups low-sodium tomato
sauce

Grated Parmesan cheese
(optional)

STAPLES

1 tablespoon olive oil

4 cloves garlic, minced

1½ cups water

¼ teaspoon freshly ground
black pepper

*This pasta-with-beans dish is a stick-to-the-ribs Italian classic.
Be sure to save any leftovers to enjoy the next day.*

1. Bring a 4-quart pot of water to a rolling boil. Add the
pasta, and cook according to package directions.

2. While the water is heating up, coat a 12-inch nonstick
skillet with cooking spray, add the oil, and preheat over
medium-low heat. Add the garlic, and cook, stirring often,
for 1 to 2 minutes, or until soft but not brown.

3. Increase the heat to high, and stir the beans, tomato
sauce, water, and black pepper into the skillet. Bring to a
boil; then reduce the heat to low, and simmer uncovered
while the pasta cooks, stirring occasionally.

4. Drain the pasta, and add it to the skillet. Toss to mix
well.

5. Spoon the pasta into individual serving dishes, and
serve immediately, as is or topped with a sprinkling of
Parmesan cheese.

NUTRITIONAL FACTS (PER SERVING)

Calories: 391 Carbohydrates: 71.5 g Cholesterol: 0 mg Fat: 5 g Fiber: 9.5 g Protein: 14.5 g Sodium: 200 mg

PENNE FROM HEAVEN

TIME: 30 minutes   YIELD: 4 servings

A light sauce made of juicy plum tomatoes and garden-fresh basil gives character to this heavenly pasta dish.

1. Bring a 4-quart pot of water to a rolling boil. Add the pasta, and cook according to package directions.

2. While the water is heating up, coat a 12-inch nonstick skillet with cooking spray, add the oil, and preheat over medium-low heat. Add the garlic, and cook, stirring often, for 1 to 2 minutes, or until soft but not brown.

3. Add the tomatoes to the skillet and mix well. Stir in the broth, increase the heat to high, and bring to a boil. Reduce the heat to low and simmer for 15 minutes, or until the pasta is cooked.

4. Drain the pasta and add it to the skillet along with the basil. Toss to mix well.

5. Spoon the pasta into individual serving dishes, and serve immediately, as is or topped with a sprinkling of Parmesan cheese.

COMPLETE MEAL

MAIN INGREDIENTS

1 pound penne pasta

8 large plum tomatoes, coarsely chopped

¼ cup coarsely chopped fresh basil

Grated Parmesan cheese (optional)

STAPLES

2 teaspoons olive oil

6 large cloves garlic, minced

2 cups reduced-sodium, fat-free vegetable broth

NUTRITIONAL FACTS (PER SERVING)

Calories: 473 Carbohydrates: 91 g Cholesterol: 0 mg Fat: 5 g Fiber: 5.5 g Protein: 16.5 g Sodium: 515 mg

Making the Most of Basil

Basil is a wonderful herb that instantly adds vivid color and a distinctive Mediterranean flavor and aroma to a wide variety of dishes. In this book, we use it in salads, sandwiches, sauces, and more. Because basil loses much of its punch and all of its color when dried, we always try to use it fresh. But like all produce, basil is perishable. These simple guidelines will help you make the most of your basil.

❏ To keep a purchased bunch of basil at its freshest, place the stems in water in a tall glass or jar as soon as you bring your produce home. Then cover the leaves with a plastic bag and refrigerate until ready to use.

❏ If you know that you're going to use the basil leaves within a few hours, remove them from the stems, and rinse them carefully under cool running water, being sure to wash away any sand or dirt. Dry the leaves completely, seal them in plastic bags, and refrigerate until ready to use.

❏ When chopped fresh basil is called for in a recipe, use the following method to get the job done quickly and easily. First, stack the fresh leaves and tightly roll them into a cylinder. Then use a very sharp knife to thinly slice the rolled

basil. Use these julienned strips as is, or chop them further, if desired.

❏ If you can't use all of the basil you've purchased—which is very often the case—don't toss that extra basil away. (It's too good!) Instead, freeze the washed and thoroughly dried leaves on baking sheets, transfer them to a sealed plastic bag, and keep them in the freezer until ready to use. Although the leaves will turn black during the freezing process, they can still add a marvelous flavor to cooked sauces and soups.

Keep in mind that basil is easy to grow in a sunny spot in your garden, or even on a sunny windowsill. By growing your own basil, you'll be able to enjoy its unique qualities at a moment's notice.

POTATO GNOCCHI WITH QUICK MEAT SAUCE

TIME: 45 minutes
YIELD: 4 servings

These plump Italian potato dumplings are light yet filling. Many major grocery stores and gourmet shops carry both fresh and frozen varieties.

1. Coat a 4-quart pot with cooking spray, add the oil, and preheat over medium heat. Add the onion and garlic, and cook, stirring often, for 2 to 3 minutes, or until the onion begins to soften.

2. Add the ground beef and cook for about 4 minutes, stirring to crumble, until no pink remains.

3. Stir in the crushed tomatoes, tomato sauce, water, oregano, garlic powder, and black pepper. Increase the heat to high, and bring to a boil. Then reduce the heat to low, and simmer uncovered for 30 minutes, stirring occasionally.

4. After the sauce has been simmering for 10 to 15 minutes, bring a 4-quart pot of water to a rolling boil. Add the gnocchi, and cook for 2 to 3 minutes, or until they float to the top.

5. Drain the gnocchi, and divide them among individual serving bowls. Top with the sauce and serve.

COMPLETE MEAL

MAIN INGREDIENTS

12 ounces 93% lean ground beef

29-ounce can crushed tomatoes in purée

2 cans (8 ounces each) low-sodium tomato sauce

1½ pounds gnocchi

STAPLES

2 teaspoons olive oil

½ cup chopped onion

2 tablespoons minced garlic

½ cup water

2 teaspoons dried oregano

2 teaspoons garlic powder

¼ teaspoon freshly ground black pepper

NUTRITIONAL FACTS (PER SERVING)

Calories: 570 Carbohydrates: 85 g Cholesterol: 71.5 mg Fat: 7.5 g Fiber: 9 g Protein: 38 g Sodium: 1,290 mg

SPAGHETTI WITH ZUCCHINI

TIME: 30 minutes

YIELD: 4 servings

COMPLETE MEAL

MAIN INGREDIENTS

1 pound spaghetti

4 medium zucchini (about 3 pounds)

½ cup chopped fresh basil

Grated Parmesan cheese (optional)

STAPLES

2 teaspoons olive oil

6 large cloves garlic, minced

¼ teaspoon freshly ground black pepper

2 cups reduced-sodium, fat-free chicken broth

Keep this simple spaghetti dish in mind when your summer garden is overflowing with ripe zucchini.

1. Bring a 4-quart pot of water to a rolling boil. Add the spaghetti, and cook according to package directions.

2. While the water is heating up, scrub the zucchini well and cut them into 1-inch-thick rounds. Set aside.

3. Coat a 12-inch nonstick skillet with cooking spray, add the oil, and preheat over medium heat. Add the garlic, and cook, stirring often, for 1 to 2 minutes, or until soft but not brown.

4. Add the zucchini, black pepper, and chicken broth to the skillet, and mix well. Increase the heat to high, and bring to a boil. Then reduce the heat to low, stir in the basil, cover, and simmer for 5 to 7 minutes, or until the zucchini is soft.

5. Drain the pasta, and add it to the skillet. Toss to mix well.

6. Spoon the pasta into individual serving dishes, and serve immediately, as is or topped with a sprinkling of Parmesan cheese.

NUTRITIONAL FACTS (PER SERVING)

Calories: 515 Carbohydrates: 96.5 g Cholesterol: 0 mg Fat: 4.5 g Fiber: 11 g Protein: 21.5 g Sodium: 95 mg

TUSCAN-STYLE FUSILLI

TIME: 30 minutes   YIELD: 4 servings

*Juicy tomatoes, plump cannellini beans, and fresh spinach
are spotlighted in this very garlicky pasta dish.*

1. Bring a 4-quart pot of water to a rolling boil. Add the
pasta, and cook according to package directions.

2. While the water is heating up, coat a 12-inch nonstick
skillet with cooking spray, add the oil, and preheat over
medium heat. Add the garlic and cook, stirring often, for 1
to 2 minutes, or until soft but not brown.

3. Add the tomatoes and beans to the skillet, and toss to
mix. Cook, stirring constantly, for 2 to 3 minutes, or until the
tomatoes begin to soften.

4. Add the spinach, broth, garlic powder, and black pepper to the skillet, and stir to mix. Increase the heat to high,
and bring to a boil. Then reduce the heat to low and simmer, stirring occasionally, for 10 to 12 minutes while the
pasta cooks.

5. Drain the pasta, and divide among individual serving
bowls. Top with the sauce and serve immediately.

COMPLETE MEAL

MAIN INGREDIENTS

12 ounces fusilli pasta

*2 cups coarsely chopped plum
tomatoes (about 4 large)*

*19-ounce can cannellini beans
(white kidney beans), rinsed
and drained*

*4 cups (packed) coarsely
chopped packaged,
prewashed spinach*

STAPLES

2 teaspoons olive oil

*6 medium cloves garlic,
halved lengthwise*

*2 cups reduced-sodium,
fat-free chicken broth*

1 tablespoon garlic powder

*¼ teaspoon freshly ground
black pepper*

NUTRITIONAL FACTS (PER SERVING)

Calories: 505 Carbohydrates: 92.5 g Cholesterol: 0 mg Fat: 4.5 g Fiber: 13.5 g Protein: 22 g Sodium: 286 mg

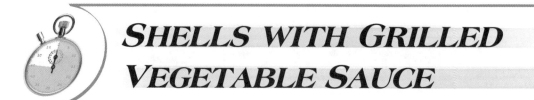

SHELLS WITH GRILLED VEGETABLE SAUCE

TIME: 45 minutes   **YIELD:** 4 servings

MAIN INGREDIENTS

1 small eggplant (about
12 ounces)

1 medium red bell pepper
(about 4 ounces)

1 medium zucchini (about
8 ounces), scrubbed well

1 pound medium pasta shells

15-ounce can crushed
tomatoes in purée

Grated Parmesan cheese
(optional)

Steaming hot pasta shells are crowned with a thick sauce of smoky grilled vegetables in this very special dish. While it is best to cook the vegetables on a barbecue, you can also enjoy delicious results by using a conventional broiler.

1. Preheat an outdoor barbecue grill or oven broiler.

2. Using a potato peeler, remove the skin from the eggplant; then cut it into $\frac{1}{4}$-inch-thick rounds. Cut the bell pepper into eighths, quarter the zucchini lengthwise, and cut the onion crosswise into $\frac{1}{4}$-inch-thick rounds.

3. Spray the vegetables with cooking spray, and sprinkle with 2 teaspoons garlic powder. Place the vegetables on the hot grill or under the broiler, about 4 to 5 inches from the

heat source. Cook the vegetables for about 5 minutes on each side, or until they are just done. Immediately transfer the hot vegetables to a plastic bag. Seal the bag, and let the vegetables steam for 10 minutes.

4. Bring a 4-quart pot of water to a rolling boil. Add the pasta, and cook according to package directions.

5. While the water is heating up, remove the onion, eggplant, and zucchini from the bag, cut into small pieces, and place in a large bowl. Peel and discard the skin from the bell pepper, cut into small pieces, and add to the bowl.

6. Place a third of the vegetables in a 2-quart saucepan, and set aside. Purée the remaining vegetables in a blender or food processor along with the broth. (If using a blender, you may have to do this in 2 batches.) Add the puréed vegetables to the saucepan along with the crushed tomatoes, black pepper, and the remaining garlic powder. Place over medium-low heat, and simmer until the sauce is heated through.

7. Drain the pasta, and divide among individual serving bowls. Top with the sauce, and serve immediately, as is or topped with a sprinkling of Parmesan cheese.

STAPLES

1 medium onion (about 6 ounces)

Cooking spray

4 teaspoons garlic powder, divided

1 cup reduced-sodium, fat-free vegetable broth

⅛ teaspoon freshly ground black pepper

NUTRITIONAL FACTS (PER SERVING)

Calories: 565 Carbohydrates: 116 g Cholesterol: 0 mg Fat: 3 g Fiber: 11 g Protein: 19.5 g Sodium: 99 mg

KITCHEN QUICKIES PASTA

TIME: 25 minutes   **YIELD:** 4 servings

COMPLETE MEAL

MAIN INGREDIENTS

1 pound small shell pasta

1 cup coarsely chopped packaged, prewashed spinach

1/3 cup grated Parmesan cheese

STAPLES

1 tablespoon olive oil

1 tablespoon minced garlic

Crushed red pepper to taste

Chop the spinach and garlic while the pasta is cooking, and this simple but satisfying meal will be on the table before you can say "Kitchen Quickies"!

1. Bring a 4-quart pot of water to a rolling boil. Add the pasta, and cook according to package directions.

2. Drain the pasta well. While the pasta is in the colander, place the pasta pot over medium-low heat and add the olive oil and garlic. Cook for only a minute or 2, stirring occasionally. Add the spinach, and cook for another minute. Remove the pot from the heat.

3. Return the pasta to the pot, and toss with the spinach mixture. Sprinkle with the cheese and crushed red pepper, and toss well.

4. Spoon the pasta into individual serving dishes and serve immediately.

NUTRITIONAL FACTS (PER SERVING)

Calories: 225 Carbohydrates: 32 g Cholesterol: 42.5 mg Fat: 7 g Fiber: 1.5 g Protein: 10 g Sodium: 171 mg

6. PERFECT POULTRY

Americans have had an enduring love affair with chicken and turkey. In many families, Sunday just isn't Sunday unless the kitchen is filled with the aroma of a chicken slowly roasting in the oven. And for most of us, Thanksgiving isn't complete without that most American of foods, the turkey. True, a busy weeknight isn't the best of times to roast a chicken. But it is a *great* time to take advantage of the many fast-cooking poultry cuts now available in your supermarket. To make these products even more attractive, it's worth noting that chicken breast cutlets, turkey breast cutlets, and lean ground turkey are the healthiest parts of the bird—low in fat, and rich in high-quality protein.

The recipes in this chapter combine chicken, turkey, and a variety of other healthful ingredients to create fast-and-easy dishes designed to suit every fancy and every occasion. Looking for a dish that even the fussiest kids will love? In no time at all, you can whip up Twenty-Minute Salsa Chicken and Rice or Turkey Slop-

py Joes, two kid-pleasing dishes that are a snap to make. Need something a bit more elegant? Serve Chicken with Mushrooms and Artichokes in Wine—a picture-pretty entrée that's perfect for even those special occasions. For those who like it hot, there is a range of dishes, from spicy Four-Alarm Chicken Dijon to our Cajun-Style Lemon Chicken. In the mood for something a bit tamer? Try Crisp Chicken Cutlets—lightly seasoned and baked crisp and brown. It's a wonderful choice, as is traditional Sliced Turkey with Orange-Cranberry Sauce.

Like all of our entrée chapters, this one includes several recipes for complete meals. Spicy South-of-the Border Skillet Dinner is one such dish. Others include Mandarin Orange Chicken and Easy Chicken and Rice. These dishes are great time-savers as they need no accompaniment other than bread or a green salad.

So don't wait until Sunday to enjoy one of your favorite foods. Instead, turn the page and learn just how easy it is to make lean, delicious poultry a part of your everyday menus.

101

CAJUN-STYLE LEMON CHICKEN

TIME: 30 minutes   YIELD: 4 servings

MAIN INGREDIENTS

4 boneless, skinless chicken breast halves (about 5 ounces each)

1 medium lemon, cut into wedges

STAPLES

¼ cup all-purpose flour

3 teaspoons Cajun spice blend, divided

2 teaspoons paprika

Cooking spray

2 teaspoons canola oil

1 cup reduced-sodium, fat-free chicken broth

1 tablespoon lemon juice

Serve these spicy chicken cutlets over a bed of hot brown rice. A crisp green salad is the perfect accompaniment.

1. Place the flour, half of the Cajun spice blend, and the paprika in a shallow plate, and stir to blend. Set aside 1 tablespoon of this flour mixture.

2. Lightly coat both sides of the chicken with cooking spray. Then dredge in the flour mixture.

3. Coat a 12-inch nonstick skillet with cooking spray, add the oil, and preheat over medium-low heat. Add the chicken and cook for 5 to 7 minutes on each side, or until no longer pink inside when cut with a knife. Transfer to a plate, and cover to keep warm.

4. Add the broth, lemon juice, and remaining Cajun spice blend to the skillet, along with the reserved tablespoon of flour mixture. Mix well, stirring constantly, over medium-low heat, for 3 to 5 minutes, or until the sauce thickens slightly.

5. Arrange the chicken breasts on a serving platter, and spoon the sauce on top. Garnish with lemon wedges, and serve immediately.

NUTRITIONAL FACTS (PER SERVING)

Calories: 228 Carbohydrates: 11 g Cholesterol: 82 mg Fat: 4.5 g Fiber: 2 g Protein: 36 g Sodium: 610 mg

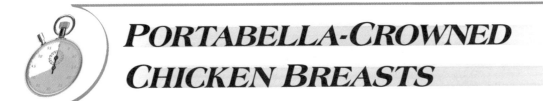

PORTABELLA-CROWNED CHICKEN BREASTS

TIME: 40 minutes

YIELD: 4 servings

Imagine a moist chicken cutlet crowned with a juicy Portabella mushroom cap, and smothered in sweet grilled onions. Forty minutes is all you need to prepare this very special dish.

1. Coat a 12-inch nonstick skillet with cooking spray, add the oil, and preheat over medium heat.

2. Layer the onion rings in the bottom of the skillet, and top with the mushroom caps. Cover and cook for 10 to 15 minutes, occasionally stirring the onions and turning the mushroom caps, until the onions begin to brown and the mushrooms start to soften.

3. Transfer the mushrooms to a plate, and push the onions to the perimeter of the skillet. Reduce the heat to medium-low, and place the chicken breasts in the center of the skillet. Cover and cook for 5 to 8 minutes. Turn the chicken breasts over, sprinkle with salt, if desired, and top with the mushroom caps. Cover and continue to simmer for 3 to 5 minutes, or until the chicken is no longer pink inside when cut with a knife.

4. Place the cooked chicken breasts on individual serving plates, top with mushroom caps, and cover with grilled onions. Serve immediately.

MAIN INGREDIENTS

4 large Portabella mushroom caps

4 boneless, skinless chicken breast halves (about 6 ounces each)

STAPLES

1 teaspoon olive oil

1 large Vidalia or other sweet onion, thinly sliced and separated into rings

Salt (optional)

NUTRITIONAL FACTS (PER SERVING)

Calories: 234 Carbohydrates: 7.5 g Cholesterol: 98.5 mg Fat: 3.5 g Fiber: 1.5 g Protein: 41.5 g Sodium: 115 mg

CHICKEN SALTIMBOCCA

TIME: 30 minutes

YIELD: 4 servings

MAIN INGREDIENTS

1½ pounds thinly sliced
chicken breast cutlets

4 ounces reduced-sodium
ham, thinly sliced

STAPLES

¼ teaspoon ground sage

¼ teaspoon freshly ground
black pepper

2 teaspoons olive oil

½ cup Marsala wine

We serve these flavorful chicken cutlets over a bed of fresh cooked spinach.

1. Sprinkle the sage and black pepper on each chicken cutlet, and top each with a slice or 2 of ham. Press the ham so it sticks to the chicken.

2. Coat a 12-inch nonstick skillet with cooking spray, add the oil, and preheat over medium heat.

3. Place the cutlets ham-side-down in the pan, and cook for 3 to 5 minutes. Then turn and continue to cook for another 2 to 3 minutes, or until the chicken is no longer pink inside when cut with a knife. Transfer the cutlets to a platter, and cover to keep warm.

4. Add the wine to the skillet, and cook for 1 to 2 minutes, stirring to mix with the pan juices. Spoon the sauce over the cutlets, and serve immediately.

NUTRITIONAL FACTS (PER SERVING)

Calories: 278 Carbohydrates: 4 g Cholesterol: 109 mg Fat: 5 g Fiber: 0 g Protein: 44.5 g Sodium: 346 mg

CHICKEN TORTILLA SQUARES

TIME: 45 minutes

YIELD: 4 servings

This dish features shredded chicken blanketed between layers of soft baked tortilla chips, spicy salsa, and shredded cheese. Serve with a cool green salad.

1. Preheat the oven to 375°F. Spray a 9-inch square baking pan with cooking spray, and set aside.

2. Place the chicken in the bottom of a 4-quart pot, add just enough water to partially cover, and bring to a boil over high heat. Reduce the heat to low, cover, and simmer for 7 to 10 minutes, or until no longer pink inside when cut with a knife. Transfer the chicken to a plate, and place in the refrigerator to cool for about 5 minutes, or until the chicken is warm to the touch. Using a fork, shred the chicken.

3. Spoon 1 cup of salsa on the bottom of the baking pan. Arrange the tortilla chips in a layer on the bottom, and top with the shredded chicken. Spoon on the remaining salsa, and sprinkle with the cheese.

4. Cover the pan with aluminum foil, and bake for 20 minutes, or until the chips are somewhat soft and the cheese has melted. Top with the crushed chips, if desired, cut into squares, and serve immediately.

COMPLETE MEAL

MAIN INGREDIENTS

1 pound thinly sliced boneless, skinless, chicken breasts

3 cups (17 ounces) low-sodium salsa,* divided

4 ounces baked tortilla chips

¾ cup shredded light Mexican cheese blend**

½ cup crushed tortilla chips (optional)

* Green Mountain Gringo Salsa is a good brand.

** Sargento brand Light 4 Cheese Mexican Recipe Blend is a good choice.

NUTRITIONAL FACTS (PER SERVING)

Calories: 327 Carbohydrates: 33 g Cholesterol: 73.5 mg Fat: 6 g Fiber: 2 g Protein: 34 g Sodium: 757 mg

CHICKEN WITH MUSHROOMS AND ARTICHOKES IN WINE

TIME: 35 minutes

YIELD: 4 servings

COMPLETE MEAL

MAIN INGREDIENTS

1 cup long grain white rice

1¼ pounds boneless, skinless chicken breasts

6-ounce can sliced mushrooms, undrained

14-ounce can artichoke hearts, drained and cut in half

Saucy and fragrant with garlic, this makes an elegant dish for company.

1. Place the water in a 1-quart saucepan, and bring to a boil over high heat. Stir in the rice and cover. Reduce the heat to medium-low, and cook for about 18 minutes, or until all of the water has been absorbed.

2. Cut the chicken into 1-x-2-inch pieces.

3. Place the flour and black pepper in a shallow bowl and stir to mix. Dredge the chicken pieces in the flour until lightly coated.

4. Coat a 12-inch nonstick skillet with cooking spray, and preheat over medium-high heat. Add the chicken to the

skillet and cook, tossing or turning the pieces occasionally, for about 7 minutes, or until the chicken is lightly browned and no longer pink inside when cut with a knife. Do not overcook the chicken.

5. Reduce the heat to medium, and add the wine to the skillet. Simmer, without stirring, for 2 to 3 minutes, or until the liquid is slightly reduced.

6. Pour off and discard about half the liquid from the mushrooms, and add the mushrooms and the remaining liquid to the pan. Add the garlic and artichokes, and stir or toss the mixture to combine. Simmer gently over medium heat for about 5 minutes, or until the vegetables are heated through and the garlic is soft.

7. Divide the rice among 4 individual serving plates. Top each serving with some of the chicken mixture, spooning some of the sauce over the chicken. Serve immediately.

STAPLES

1½ cups water

¼ cup all-purpose flour

¼ teaspoon freshly ground black pepper

½ cup dry white wine

3 large cloves garlic, chopped

NUTRITIONAL FACTS (PER SERVING)

Calories: 446 Carbohydrates: 59 g Cholesterol: 82 mg Fat: 2.5 g Fiber: 7.5 g Protein: 41 g Sodium: 316 mg

CRISP CHICKEN CUTLETS

TIME: 30 minutes

YIELD: 4 servings

MAIN INGREDIENTS

½ cup fat-free egg substitute

1½ pounds thinly sliced chicken breast cutlets

2 medium lemons, cut into wedges

STAPLES

1¼ cups plain bread crumbs

¾ teaspoon dried oregano

½ teaspoon freshly ground black pepper

¼ teaspoon paprika

Although made with virtually no oil, these lightly seasoned cutlets are crisp and brown. Delicious!

1. Preheat an oven broiler.

2. Place the bread crumbs and all of the spices in a medium-sized shallow bowl, and stir to mix well. Set aside.

3. Place the egg substitute in a second shallow bowl, and set aside.

4. Spray a 9-x-13-inch baking pan with cooking spray. Dip each cutlet first in the egg substitute and then in the bread crumb mixture, coating well. Arrange the cutlets on the prepared pan. Squeeze the juice of 1 lemon over the chicken.

5. Place the chicken under the broiler, about 4 inches below the heat source. Broil for about 3 minutes, or until the chicken is lightly browned. Turn the cutlets over, and squeeze the juice of the remaining lemon over them. Broil for 3 additional minutes, or until lightly browned and no longer pink inside when cut with a knife. Serve immediately.

Variation

For a change of pace, make Tarragon Chicken by replacing the paprika and oregano with ¼ cup dried tarragon.

NUTRITIONAL FACTS (PER SERVING)

Calories: 358 Carbohydrates: 31 g Cholesterol: 99 mg Fat: 5 g Fiber: 3.5 g Protein: 48 g Sodium: 456 mg

EASY CHICKEN AND RICE

TIME: 30 minutes   YIELD: 4 servings

What a terrific one-pot meal. It's quick, requires minimum preparation, and tastes great!

1. Place the chicken strips in a medium-sized bowl, and sprinkle with the paprika, salt, if desired, and black pepper. Stir to coat.

2. Place the broth in a 4-quart pot, and bring to a boil over high heat. Add the chicken, onion, garlic, and rice. Stir the ingredients, reduce the heat to low, and cover. Simmer for 15 minutes.

3. Toss the bell pepper into the rice mixture. Cover and continue to simmer for another 5 to 7 minutes, or until the liquid has been absorbed and the rice is tender.

4. Spoon the chicken and rice into bowls, and serve.

COMPLETE MEAL

MAIN INGREDIENTS

1 pound boneless, skinless chicken breast, cut into thin strips

1½ cups long grain white rice

½ cup coarsely chopped green bell pepper

STAPLES

1 teaspoon paprika

½ teaspoon salt (optional)

½ teaspoon freshly ground black pepper

2 cups reduced-sodium, fat-free chicken broth

1 small onion, coarsely chopped

3 cloves garlic, minced

NUTRITIONAL FACTS (PER SERVING)

Calories: 416 Carbohydrates: 61 g Cholesterol: 66 mg Fat: 2 g Fiber: 2 g Protein: 35 g Sodium: 164 mg

EASY GRILLED CHICKEN FAJITAS

TIME: 20 minutes   YIELD: 4 fajitas

MAIN INGREDIENTS

¼ cup lime juice

1 pound boneless, skinless chicken breasts

4 fat-free flour tortillas (10-inch rounds)

1 cup low-sodium salsa*

8 cups (loosely packed) shredded romaine lettuce

STAPLES

2 teaspoons canola oil

2 teaspoons honey

¼ teaspoon freshly ground black pepper

* Green Mountain Gringo Salsa is a good brand.

Although this chicken tastes best when grilled on an outdoor barbecue, you can also cook it under an oven broiler.

1. Preheat an outdoor barbecue grill or oven broiler.

2. Place the lime juice, oil, honey, and black pepper in a shallow dish, and stir to mix. Add the chicken, and turn to coat. Let stand for 5 minutes.

3. Place the chicken on the heated grill or under the broiler, about 4 to 5 inches from the heat source. Cook for about 5 minutes on each side, or until brown on the outside and no longer pink inside when cut with a knife. While the chicken cooks, wrap the tortillas in foil and warm on the edge of the grill or in the oven.

4. Cut the chicken into thin strips, and place an even amount in the center of each tortilla. Top each with ¼ cup of salsa and 2 cups of lettuce. Roll up and serve immediately.

NUTRITIONAL FACTS (PER FAJITA)

Calories: 308 Carbohydrates: 35 g Cholesterol: 66 mg Fat: 4 g Fiber: 3 g Protein: 31 g Sodium: 593 mg

Top Left: Linguine with White Clam Sauce (page 91)
Top Right: Chicken and Mushroom Marinara (page 82)
Bottom: Tuscan-Style Fusilli (page 97)

Top Left: Sliced Turkey with Orange-Cranberry Sauce (page 126)

Center Left: Corn Skillet Scramble (page 184)

Center Right: Lemony Greek Chicken (page 114)

Bottom: Portabella-Crowned Chicken Breast (page 103)

Top Right: Crisp Chicken Cutlets (page 108)

Top Left: Orange and Ginger Glazed Carrots (page 189)

Bottom Right: Spicy Island Chicken with Red Beans and Rice (page 121)

Bottom Left: Garlic and Herb Mashed Potatoes (page 193)

Top Right: Stir-Fried Spinach with Garlic (page 197)

Center Right: Meat and Potato Lover's Stir-Fry (page 132)

Bottom Left: Filet Mignons with Mushrooms Marsala (page 130)

Bottom Right: Stuffed Bell Peppers (page 134)

The Versatile Chicken Cutlet

As every kitchen-quickies cook knows, when you're pressed for time, there's nothing more versatile than a cooked chicken breast or cutlet. Once you have cubed or shredded the chicken, you can add it to simmering broth for a fast soup, toss it with fresh greens for a main-dish salad, combine it with chopped celery and low-fat mayonnaise for a quick chicken salad—the possibilities are endless. And, of course, whole cooked cutlets and chicken breasts can be tucked into a roll along with crisp lettuce and a slice of tomato for a satisfying sandwich, or blanketed with tomato sauce and a sprinkling of cheese for a quick chicken Parmesan.

While cooked cutlets are readily available in most delis and grocery stores—and, certainly, nothing could be faster—it's great to know that with a minimum of fuss, you can prepare them yourself in about fifteen minutes. You can then use them immediately or keep them on hand to speed the preparation of future meals. Properly stored in a sealed plastic container in the refrigerator, cooked chicken will keep for up to four days.

When grilling or broiling, feel free to flavor the chicken with your choice of seasonings, or to baste them with your favorite marinade or sauce as they cook. Poached chicken may be seasoned after it is cooked, or you may add herbs or other seasoning to the cooking liquid.

When preparing chicken cutlets, we suggest any of the following easy and convenient cooking methods:

Broiling. The closest thing to grilling, broiling under an intense heat source quickly sears the chicken, browning it on the outside, while keeping it moist and juicy inside. Arrange the cutlets on a broiler pan and place in a preheated broiler about 4 to 5 inches from the heat source. Depending on their thickness, cook the cutlets for 3 to 5 minutes on each side, or until they are browned on the outside and no longer pink inside when cut with a knife.

Grilling. Nothing is more irresistible than the smoky taste of chicken that has been cooked over an open flame. Place the cutlets on a preheated barbecue grill, about 4 to 5 inches from the heat source. Depending on their thickness, cook the cutlets for 3 to 5 minutes on each side, or until they are no longer pink inside when cut with a knife.

Poaching on the Stove. Poached foods are gently simmered in a small amount of water or seasoned liquid. Place the cutlets in a pot or skillet that is just large enough to hold them. Add enough water or broth to partially cover the chicken, then bring to a boil over high heat. Immediately reduce the heat to low, cover, and simmer for 7 to 10 minutes, or until no longer pink inside when cut with a knife. The poaching time will depend on the thickness of the cutlets. This effective cooking method is also a wonderful way of preparing fish, eggs, and shellfish.

Poaching in a Microwave Oven. Here is yet another way to poach chicken. Simply place skinless, boneless breast halves in a large microwave-safe dish, arranging them in a single layer so that the thin ends point towards the center. Add chicken broth, using about $1/4$ cup for two to six breast halves, and about $1/2$ cup for eight breast halves. Cover tightly with microwave-safe plastic wrap, and cook on high power until no longer pink inside when cut with a knife. Depending on the thickness of the breasts, this will take about 5 minutes for two breast halves; just add an additional minute of cooking for every two additional halves. Remember to remove the plastic wrap carefully to prevent a steam burn.

FOUR-ALARM CHICKEN DIJON

TIME: 25 minutes

YIELD: 4 servings

MAIN INGREDIENTS

4 boneless, skinless chicken
  breast halves (about
  6 ounces each)

STAPLES

3 tablespoons Dijon-style
  mustard

1 teaspoon canola oil

½ teaspoon dried thyme

½ cup flavored bread crumbs

¾ teaspoon cayenne pepper

¼ teaspoon freshly ground
  black pepper

Cooking spray

Cayenne pepper and Dijon mustard put a real spark in these fiery chicken cutlets.

1. Preheat the oven to 475°F. Coat a baking sheet with cooking spray, and set aside.

2. Place the mustard, oil, and thyme in a shallow plate, and mix together with a whisk. In another plate, combine the bread crumbs, cayenne pepper, and black pepper.

3. Pat the cutlets dry with paper towels. Coat with a thin layer of the mustard mixture, spreading it evenly with the back of a spoon; then roll in the bread crumbs to coat completely. Arrange on the baking sheet, and spray each cutlet lightly with cooking spray.

4. Bake for 12 to 14 minutes, or until no longer pink inside when cut with a knife. To brown the bread crumbs further, place the chicken under the broiler for a minute or 2. Serve immediately.

NUTRITIONAL FACTS (PER SERVING)

Calories: 287 Carbohydrates: 15 g Cholesterol: 98.5 mg Fat: 5.5 g Fiber: 1 g Protein: 43 g Sodium: 683 mg

MANDARIN ORANGE CHICKEN

TIME: 30 minutes   **YIELD:** 4 servings

Sweet Mandarin oranges give this chicken its delightfully light flavor. For tips on quick thawing, see page 10.

1. Place the orange juice in a $1\frac{1}{2}$- or 2-quart pot, and bring to a boil over high heat. Stir in the couscous and cover. Remove from the heat and allow to sit for 5 minutes, or until all of the orange juice has been absorbed.

2. Coat a large nonstick wok or 12-inch skillet with cooking spray, add the oil, and preheat over medium heat. Add the onion and cook, stirring often, for 2 to 3 minutes, or until soft.

3. Toss the chicken strips into the skillet, increase the heat to medium-high, and cook, stirring or tossing constantly, for 5 to 6 minutes, or until no longer pink inside when cut with a knife.

4. Add the peas and Mandarin oranges to the skillet, and stir to mix. Reduce the heat to medium-low and cook, stirring frequently, for about 3 minutes.

5. Fluff the cooked couscous and add it to the skillet, along with the almonds, if desired. Mix well, and serve immediately.

COMPLETE MEAL

MAIN INGREDIENTS

$1\frac{1}{2}$ cups orange juice

1 cup couscous

$1\frac{1}{2}$ pounds chicken breast cutlets, cut into thin strips

1 cup frozen peas, thawed

2 cans (11 ounces each) Mandarin oranges, undrained

2 tablespoons sliced almonds (optional)

STAPLES

2 teaspoons canola oil

$\frac{1}{2}$ cup finely chopped onion

NUTRITIONAL FACTS (PER SERVING)

Calories: 542 Carbohydrates: 75 g Cholesterol: 98.5 mg Fat: 5 g Fiber: 5.5 g Protein: 48.5 g Sodium: 166 mg

LEMONY GREEK CHICKEN

TIME: 45 minutes   **YIELD:** 4 servings

COMPLETE MEAL

MAIN INGREDIENTS

1½ pounds thinly sliced
  chicken breast cutlets

1 cup (loosely packed) chopped
  packaged, prewashed spinach

¼ cup chopped red bell pepper

¾ cup orzo pasta

2 ounces reduced-fat feta
  cheese, crumbled (about
  ⅔ cup)

Orzo pasta that's flecked with bits of red bell pepper and chopped spinach makes the perfect bed for these lemon-and-oregano-flavored chicken cutlets. A light sprinkling of crumbled feta cheese adds the final touch.

1. Preheat an outdoor barbecue grill or oven broiler.

2. Place the lemon juice, olive oil, garlic, oregano, and black pepper in a medium-sized shallow bowl, and stir to mix well. Add the cutlets to the bowl, and turn well to coat. Marinate at room temperature for at least 15 minutes, turning the cutlets occasionally.

3. As the cutlets marinate, place the chicken broth, spinach, and bell pepper in a 2-quart pot, and bring to a boil

over high heat. Stir in the orzo, cover, and reduce the heat to low. Cook, stirring once or twice, for 20 to 25 minutes, or until the broth is absorbed and the orzo is tender.

4. After the orzo has been cooking for about 15 minutes, remove the cutlets from the bowl. Place the marinade in a 1-quart saucepan, and bring to a rolling boil. Boil for 1 minute, then remove from the heat.

5. Place the cutlets on a barbecue grill or under the broiler, about 4 to 5 inches from the heat source. Cook, basting several times with the reserved marinade, for 3 to 4 minutes on each side, or until the chicken is lightly browned and no longer pink inside when cut with a knife.

6. Divide the orzo among individual serving plates. Top each serving with an equal amount of chicken and a sprinkling of feta cheese. Serve immediately.

STAPLES

⅓ cup lemon juice

1 teaspoon olive oil

1 teaspoon minced garlic

¾ teaspoon dried oregano

⅛ teaspoon freshly ground black pepper

2 cups reduced-sodium, fat-free chicken broth

NUTRITIONAL FACTS (PER SERVING)

Calories: 371 Carbohydrates: 27 g Cholesterol: 103 mg Fat: 7 g Fiber: 1.5 g Protein: 50 g Sodium: 394 mg

MARGARITA CHICKEN

TIME: 35 minutes   **YIELD:** 4 servings

MAIN INGREDIENTS

⅓ cup tequila

Grated zest and juice of 1 lime

1½ pounds thinly sliced
  chicken breast cutlets

STAPLES

2 tablespoons honey

¼ teaspoon ground cumin

This sweet and tangy chicken is a snap to make.

1. Preheat an oven broiler.

2. Place the tequila, lime zest and juice, honey, and cumin in a medium-sized shallow bowl, and stir to mix well. Add the cutlets, and turn well to coat. Allow to marinate at room temperature for 10 minutes, turning the cutlets occasionally.

3. Reserving the marinade, remove the cutlets and place on a broiler pan. Transfer the marinade to a 1-quart saucepan, and bring it to a rolling boil. Boil for 1 minute, and remove from the heat.

4. Place the cutlets under the broiler, about 4 inches below the heat source. Broil for about 4 minutes, basting several times with the marinade. Turn, baste once more, and broil for 2 to 4 additional minutes, or until lightly browned and no longer pink inside when cut with a knife. Serve hot.

NUTRITIONAL FACTS (PER SERVING)

Calories: 268 Carbohydrates: 11 g Cholesterol: 99 mg Fat: 2 g Fiber: 0.5 g Protein: 39.5 g Sodium: 112 mg

Marinade Musts

Marinades allow you to infuse meat, poultry, seafood, and vegetables with tantalizing flavors and aromas, adding a whole new dimension to your entrée or side dish. And, depending on your mood, you can choose from among a range of different marinade ingredients. Begin with your favorite wine, aromatic vinegar, citrus juice, tomato juice, or salsa; then stir in the herbs and spices of your choice, and perhaps a clove or two of garlic. Once your mixture is ready, the fun begins, because, in addition to using the liquid as a marinade by immersing your food in it, you can also use it as a basting sauce while the food is cooking, or as a topping when the food is served. But, to ensure that your meal is as healthy as it is delicious, certain guidelines should be kept in mind. Just follow these simple marinade musts:

❒ If you're leaving your ingredients in the marinade for only 10 to 15 minutes, the food can remain at room temperature. If you're marinating for longer than that, though, be sure to place the food in the refrigerator until you're ready to begin cooking.

❒ Place the food and the marinade in a nonreactive bowl—one made of stainless steel, glass, glazed ceramic, or plastic, for instance. Remember that the smaller the container, the less marinade you'll need.

❒ Because the recipes in this book are designed for speed, we never marinate our ingredients for more than a few minutes. However, you may sometimes want to leave your ingredients in the marinade longer to intensify the flavors. Just avoid marinating meats for longer than twenty-four hours, as this may make the meat mushy. Never marinate seafood for more than an hour, as the acid in the marinade will "cook" the fish.

❒ If, after removing the meat, seafood, or poultry from the marinade, you want to use the liquid as a basting sauce or a table sauce, first transfer the marinade to a 1-quart saucepan and bring it to a rolling boil over high heat. Allow it to remain at a boil for at least one minute before continuing with your recipe. This will destroy any bacteria it may have picked up from the meat. Now you're cooking!

MUSTARD CHICKEN WITH SHERRIED MUSHROOMS AND ONIONS

TIME: 45 minutes   **YIELD:** 4 servings

MAIN INGREDIENTS

8 ounces packaged, presliced
  mushrooms (about 2½ cups)

4 chicken breast cutlets,
  pounded thin (about
  4 ounces each)

4 slices beefsteak tomato
  (each about ¼ inch thick)

½ cup shredded light
  mozzarella cheese

STAPLES

1 medium onion, thinly sliced

⅓ cup dry sherry

¼ teaspoon freshly ground
  black pepper, divided

4 teaspoons Dijon-style
  mustard

*A few simple ingredients turn these chicken cutlets into a
special treat.*

1. Coat a 12-inch nonstick skillet with cooking spray, and
preheat over medium-high heat. Add the onion and mushrooms, and cook, stirring frequently, for about 7 minutes, or
until soft.

2. Add the sherry to the skillet, bring the ingredients to a
boil, and cook for a minute or 2, or until the liquid is slightly reduced. Transfer the mixture to a bowl, and set aside.

3. Spray the same skillet with cooking spray, and place
over medium-high heat. Arrange the chicken in the pan,
and sprinkle lightly with about half of the black pepper.
(Depending on the size of the cutlets, you may have to use
2 pans.) Cook for about 2 minutes, or until the cutlets are
lightly browned on the bottom. Turn the cutlets over, sprinkle lightly with the remaining pepper, and cook for an additional 2 to 3 minutes, or just until no longer pink inside
when cut with a knife.

4. Reduce the heat under the chicken to medium, and
spread each cutlet with 1 teaspoon of mustard. Top each
with a slice of tomato followed by a portion of the mushroom mixture and 2 tablespoons of the cheese. Cover the
skillet and cook for 2 to 3 minutes, or just until the cheese is
melted. Serve immediately.

NUTRITIONAL FACTS (PER SERVING)

Calories: 209 Carbohydrates: 7.5 g Cholesterol: 73.5 mg Fat: 3.5 g Fiber: 1.5 g Protein: 31.5 g Sodium: 316 mg

SCALLION CHICKEN WITH RASPBERRY SAUCE

TIME: 25 minutes   YIELD: 4 servings

Juicy scallion-studded chicken cutlets bask in a sea of raspberry-balsamic sauce in this very special entrée.

1. Place the thyme, onion powder, salt, and black pepper in a small bowl, mix well, and set aside.

2. Coat a 12-inch nonstick skillet with cooking spray, add the oil, and preheat over medium heat. Add the scallions and cook, stirring occasionally, for 3 minutes, or until they begin to soften.

3. While the scallions are cooking, sprinkle both sides of the chicken cutlets with the dry spice mixture, and rub to coat. Add the cutlets to the skillet, and cook along with the scallions for 3 to 5 minutes on each side, or until no longer pink inside when cut with a knife. Transfer to a serving plate, and cover to keep warm.

4. Add the raspberry preserves and vinegar to the skillet, stirring to combine well with the pan juices. Cook for 1 to 2 minutes, or until the preserves are melted and the sauce is heated through.

5. Spoon the hot raspberry sauce over the cutlets, and serve immediately.

MAIN INGREDIENTS

4 large scallions, chopped

1½ pounds thinly sliced chicken breast cutlets

¼ cup red or black raspberry preserves

STAPLES

½ teaspoon dried thyme

½ teaspoon onion powder

¼ teaspoon salt

¼ teaspoon freshly ground black pepper

2 teaspoons canola oil

2 tablespoons balsamic vinegar

NUTRITIONAL FACTS (PER SERVING)

Calories: 274 Carbohydrates: 17 g Cholesterol: 99 mg Fat: 4.5 g Fiber: 1 g Protein: 40 g Sodium: 272 mg

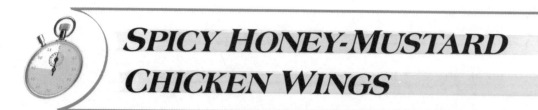

SPICY HONEY-MUSTARD CHICKEN WINGS

TIME: 45 minutes

YIELD: 4 servings

MAIN INGREDIENTS

12 chicken wings, separated at the joints (tips discarded), to yield 24 "wingettes"

2 tablespoons bottled sweet-and-sour sauce

STAPLES

2 tablespoons honey

2 teaspoons Dijon-style mustard

1 teaspoon minced garlic

½ teaspoon cayenne pepper

Paprika

Instead of the honey-mustard sauce, feel free to use your favorite barbecue or teriyaki sauce. To save time, be sure to buy chicken wings that are already separated.

1. Preheat the oven to 450°F. Coat a nonstick baking sheet with cooking spray.

2. With a sharp knife, carefully cut away as much excess skin as possible from the wingettes. Rinse and pat dry.

3. Place all of the remaining ingredients, except the paprika, in a small bowl, and stir to mix. Brush the mixture liberally on both sides of the wings, and arrange the wings on the baking sheet. Sprinkle with the paprika.

4. Bake for about 15 minutes. Then turn and bake for 15 additional minutes, or until brown and crisp. Serve immediately.

NUTRITIONAL FACTS (PER SERVING)

Calories: 186 Carbohydrates: 14.5 g Cholesterol: 53.5 mg Fat: 5.5 g Fiber: 0.5 g Protein: 19.5 g Sodium: 187 mg

SPICY ISLAND CHICKEN WITH RED BEANS AND RICE

TIME: 30 minutes   YIELD: 4 servings

You can almost hear the gentle music of steel drums and feel the warmth of hot tropical sun when you taste this spicy Jamaican-style chicken. We suggest wedges of fresh pineapple to accompany this island treat.

1. Place all of the dry spices and the chili pepper in a small bowl, and stir to mix well. Add the lime juice, and stir into a thin paste.

2. Rub the spice mixture on both sides of the chicken breasts, and set aside.

3. Coat a 12-inch nonstick skillet with cooking spray, add the oil, and preheat over medium heat. Add the chicken, cover, and cook for about 6 minutes on each side, or until the chicken is no longer pink inside when cut with a knife.

4. While the chicken is cooking, bring the water to boil in a 2-quart pot. Add the rice, stir, and cover. Remove from the heat, and let stand for 5 minutes, or until the water is absorbed and the rice is tender.

5. When the rice is cooked, add the beans and mix well. Cover and keep warm.

6. Transfer the cooked chicken to individual dishes, spooning some of the beans and rice next to the cutlets. Serve immediately.

COMPLETE MEAL

MAIN INGREDIENTS

½ small fresh jalapeño or serrano chili pepper, seeded, deveined, and minced

1 tablespoon lime juice

4 boneless, skinless chicken breast halves (about 6 ounces each)

2 cups instant white rice

7.5-ounce can small red beans, rinsed and drained

STAPLES

1 teaspoon dried thyme

½ teaspoon ground cinnamon

½ teaspoon ground ginger

½ teaspoon dry mustard

½ teaspoon paprika

¼ teaspoon cayenne pepper

2 teaspoons canola oil

2 cups water

NUTRITIONAL FACTS (PER SERVING)

Calories: 441 Carbohydrates: 50.5 g Cholesterol: 98.5 mg Fat: 5 g Fiber: 4.5 g Protein: 46.5 g Sodium: 207 mg

TWENTY-MINUTE SALSA CHICKEN AND RICE

TIME: 20 minutes   YIELD: 4 servings

COMPLETE MEAL

MAIN INGREDIENTS

1 pound boneless, skinless
chicken breasts

2 cups instant brown or white
rice

1½ cups low-sodium salsa*

STAPLES

1 teaspoon garlic powder

1 cup reduced-sodium, fat-free
chicken broth

* Green Mountain Gringo Salsa
  is a good brand.

*Choose a mild, medium, or hot salsa to enliven this quick
and easy one-pot meal.*

1. Cut the chicken into bite-sized pieces, and sprinkle
with the garlic powder.

2. Coat a 4-quart pot with cooking spray, and preheat over
medium heat. Add the chicken and cook, turning the pieces
occasionally, for about 7 minutes, or until the chicken is no
longer pink inside when cut with a knife. Transfer the
chicken to a bowl.

3. Place the rice, salsa, and broth in the pot, and stir to
mix. Increase the heat to high, and bring to a boil.

4. Return the chicken to the pot, reduce the heat to low,
and cover. Simmer for 5 to 10 minutes, or until the liquid
has been absorbed and the rice is tender. Serve immediately.

NUTRITIONAL FACTS (PER SERVING)

Calories: 345 Carbohydrates: 46 g Cholesterol: 66 mg Fat: 1.5 g Fiber: 1 g Protein: 31.5 g Sodium: 374 mg

SOUTH-OF-THE-BORDER SKILLET DINNER

TIME: 30 minutes

YIELD: 4 servings

You can really spice up this savory dish by adding a pinch or two of cayenne or chili pepper.

1. Coat a deep 12-inch nonstick skillet or a 4-quart saucepan with cooking spray, and preheat over medium heat. Add the turkey and cook, stirring constantly, for about 4 minutes, or until no longer pink.

2. Stir in all of the remaining ingredients, except the macaroni and the cheese, and mix well. Increase the heat to high, and bring to a boil. Stir in the macaroni, and reduce the heat to low. Cover and simmer, stirring occasionally, for 10 to 12 minutes, or until the pasta is tender.

3. Divide the mixture among individual serving bowls and serve immediately, as is or topped with the Cheddar cheese.

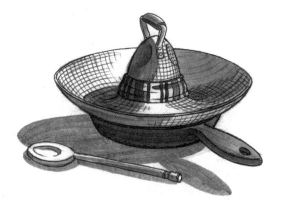

COMPLETE MEAL

MAIN INGREDIENTS

1 pound 99% lean ground turkey

15-ounce can low-sodium tomato sauce

1.5-ounce package burrito seasoning mix

¼ cup chopped green and/or red bell pepper

1¼ cups elbow macaroni

Shredded low-fat Cheddar cheese (optional)

STAPLES

1 cup water

NUTRITIONAL FACTS (PER SERVING)

Calories: 377 Carbohydrates: 54.5 g Cholesterol: 55.5 mg Fat: 2.5 g Fiber: 5.5 g Protein: 36.5 g Sodium: 750 mg

TURKEY SLOPPY JOES

TIME: 35 minutes   **YIELD:** 4 servings (2 sloppy Joes each)

MAIN INGREDIENTS

1 pound 99% lean ground turkey

½ cup frozen chopped onion

½ cup frozen chopped green bell pepper

½ cup chopped celery

1-pound can no-salt-added tomato sauce

8 hamburger buns, toasted

STAPLES

1 tablespoon plus 2 teaspoons white wine vinegar

2 tablespoons brown sugar

1 teaspoon dry mustard

½ teaspoon freshly ground black pepper

¼ teaspoon crushed red pepper

¼ teaspoon salt (optional)

Frozen chopped green pepper and onions speed up the preparation of this satisfyingly saucy dish.

1. Coat a 4-quart pot with nonstick cooking spray, and preheat over medium-high heat. Crumble the turkey into the pot, and add the onion, green pepper, and celery. Cook, stirring constantly, for about 4 minutes, or until the turkey is no longer pink.

2. Add the tomato sauce, vinegar, brown sugar, mustard, black and red pepper, and salt, if desired, and stir to mix. Reduce the heat to medium-low and cook uncovered, stirring occasionally, for 20 to 25 minutes, or until the mixture has thickened to the desired consistency.

3. Spoon even amounts of the sloppy Joe mixture over the bottom halves of the buns. Cover with the top halves, and serve immediately.

NUTRITIONAL FACTS (PER SERVING)

Calories: 366 Carbohydrates: 54 g Cholesterol: 55.5 mg Fat: 4 g Fiber: 8 g Protein: 36.5 g Sodium: 475 mg

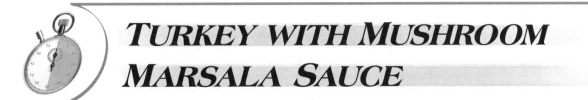

TURKEY WITH MUSHROOM MARSALA SAUCE

TIME: 30 minutes   **YIELD:** 4 servings

This is a great way to make leftover turkey moist and flavorful, or to turn deli-bought turkey into a delicious hot dish.

1. Coat a 12-inch skillet or wok with nonstick cooking spray, and preheat over medium-high heat. Add the onions, and cook, stirring frequently, for about 4 minutes. Add the mushrooms, and continue to cook for about 5 minutes, or until the mushrooms become browned and tender.

2. Cut any large turkey slices in half to make handling easier. Reduce the heat to medium, and add the turkey. Cook, tossing occasionally, for a minute or 2, or just until the turkey is hot.

3. Add all of the remaining ingredients to the skillet, and toss well. Transfer the turkey to a serving dish, and cover to keep warm.

4. Increase the heat to high, and bring the skillet mixture to a boil. Cook a minute or 2, until slightly reduced, pour over the turkey, and serve immediately.

MAIN INGREDIENTS

8 ounces packaged, presliced mushrooms (about 2½ cups)

1 pound sliced, cooked turkey

STAPLES

1½ cups slivered onions

¼ cup Marsala wine

1 cup reduced-sodium, fat-free chicken broth

¼ teaspoon freshly ground black pepper

¼ teaspoon garlic powder

2 pinches salt

NUTRITIONAL FACTS (PER SERVING)

Calories: 215 Carbohydrates: 8.5 g Cholesterol: 94 mg Fat: 1 g Fiber: 1.5 g Protein: 37.5 g Sodium: 194 mg

SLICED TURKEY WITH ORANGE-CRANBERRY SAUCE

TIME: 15 minutes   YIELD: 4 servings

MAIN INGREDIENTS

1-pound can whole berry
  cranberry sauce

½ cup orange juice

1 tablespoon grated orange
  peel

1½ pounds thinly sliced
  turkey breast cutlets

4 orange slices, quartered

STAPLES

2 teaspoons canola oil

½ cup reduced-sodium,
  fat-free chicken broth

Fifteen minutes is all you need to prepare this cranberry-sweetened turkey dish. For a perfect autumn meal, serve it with Harvest Pumpkin Soup (page 22) and Green Beans with Caramelized Onions (page 186).

1. Place the cranberry sauce, orange juice, and orange peel in a medium-sized bowl, and stir well to combine. Set aside.

2. Coat a 12-inch nonstick skillet with cooking spray, add the oil, and preheat over medium heat. Add the turkey slices, and cook for about 2 minutes on each side, or until no longer pink inside when cut with a knife. Transfer to a platter, and cover to keep warm.

3. Add the chicken broth to the skillet, and stir over medium heat for about 2 minutes. Stir in the cranberry mixture, and cook until heated through.

4. Spoon the cranberry mixture over the hot turkey slices, garnish with the oranges, and serve immediately.

NUTRITIONAL FACTS (PER SERVING)

Calories: 417 Carbohydrates: 51.5 g Cholesterol: 105.5 mg Fat: 3.5 g Fiber: 2.5 g Protein: 43 g Sodium: 162 mg

7. Hearty Beef and Pork

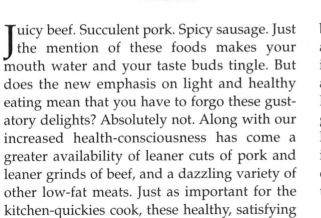

Juicy beef. Succulent pork. Spicy sausage. Just the mention of these foods makes your mouth water and your taste buds tingle. But does the new emphasis on light and healthy eating mean that you have to forgo these gustatory delights? Absolutely not. Along with our increased health-consciousness has come a greater availability of leaner cuts of pork and leaner grinds of beef, and a dazzling variety of other low-fat meats. Just as important for the kitchen-quickies cook, these healthy, satisfying foods can be prepared *fast*, with no fuss and with great results.

This chapter uses a variety of super-lean meats to make a variety of super-delicious dishes—dishes that range from the casual to the formal, from the familiar to the unexpected. Of course, we've included our favorite chili recipe, and Chili con Carne will delight you both with its ease of preparation and its saucy savor. But if you are looking for something a little different, you might want to try Picadillo over Rice, a delightfully sweet and spicy Brazilian dish that's a welcome change from the usual ground

beef entrées. Stir-fries are great when you're in a rush, and this chapter offers two—Asian-inspired Pork Stir-Fry over Sesame Noodles, and all-American Meat and Potato Lover's Stir-Fry. And for those special occasions, we suggest you try Filets Mignons with Mushrooms Marsala, a simple yet elegant dish that is sure to impress. We've even found a way to make a delectable company-perfect pork roast in well under an hour!

As always, we've included several recipes that serve as complete meals—dishes that need no accompaniment other than a hearty loaf of bread. The stir-fries mentioned above are both complete meals, as is our chili. Others include satisfying Sausage and Cannellini over Baby Greens, Pork Chops with Cabbage and Apples, and Ground Beef Stroganoff.

So the next time you long for a hearty entrée, don't let your low-fat lifestyle *or* your hectic schedule keep you from indulging in the glories of beef and pork. Lean, luscious, and fuss-free, our recipes will help you make these wonderful foods a part of your fast and easy menus.

CHILI CON CARNE

TIME: 45 minutes   YIELD: 4 servings

COMPLETE MEAL

MAIN INGREDIENTS

1 pound 93% lean ground beef

8-ounce can stewed tomatoes

1-pound can red kidney beans, rinsed and drained (about 2 cups)

8-ounce can no-salt-added tomato sauce

STAPLES

2 medium onions, chopped

2 tablespoons red wine vinegar

1½–2 tablespoons chili powder

¼ teaspoon garlic powder

Hot and hearty, this is the perfect dish to enjoy on a cold winter's day.

1. Coat a 4-quart pot with cooking spray, and preheat over medium-high heat. Add the beef, and cook, stirring constantly to crumble, for about 4 minutes, or until no pink remains. Drain off any excess fat.

2. Pour off and reserve about half of the liquid from the stewed tomatoes. Then add the tomatoes and all of the remaining ingredients to the pot, and stir to mix. Reduce the heat to medium-low, cover, and cook, stirring occasionally, for at least 25 minutes. If the chili seems too thick, add some of the reserved liquid from the tomatoes. Enjoy as is, or topped with chopped raw onion, chopped green or red bell peppers, or low-fat shredded Cheddar cheese.

NUTRITIONAL FACTS (PER SERVING)

Calories: 312 Carbohydrates: 32.5 g Cholesterol: 70.5 mg Fat: 5.5 g Fiber: 10.5 g Protein: 35 g Sodium: 378 mg

PICADILLO OVER RICE

TIME: 35 minutes   YIELD: 4 servings

This sweet and spicy Brazilian dish makes a great change of pace from chili. Serve it over rice, as we do, or omit the rice and use the stew as an unusual sloppy Joe topping.

1. Coat a 12-inch nonstick skillet with cooking spray, and preheat over medium-high heat. Add the beef and onion and cook, stirring constantly to crumble, for about 4 minutes, or until no pink remains. Drain off any excess fat.

2. Add the apple and all of the spices, and cook, stirring constantly, for 1 minute.

3. Add the tomatoes, raisins, and vinegar to the skillet, and bring to a boil. Reduce the heat to medium-low, and simmer uncovered, stirring occasionally, for about 10 minutes, or until the flavors have blended and the mixture has thickened.

4. While the picadillo is simmering, place the water in a 1-quart saucepan and bring to a boil over high heat. Stir in the rice, cover, and reduce the heat to medium-low. Cook for 10 minutes, or until all the water has been absorbed.

5. Divide the rice among individual serving plates, and top with the picadillo. Serve immediately.

COMPLETE MEAL

MAIN INGREDIENTS

1 pound 93% lean ground beef

⅔ cup peeled and chopped sweet apple, such as Fuji

14.5-ounce can no-salt-added diced tomatoes, undrained

¼ cup dark raisins

1 cup instant brown rice

STAPLES

1 large onion, chopped

1½ teaspoons chili powder

½ teaspoon dried oregano

½ teaspoon ground cumin

¼ teaspoon cayenne pepper

⅛ teaspoon ground cinnamon

2 tablespoons red wine vinegar

1 cup water

NUTRITIONAL FACTS (PER SERVING)

Calories: 368 Carbohydrates: 36.5 g Cholesterol: 95.5 mg Fat: 6.5 g Fiber: 4.5 g Protein: 40 g Sodium: 95 mg

FILETS MIGNONS WITH MUSHROOMS MARSALA

TIME: 25 minutes   **YIELD:** 4 servings

MAIN INGREDIENTS

4 filet mignon steaks (about
   6 ounces each)

12 ounces packaged, presliced
   mushrooms (about 4 cups)

STAPLES

4 pinches salt

4 pinches freshly ground black
   pepper

4 pinches garlic powder

4 cloves garlic, chopped

¼ cup plus 2 tablespoons
   Marsala wine

Simple and elegant, this is the perfect entrée for that special dinner.

1. Preheat an oven broiler.

2. Trim any excess fat from the steaks. Sprinkle each steak with a pinch each of salt, black pepper, and garlic powder, and set aside.

3. Coat a 10-inch nonstick skillet with cooking spray, and preheat over medium-high heat. Add the mushrooms and garlic, and cook, stirring frequently, for about 5 minutes, or until the mushrooms are lightly browned. Remove from the heat, and set aside.

4. Arrange the steaks on a broiler pan, and place under the preheated broiler, about 4 inches below the heat source. Broil for about 4 minutes on each side, depending on the thickness of the steaks and the desired degree of doneness.

5. A few minutes before the steaks are done, reheat the mushrooms over medium-high heat. Add the Marsala, bring to a boil, and cook for about 2 minutes, or until the wine is slightly reduced.

6. Place each steak on an individual serving plate, top with some of the mushrooms, and serve immediately.

NUTRITIONAL FACTS (PER SERVING)

Calories: 326 Carbohydrates: 8 g Cholesterol: 105.5 mg Fat: 13 g Fiber: 1 g Protein: 37.5 g Sodium: 230 mg

GROUND BEEF STROGANOFF

TIME: 35 minutes   YIELD: 4 servings

This fast-and-easy Stroganoff is just as creamy and delicious as the classic version.

1. Bring a 4-quart pot of water to a rolling boil, and cook the noodles according to package directions.

2. While the water is heating up, coat a 12-inch nonstick skillet with cooking spray, and preheat over medium-high heat. Add the mushrooms, onion, and garlic, and cook, stirring frequently, for about 7 minutes, or until the onion is soft and the mushrooms are lightly browned. Transfer the mixture to a bowl and set aside.

3. Place the beef in the skillet, and cook over medium-high heat, stirring constantly to crumble, for about 4 minutes, or until no pink remains. Drain off any excess fat.

4. Stir the mushroom mixture into the beef. Sprinkle with the black pepper and flour, and cook, stirring constantly, for 2 minutes.

5. Stir the broth into the beef, and bring to a boil. Cook, stirring frequently, for 3 to 4 minutes, or until the mixture has thickened. Stir in the Worcestershire sauce.

6. Reduce the heat under the skillet to low, and wait until the mixture is no longer boiling. Slowly stir in the sour cream, and heat for a minute or 2, or just until hot.

7. Drain the noodles well, and divide among individual serving plates. Top with the Stroganoff, and serve immediately.

COMPLETE MEAL

MAIN INGREDIENTS

8 ounces "no-yolk" noodles

6 ounces packaged, presliced mushrooms (about 2 cups)

1 pound 93% lean ground beef

¾ cup nonfat sour cream

STAPLES

1 medium onion, coarsely chopped

2 cloves garlic, chopped

½ teaspoon freshly ground black pepper

2 tablespoons all-purpose flour

1¼ cups reduced-sodium, fat-free beef broth

2 teaspoons Worcestershire sauce

NUTRITIONAL FACTS (PER SERVING)

Calories: 515 Carbohydrates: 57.5 g Cholesterol: 95.5 mg Fat: 7.5 g Fiber: 3 g Protein: 50 g Sodium: 176 mg

MEAT AND POTATO LOVER'S STIR-FRY

TIME: 45 minutes   **YIELD:** 4 servings

MAIN INGREDIENTS

*4 medium potatoes, scrubbed
and cut into ¼-inch slices*

*1 pound London broil shoulder
cut, cut into ¼-inch slices*

*1 medium green bell pepper,
cut into thin strips*

STAPLES

Cooking spray

½ teaspoon garlic powder

*½ teaspoon freshly ground
black pepper*

*½ large onion, cut into thin
strips*

¼ teaspoon salt

*This unusual stir-fry will surely delight the meat and potato
lovers in your house.*

1. Layer the potato slices in a medium-sized microwave-safe bowl, lightly spraying each layer with cooking spray to prevent the slices from sticking to one another as they cook. Cover the bowl tightly with plastic wrap, and microwave on high power for 5 to 6 minutes, or just until the potatoes are tender when pierced with a fork. Carefully remove the plastic wrap and set aside.

2. Sprinkle the beef with the garlic powder and black pepper, and toss to coat evenly. Coat a large nonstick wok or 12-inch skillet with cooking spray, and preheat over high heat. Add the beef and cook, tossing constantly, for 3 minutes. Transfer the beef to a bowl, and set aside.

3. Add the green pepper and onion to the wok or skillet, and cook, tossing constantly, for 3 minutes. Add the potatoes, and continue to cook and toss for 5 minutes, or until the potatoes are browned.

4. Add the beef, and toss until heated through. Sprinkle with the salt, toss to mix, and serve.

NUTRITIONAL FACTS (PER SERVING)

Calories: 325 Carbohydrates: 35 g Cholesterol: 56 mg Fat: 8.5 g Fiber: 4 g Protein: 26 g Sodium: 226 mg

Stir-Fry Crazy

Stir-fries can be the best friend of the kitchen-quickies cook. By cutting up your ingredients into small pieces, you greatly reduce cooking time. Just as important, most stir-fries are complete meals—packed with both meat and plenty of nutrient-rich veggies—so that you don't have to spend time cooking side dishes.

But some stir-fry recipes can be time-consuming. Why? Prep time! You can spend literally hours cutting up the stir-fry vegetables required by some recipes. In addition, some recipes direct you to marinate the meat for hours so that, despite the short cooking time, it will be sufficiently tender. Fortunately, for each of these problems, we have a solution. The following simple tips and guidelines will help you create delicious low-fat stir-fries that can be prepared quickly and with a minimum of fuss.

❒ To minimize the prep time needed to wash and cut up vegetables, make use of convenience foods like packaged broccoli florets and sliced fresh mushrooms. A good salad bar, too, can be a source of precut, prewashed vegetables—just be sure to cut the veggies into bite-sized pieces before cooking. You'll also want to try some of the frozen vegetable mixtures created just for stir-fries.

❒ If you are including meat in your stir-fry, start off with a tender cut, such as pork tenderloin or London broil shoulder cut. Then further minimize the chance of "chewiness" by slicing the meat as thin as possible. This is most easily done when the meat is partially frozen, so if you have time, wrap the raw meat in plastic wrap and pop it into the freezer for twenty to thirty minutes before slicing. For maximum tenderness, be sure to slice the meat against the grain.

❒ For best results, use a large nonstick wok. This will allow you to stir and toss the ingredients constantly without tossing them out of the pan. And because the ingredients have room to "spread out," they'll cook more quickly. If you don't have a wok, choose your largest, deepest skillet.

❒ When you're ready to cook, first coat the wok or skillet with cooking spray and preheat over medium-high to high heat. Cook the meat, poultry, or seafood first, tossing it constantly just until done. Then remove it from the pan so that you can cook the vegetables. Start stir-frying the slow-cooking vegetables first—the carrots and broccoli, for instance. After a couple of minutes, toss in the quick-cooking vegetables, like sliced mushrooms and onions. If using any very long-cooking vegetable, like potatoes, reduce your stir-frying time by microwaving the vegetable just until tender before adding it to the wok. When the vegetables are done to taste, return the meat to the wok and toss to mix and to heat through. This method will prevent you from ending up with a mixture of overcooked and undercooked ingredients.

❒ Don't think that you have to devise a complicated stir-fry sauce to add savor to your creation. Our Meat and Potato Lover's Stir-Fry (page 132) is seasoned only with spices—and it's anything but dull. Stir-Fried Vegetable Rice (page 180) owes its distinctive flavor to fresh ginger and a splash of light soy sauce. And Pork Stir-Fry over Sesame Noodles (page 140) makes good use of a commercial stir-fry sauce. Use your imagination, and you're sure to come up with other fast-and-easy stir-fry sauces and seasonings. Soon, you'll be as crazy about stir-fries as we are!

STUFFED BELL PEPPERS

TIME: 45 minutes

YIELD: 4 servings (2 pepper halves each)

MAIN INGREDIENTS

¼ cup instant brown rice

4 medium green or red bell peppers (4 ounces each)

1 pound 93% lean ground beef

2 egg whites

15-ounce can tomato sauce

STAPLES

½ cup water, divided

⅓ cup finely chopped onion

¼ cup flavored bread crumbs

Really hungry? Try serving these savory stuffed peppers with Garlic and Herb Mashed Potatoes (page 193) for a satisfying meal.

1. Place ¼ cup of the water in a 1-quart saucepan, and bring to a boil over high heat. Stir in the rice and cover. Reduce the heat to medium-low and cook for 10 minutes, or until the water has been absorbed and the rice is tender.

2. While the rice is cooking, cut the peppers in half crosswise, and remove the stems and seeds. Set aside.

3. Place the beef, onion, cooked rice, bread crumbs, and egg whites in a large bowl, and mix well with your hands. Divide the mixture among the pepper halves.

4. Place the filled peppers in a deep 12-inch nonstick skillet with a cover. Add the remaining ¼ cup water to the bottom of the skillet, cover, and cook over medium heat for 10 minutes.

5. Pour the tomato sauce over the peppers. Reduce the heat to low, cover, and simmer for another 20 minutes, or until the peppers are soft and the beef is cooked.

6. Serve immediately, topping each pepper with some of the sauce.

NUTRITIONAL FACTS (PER SERVING)

Calories: 335 Carbohydrates: 27.5 g Cholesterol: 95.5 mg Fat: 6.5 g Fiber: 4.5 g Protein: 42 g Sodium: 1,040 mg

SPICY BEEF AND SPINACH BURRITOS

TIME: 20 minutes

YIELD: 4 servings (2 burritos each)

Super-fast to make, these hearty burritos—bursting with beef, spinach, cheese, and spicy salsa—are sure to delight every member of your family. For tips on quick thawing, see page 10.

1. Preheat the oven to 350°F.

2. Wrap the tortillas in aluminum foil, and warm in the oven for about 10 minutes. Keep warm until ready to use.

3. Coat a 12-inch nonstick skillet with cooking spray, and preheat over medium-high heat. Add the beef and garlic, and cook, stirring constantly to crumble, for about 7 minutes, or until no pink remains. Drain off any excess fat.

4. Add the spinach, salsa, chili powder, and cumin to the beef, and stir to mix well. Cook for 3 to 5 additional minutes, or until heated through.

5. Remove the skillet from the heat, and stir in the cheese.

6. Place about ½ cup of the beef mixture in the center of each tortilla. Fold the bottom edge up over the filling, and fold the sides to the center, overlapping them. Serve immediately.

COMPLETE MEAL

MAIN INGREDIENTS

8 fat-free flour tortillas (8-inch rounds)

1¼ pounds 93% lean ground beef

10-ounce package frozen spinach, thawed and squeezed dry

1 cup hot low-sodium chunky-style salsa*

½ cup shredded light Mexican cheese blend**

STAPLES

2 cloves garlic, chopped

1 tablespoon plus 1 teaspoon chili powder

½ teaspoon ground cumin

* Green Mountain Gringo Salsa is a good brand.

** Sargento brand Light 4 Cheese Mexican Recipe Blend is a good choice.

NUTRITIONAL FACTS (PER SERVING)

Calories: 558 Carbohydrates: 57.5 g Cholesterol: 124 mg Fat: 10 g Fiber: 5 g Protein: 57.5 g Sodium: 1,115 mg

PORK CUTLETS WITH CABBAGE AND APPLES

TIME: 45 minutes   **YIELD:** 4 servings

COMPLETE MEAL

MAIN INGREDIENTS

1½ pounds thinly sliced pork cutlets

6 cups packaged shredded cabbage (loosely packed)

1 medium apple (any variety), cored, peeled, and cut into thin wedges

2 cups apple juice

Be sure to use finely shredded cabbage and thinly cut apples for quicker cooking.

1. Preheat the oven to warm or low.

2. Trim any visible fat from the cutlets. Coat a 12-inch nonstick skillet with cooking spray, and preheat over medium heat. Add the cutlets, and brown for about 2 minutes on each side, or until no longer pink inside when cut with a knife. Transfer the cutlets to a serving platter, cover, and place in the warm oven.

3. Add the cabbage, onion, apple wedges, and apple juice to the skillet. Increase the heat to high, and bring to a boil. Then reduce the heat to low, cover, and simmer, stirring occasionally, for 20 to 25 minutes, or until the cabbage and apples are tender.

4. Using a slotted spoon, scoop up the cabbage-apple mixture and place on top of the cutlets. Cover to keep warm.

5. Transfer 1 or 2 tablespoons of the cooking liquid to a small bowl, add the cornstarch, and stir to dissolve. Stir the cornstarch mixture into the cooking liquid along with the brown sugar and black pepper. Cook over medium heat, stirring constantly, for a minute or 2, or until the sugar is dissolved and the sauce has thickened.

6. Serve the cutlets and apple-cabbage mixture with the piping hot sauce on the side.

STAPLES

1 medium onion, cut into wedges

2 tablespoons cornstarch

1 tablespoon brown sugar

¼ teaspoon freshly ground black pepper

NUTRITIONAL FACTS (PER SERVING)

Calories: 347 Carbohydrates: 34.5 g Cholesterol: 98 mg Fat: 7.5 g Fiber: 4 g Protein: 35 g Sodium: 85 mg

GARLIC AND ROSEMARY ROASTED PORK TENDERLOIN

TIME: 40 minutes   YIELD: 4 servings

MAIN INGREDIENTS

2 pork tenderloin roasts
 (12 ounces each), trimmed

STAPLES

4 large cloves garlic, crushed

¾ teaspoon dried rosemary

¾ teaspoon freshly ground
 black pepper

½ teaspoon salt

Cooking spray

Always tender and succulent, pork tenderloins are as perfect for company dinners as they are for weekday meals. And this cooking method allows you to prepare a flavorful roast fast!

1. Preheat the oven to 500°F.

2. Place the garlic, rosemary, black pepper, and salt in a small dish, and stir to mix well. Rub the mixture evenly over the tenderloins.

3. Place the roasts in a baking pan, and spray the tops lightly with cooking spray. Place the pan in the oven, and reduce the oven temperature to 475°F.

4. Roast for about 25 minutes, or just until the center of the roast is no longer pink when cut with a knife.

5. Slice the roasts thinly on the diagonal, and serve immediately.

NUTRITIONAL FACTS (PER SERVING)

Calories: 215 Carbohydrates: 1.5 g Cholesterol: 101 mg Fat: 6 g Fiber: < 1 g Protein: 36 g Sodium: 363 mg

PORK PAPRIKASH

TIME: 40 minutes   YIELD: 4 servings

Lean, tender pork tenderloin is the best cut to use for this complete-meal dish.

1. Bring a 4-quart pot of water to a rolling boil. Add the noodles, and cook according to package directions.

2. While the water is heating up, coat a deep 12-inch non-stick skillet with cooking spray, and preheat over medium heat. Add the pork and cook, stirring and tossing constantly, for 3 to 4 minutes, or until no longer pink inside when cut with a knife.

3. Add the garlic, onion, carrot, mushrooms, paprika, and half the broth to the skillet. Increase the heat to high, and bring to a boil. Then reduce the heat to medium and simmer uncovered, stirring occasionally, for 12 to 15 minutes, or until the vegetables are tender.

4. Place the remaining broth in a bowl, and stir in the cornstarch until dissolved. Drain the noodles well, and add to the skillet along with the cornstarch mixture and the sour cream. Toss well to mix.

5. Transfer the paprikash to a serving platter and serve immediately.

COMPLETE MEAL

MAIN INGREDIENTS

8 ounces "no-yolk" noodles, medium or wide

12 ounces pork tenderloin, cut into bite-sized pieces

1 large carrot, thinly sliced

1½ cups packaged, presliced mushrooms

1 cup nonfat sour cream

STAPLES

4 cloves garlic, minced

1 cup thinly sliced onion

1 tablespoon paprika

1½ cups reduced-sodium, fat-free chicken broth, divided

1 tablespoon cornstarch

NUTRITIONAL FACTS (PER SERVING)

Calories: 430 Carbohydrates: 60.5 g Cholesterol: 55.5 mg Fat: 4.5 g Fiber: 4 g Protein: 33.5 g Sodium: 180 mg

PORK STIR-FRY OVER SESAME NOODLES

TIME: 45 minutes   **YIELD**: 4 servings

COMPLETE MEAL

MAIN INGREDIENTS

6 ounces angel hair pasta

1 pound pork tenderloin, sliced into thin strips

2 tablespoons commercial stir-fry sauce, divided

2 celery stalks, thinly sliced

1 medium red or green bell pepper, cut into thin strips

6-ounce can sliced mushrooms, drained

STAPLES

1 tablespoon garlic powder

1 tablespoon light soy sauce

1 tablespoon sesame oil

Feel free to add other vegetables to this dish according to your taste. Peeled baby carrots, scallions, and sliced water chestnuts are good choices.

1. Bring a 4-quart pot of water to a rolling boil. Add the pasta, and cook according to package directions.

2. While the water is heating up, sprinkle the pork slices with garlic powder. Coat a 12-inch nonstick skillet with cooking spray, and preheat over medium-high heat. Add the pork, and cook, tossing constantly, for 3 to 4 minutes, or until no longer pink inside when cut with a knife. Transfer to a bowl, and toss with half of the stir-fry sauce. Cover and set aside.

3. Recoat the skillet with cooking spray, and place over medium-high heat. Add the celery and bell pepper, and stir-fry for 3 minutes. Toss in the mushrooms, soy sauce, and remaining stir-fry sauce. Continue to stir-fry for another minute; then return the cooked pork to the skillet, and toss with the other ingredients.

4. Drain the cooked pasta, and return it to the pot. Add the sesame oil, and toss well to coat. Transfer to a serving platter, and top with the stir-fry. Serve immediately.

NUTRITIONAL FACTS (PER SERVING)

Calories: 375 Carbohydrates: 41.5 g Cholesterol: 73.5 mg Fat: 9 g Fiber: 5.5 g Protein: 31 g Sodium: 551 mg

QUICK HOPPING JOHN

TIME: 35 minutes   **YIELD:** 4 servings

In the South, many believe that eating Hopping John on New Year's Day before noon insures a year of good luck. While we can't promise that this recipe will bring good luck, we can promise that this streamlined version will allow you to sleep late and still enjoy a delicious meal by the twelve o'clock deadline.

1. Place the water in a 1-quart saucepan, and bring to a boil over high heat. Stir in the rice and cover. Reduce the heat to medium-low, and cook for 10 minutes, or until all of the water has been absorbed.

2. While the rice is cooking, coat a 4-quart pot with cooking spray, and preheat over medium-high heat. Add the garlic and 1 cup of the onion, and cook, stirring constantly, for about 4 minutes, or until the onion is soft.

3. Add the peas, Canadian bacon, cooked rice, oregano, and Tabasco sauce to the onion mixture, and stir to mix. Add enough broth to moisten the mixture without making it soupy, and continue to cook until heated through.

4. Divide the mixture among individual serving bowls. Top each serving with 2 tablespoons of the remaining onion, and serve.

MAIN INGREDIENTS

1 cup instant brown rice

4 cans (10 ounces each) black-eyed peas (about 4 cups), rinsed and drained

1 cup diced lean Canadian bacon (about 4 ounces)

STAPLES

1 cup water

4 cloves garlic, minced

1½ cups chopped onion, divided

1 teaspoon dried oregano

¼ teaspoon Tabasco sauce

½ cup reduced-sodium, fat-free chicken broth

NUTRITIONAL FACTS (PER SERVING)

Calories: 374 Carbohydrates: 62 g Cholesterol: 16.5 mg Fat: 4 g Fiber: 11.5 g Protein: 23.5 g Sodium: 795 mg

SAUSAGE AND CANNELLINI OVER BABY GREENS

TIME: 30 minutes

YIELD: 4 servings

COMPLETE MEAL

MAIN INGREDIENTS

1 pound low-fat smoked sausage*

1 large red bell pepper, chopped

2 cans (1 pound each) cannellini beans (white kidney beans), rinsed and drained

4 handfuls packaged, precut baby greens

STAPLES

2 medium onions, chopped

1 teaspoon dried thyme

1 cup dry white wine

* Hillshire Farms Lite Polska Kielbasa is a good choice.

Hearty and satisfying, this one-pot dish is also wonderfully easy to make.

1. Thinly slice the sausage on the diagonal.

2. Lightly coat a 12-inch nonstick skillet with cooking spray, and preheat over medium-high heat. Add the sausage, and cook, stirring frequently, for about 5 minutes, or until lightly browned. Transfer the sausage to a bowl and set aside.

3. Add the red pepper, onions, and thyme to the skillet, and cook, stirring frequently, for about 8 minutes, or until the vegetables are soft and lightly browned.

4. Add the wine to the skillet, increase the heat to high, and bring to a boil. Cook at a boil for 3 minutes, or until the liquid is reduced by about half.

5. Add the sausage and beans to the skillet, and stir to mix. Cook, stirring occasionally, for about 3 minutes, or just until heated through.

6. Line individual serving plates with the salad greens, spoon the sausage-bean mixture over the greens, and serve immediately.

NUTRITIONAL FACTS (PER SERVING)

Calories: 393 Carbohydrates: 52.5 g Cholesterol: 40.5 mg Fat: 4 g Fiber: 11 g Protein: 24.5 g Sodium: 1,267 mg

8. SIZZLING SEAFOOD

What's the fastest food in the West—and the East, North, and South? Seafood! Just how fast and easy is it? Well, swordfish kabobs cook in about twelve minutes. Salmon burgers, in about ten. Shrimp and scallops, in about three. We're talking *fast*.

But as you probably already know, fish and shellfish are more than just quick-cooking. They're among the healthiest of foods because they're a rich source of essential fatty acids, a type of fat that's not only good for you, but actually a necessary part of your diet. Just as important, seafood is a versatile food that can be prepared in so many ways, it need never become boring or ho-hum.

This chapter explores just a few of the ways in which seafood can become a part of your fast-and-easy menus. Shrimp, one of the fastest-cooking foods, is featured in several recipes, from lemony Shrimp Piccata over Rice to festive Spicy Shrimp Stew. Prefer scallops? Scallops with Mushrooms and Sundried Tomatoes are unbelievably quick to make and delightfully

saucy, too. Salmon is certainly a favorite these days—moist and flavorful. To satisfy the salmon lovers in your house, whip up some Super Salmon Burgers, a super-fast, super-delicious dish that's sure to please. Or delight family and friends with Savory Crab Cakes—crisp and spicy cakes that will easily rival any you've enjoyed in restaurants. Other great choices include Crab-Stuffed Flounder Roll-Ups, garlicky Clams Marinara, and Cajun Flounder in Foil Pouches.

To speed meal preparation on those extra-hectic evenings, this chapter includes a number of complete meals—dishes that need no accompaniment except, perhaps, a crisp salad or a loaf of your favorite bread. Many of the selections mentioned above are complete meals. Other choices include Simple Seafood Paella, Garlic Shrimp Florentine, and Poached Salmon with Vegetable Couscous.

So the next time you think there's no time to cook, cook up some seafood—the fast food that's as low in fat as it is high in satisfaction.

CAJUN FLOUNDER IN FOIL POUCHES

TIME: 20 minutes   YIELD: 4 servings

MAIN INGREDIENTS

8 flounder fillets (about
   3 ounces each)

2 cups Cajun-style stewed
   tomatoes

This dish is as quick and easy as they come. Serve with brown rice and a fresh green salad.

1. Preheat the oven to 400°F.

2. Tear off 4 pieces of heavy-duty aluminum foil, each 14 x 20 inches in size. Coat each with cooking spray.

3. Place 2 flounder fillets in the center of each piece of foil, and top with $\frac{1}{2}$ cup of tomatoes. Fold the upper half of the foil over the fish and tomatoes to meet the bottom half. Seal the edges together by making a tight $\frac{1}{2}$-inch fold; then fold again to double-seal. Allow space for heat circulation and expansion. Use this technique to seal the remaining sides.

4. Arrange the pouches on a cookie sheet, and bake for 15 minutes, or until the fish is opaque and can be flaked easily with a fork. When checking for doneness, open the foil pouches carefully to allow the steam to escape.

5. Place the contents of each pouch on an individual plate, and serve immediately.

NUTRITIONAL FACTS (PER SERVING)

Calories: 190 Carbohydrates: 9 g Cholesterol: 81.5 mg Fat: 2 g Fiber: 2 g Protein: 33 g Sodium: 598 mg

HALIBUT-MUSHROOM MEDLEY IN FOIL POUCHES

TIME: 25 minutes   YIELD: 4 servings

Garlic, dill, and lemon give this halibut-mushroom combination its delightful flavor. We enjoy it over a bed of rice.

1. Preheat the oven to 450°F. Tear off 4 pieces of heavy-duty aluminum foil, each 14 x 20 inches in size. Coat each with cooking spray.

2. Place 1 halibut steak in the center of each piece of foil. Spread 1 teaspoon of garlic on each steak; then sprinkle with dill and black pepper. Top with even amounts of mushrooms and tomato halves. Spoon 1 tablespoon of lemon juice over each.

3. Fold the upper half of the foil over the fish and tomatoes to meet the bottom half. Seal the edges together by making a tight $1/2$-inch fold; then fold again to double-seal. Allow space for heat circulation and expansion. Use this technique to seal the remaining sides.

4. Arrange the pouches on a cookie sheet, and bake for 15 minutes, or until the fish is opaque and can be flaked easily with a fork. When checking for doneness, open the foil pouches carefully to allow the steam to escape.

5. Place the contents of each pouch on an individual plate. Garnish with lemon wedges and serve.

MAIN INGREDIENTS

4 halibut steaks (about 6 ounces each)

$1\frac{1}{2}$ cups packaged, presliced mushrooms

8 cherry tomatoes, halved

1 lemon, cut into wedges

STAPLES

4 teaspoons minced garlic

1 teaspoon dried dill

$\frac{1}{2}$ teaspoon freshly ground black pepper

4 tablespoons lemon juice

NUTRITIONAL FACTS (PER SERVING)

Calories: 215 Carbohydrates: 6.5 g Cholesterol: 54.5 mg Fat: 4 g Fiber: 1 g Protein: 37 g Sodium: 98 mg

POACHED SALMON WITH VEGETABLE COUSCOUS

TIME: 20 minutes   YIELD: 4 servings

COMPLETE MEAL

MAIN INGREDIENTS

½ cup finely diced red bell pepper

4 salmon fillets (about 6 ounces each)

½ cup frozen peas, thawed

1 cup couscous

½ cup nonfat sour cream

STAPLES

2 cups reduced-sodium, fat-free vegetable broth

½ cup finely diced onion

½ teaspoon dried parsley

½ teaspoon dried dill

Moist, succulent salmon is placed atop a bed of light, flavorful couscous, and then crowned with a dollop of sour cream-dill dressing. If you prefer a creamy honey-mustard dressing, simply mix 2 tablespoons of Dijon-style mustard and 1 teaspoon of honey with the sour cream. For tips on quick thawing, see page 10.

1. Place the broth, onion, bell pepper, and parsley in a 4-quart pot, and bring to a boil over high heat. Add the salmon fillets, cover, and reduce the heat to low. Simmer for 5 to 8 minutes, or until the fish can be easily flaked with a fork.

2. Transfer the fish to a plate, and cover to keep warm.

3. Bring the poaching liquid to a second boil over high heat, and stir in the peas and couscous. Cover and remove from the heat. Let sit for 5 minutes.

4. Place the sour cream and dill in a small bowl, and stir to mix well. Set aside.

5. Divide the cooked couscous among individual plates. Top each portion with a salmon fillet and a dollop of dill dressing, and serve immediately.

NUTRITIONAL FACTS (PER SERVING)

Calories: 438 Carbohydrates: 48.5 g Cholesterol: 88.5 mg Fat: 6.5 g Fiber: 4 g Protein: 43 g Sodium: 205 mg

The Freshest Catch of the Day

Whenever you select fish for your entrée, you've made a great choice. Fish is low in fat, high in important nutrients, quick-cooking, and, of course, delicious. Keep in mind, though, that fish is also highly perishable. For that reason, it's important to buy and store seafood properly. To make sure that your catch is as fresh as it is tasty, follow these guidelines:

❒ Buy fish from a reliable and busy fish store. The faster the turnover rate, the fresher the fish is likely to be.

❒ Make sure that the fish is displayed on ice. This helps keep fish at its freshest.

❒ Use your nose to select the best fish. All seafood should smell fresh and clean—not strong or "fishy."

❒ When buying fish whole, select a fish with eyes that are bright, clear, and full, not cloudy or sunken. Make sure that the scales are shiny and tightly packed, and that the flesh is firm and springy when touched. Also look for gills that are bright pink or red, rather than dull and brown. Finally, check the tail; if it's dried out, that's a good indication that the fish is not as fresh as it should be.

❒ When selecting fish fillets, look for firm fillets that are moist and dense, without any visible gaps. The flesh should be translucent, not opaque.

❒ When buying packaged fish, carefully examine the package to make sure that it contains no visible liquid. Keep in mind, though, that it's best to avoid packaged fish, as the plastic can lead to bacterial growth. Instead, whenever possible, have your fillets cut fresh for you.

❒ When choosing shrimp, remember that, depending on the variety, shrimp can be light gray, brownish pink, or red when raw. For this reason, you should not use color as an indication of freshness. Do, however, choose shrimp that are dry and firm. And when selecting unshelled shrimp, look for shiny shells.

❒ When buying shellfish such as clams and mussels, make sure that the shells are firmly closed. And, again, use your nose to avoid any strong-smelling mollusks.

❒ Choose scallops that are firm, free of cloudy liquid, and sweet smelling. An ammonia- or sulfur-like odor is a clear sign that the scallops are not at their freshest.

❒ As soon as you get your fish home, place it in the coldest part of the refrigerator, and keep it there until you're ready to prepare it. Many experts suggest placing the fish on ice in the refrigerator. Avoid freezing your fish, though. Whenever possible, use it within twenty-four hours of purchase.

SUPER SALMON BURGERS

TIME: 20 minutes

YIELD: 4 burgers

MAIN INGREDIENTS

½ cup plain nonfat yogurt

1 scallion, chopped

15-ounce can salmon, well drained and bones removed

4 egg whites, or ½ cup fat-free egg substitute

4 whole wheat mini pita pockets (4-inch rounds)

6 cups shredded romaine lettuce

STAPLES

1 teaspoon dried dill

½ cup plain bread crumbs

⅔ cup chopped onion

¼ teaspoon freshly ground black pepper

We stuff these thick, tasty salmon burgers into pita pockets along with crisp, shredded romaine lettuce. Yogurt sauce flavored with dried dill and bits of chopped scallion adds the crowning touch.

1. Place the yogurt, scallion, and dill in a small bowl, and stir to mix well. Cover and chill until ready to serve.

2. Place the salmon, egg whites, bread crumbs, onion, and black pepper in a medium-sized bowl, and mix well. Shape into 4 patties about 1 inch thick.

3. Coat a 12-inch nonstick skillet with cooking spray, and preheat over medium-high heat. Add the patties and cook for 4 to 5 minutes on each side, or until browned.

4. Cut a thin slice off the top of each pita round, and carefully open the round without separating the halves. Place 1 burger in each pita pocket, and top with 1 tablespoon of yogurt sauce and 1½ cups of shredded lettuce. Serve immediately with extra sauce on the side.

NUTRITIONAL FACTS (PER BURGER)

Calories: 330 Carbohydrates: 32 g Cholesterol: 68 mg Fat: 10 g Fiber: 5 g Protein: 32.5 g Sodium: 802 mg

SWORDFISH KABOBS

TIME: 30 minutes   YIELD: 4 servings

A side dish of Rice with Mushrooms and Onions (page 190) is the perfect accompaniment.

1. Preheat an outdoor barbecue grill or oven broiler.

2. Remove and discard the skin from the swordfish; then cut the fish into 1-inch cubes.

3. In a shallow bowl, combine the lemon juice, oil, garlic, dill, and black pepper. Add the swordfish cubes, and toss to coat. Marinate for 10 minutes.

4. Remove the fish from the marinade, and set aside. Place the marinade in a small saucepan and bring to a rolling boil. Boil for 1 minute and remove from the heat.

5. Alternating the ingredients, thread the fish, green peppers, and onions onto either 4 or 8 skewers,* depending on the length of the skewers. Place 1 or 2 cherry tomatoes in the middle of each.

6. Place the kabobs on the heated grill or under the broiler, about 4 to 5 inches from the heat source. Cook, basting several times with the remaining marinade, for 2 to 3 minutes on each side, or until the fish is opaque and easily flaked with a fork.

7. Transfer the kabobs to a platter and serve immediately with the lemon wedges.

* If using wooden skewers, be sure to soak them in water for about 30 minutes before broiling.

MAIN INGREDIENTS

1½ pounds swordfish steak

1 medium green bell pepper, cut into 2-inch squares

8 cherry tomatoes

2 small lemons, cut into wedges

STAPLES

¼ cup lemon juice

2 teaspoons canola oil

1 tablespoon minced garlic

1 teaspoon dried dill

¼ teaspoon freshly ground black pepper

2 small onions, cut into wedges

NUTRITIONAL FACTS (PER SERVING)

Calories: 212 Carbohydrates: 15.5 g Cholesterol: 45.5 mg Fat: 7.5 g Fiber: 4 g Protein: 25 g Sodium: 112 mg

CRAB-STUFFED FLOUNDER ROLL-UPS

TIME: 25 minutes

YIELD: 4 servings

MAIN INGREDIENTS

6-ounce can crab meat

4 flounder fillets (about 4 ounces each)

1 medium lemon, cut into wedges

STAPLES

½ cup flavored bread crumbs, divided

½ teaspoon crushed red pepper

2 tablespoons fat-free mayonnaise

Cooking spray

Paprika

Crushed red pepper adds a spark of flavor to the crab stuffing used in these delicious flounder roll-ups. Try this dish with Creamy Caraway Cole Slaw (page 66) and steaming brown rice.

1. Preheat the oven to 425°F. Coat a large baking sheet with cooking spray, and set aside. Place half the bread crumbs on a shallow plate, and set aside.

2. Place the crab meat in a wire mesh strainer, and rinse under cool running water. Pick over the crab, removing any cartilage. Carefully press out all of the water. Pat dry with paper towels, and transfer to a large bowl. Add the remaining bread crumbs, crushed red pepper, and mayonnaise. Mix well and set aside.

3. Lightly spray each fillet with cooking spray, and coat both sides with the reserved bread crumbs. Spread even amounts of the crab mixture onto each fillet; then roll up and secure with a toothpick.

4. Arrange the roll-ups on the baking sheet, sprinkle with the paprika, and bake for 12 to 15 minutes, or until the fish is no longer translucent. Squeeze the fresh lemon over the roll-ups, and serve immediately.

NUTRITIONAL FACTS (PER SERVING)

Calories: 194 Carbohydrates: 14.5 g Cholesterol: 90 mg Fat: 2 g Fiber: 2 g Protein: 30 g Sodium: 713 mg

SAVORY CRAB CAKES

TIME: 45 minutes   YIELD: 4 servings (2 cakes each)

These flavorful crab cakes will rival any you've enjoyed in restaurants. Accompany them with Chili-Lime Tabbouleh (page 60) or Black Bean Salad with Corn and Peppers (page 56).

1. Place the crab meat in a wire mesh strainer, and rinse under cool running water. Pick over the crab, removing any cartilage. Carefully press out all of the water. Pat dry with paper towels, and transfer to a large bowl.

2. Add 1 cup of the bread crumbs and the scallions, red pepper, egg substitute, Old Bay seasoning, and black pepper to the crab meat, and stir to mix well. Divide the mixture into 8 equal portions, and shape into ¾-inch-thick cakes.

3. Place the reserved crumbs in a shallow bowl, and press each cake into the crumbs to coat completely.

4. Coat a 12-inch nonstick skillet with cooking spray, and preheat over medium-high heat. Add the crab cakes, and cook for about 6 minutes, or until browned on the bottom. Lightly spray the tops with cooking spray and turn. Cook for 6 additional minutes, or until browned on the second side.

5. Serve immediately with lemon wedges and Tabasco sauce, if desired.

MAIN INGREDIENTS

4 cans (6 ounces each) crab meat

1 cup minced scallions

1 cup minced red bell pepper

1 cup fat-free egg substitute

2 lemons, cut into wedges (optional)

STAPLES

1½ cups plain bread crumbs, divided

2 teaspoons Old Bay seasoning or other seafood seasoning

½ teaspoon freshly ground black pepper

Cooking spray

Tabasco sauce (optional)

NUTRITIONAL FACTS (PER SERVING)

Calories: 331 Carbohydrates: 34 g Cholesterol: 140.5 mg Fat: 4.5 g Fiber: 2.5 g Protein: 38 g Sodium: 1,392 mg

CRAB-SCALLION FOO YOUNG

TIME: 40 minutes

YIELD: 4 servings

MAIN INGREDIENTS

2 cans (6 ounces each) crab meat

4 large scallions, finely chopped

1 teaspoon grated fresh ginger

2 cups fat-free egg substitute

STAPLES

2 teaspoons Old Bay seasoning or Mrs. Dash extra-spicy seasoning blend

½ teaspoon freshly ground black pepper

Serve these Chinese-inspired mini-omelets with a sprinkling of soy sauce.

1. Place the crab meat in a wire mesh strainer, and rinse under cool running water. Pick over the crab, removing any cartilage. Carefully press out all of the water. Pat dry with paper towels, and transfer to a large bowl.

2. Add the scallions, ginger, seasoning blend, and black pepper to the crab meat, and toss together well to blend. Add the egg substitute to the crab mixture, and mix well. The mixture will be somewhat thick (not runny).

3. Coat a 12-inch nonstick skillet with cooking spray, and preheat over medium heat. Drop ¼-cup amounts of the mixture on the hot surface (you can make 2, possibly 3 at a time). Cook until lightly browned, turn, and cook until the second side is brown and the omelet is cooked through, about 1 minute per side. Transfer to a platter, and cover to keep warm. Repeat with the remaining mixture, and serve immediately.

NUTRITIONAL FACTS (PER SERVING)

Calories: 165 Carbohydrates: 4 g Cholesterol: 71.5 mg Fat: 4 g Fiber: 1 g Protein: 29 g Sodium: 896 mg

CLAMS MARINARA

TIME: 30 minutes   YIELD: 4 servings

These plump, juicy clams are best served over a bed of spaghetti, linguine, or other long pasta.

1. Preheat the oven to 450°F.

2. Arrange the clams in a large, deep casserole dish. Set aside. Coarsely chop the tomatoes, and place them in a large bowl along with the basil, garlic, oregano, black pepper, and salt if desired. Stir to mix, and spoon over the clams.

3. Cover and bake for 20 to 25 minutes, or until the clams open. Do not overcook, or the clams will become tough and rubbery. Garnish with the lemon wedges, and serve immediately.

MAIN INGREDIENTS

24 cherrystone clams, scrubbed well

2 cans (14.5 ounces each) no-salt-added peeled tomatoes

1 cup (loosely packed) coarsely chopped fresh basil leaves

1 medium lemon, cut into wedges

STAPLES

6 cloves garlic, thinly sliced

1 teaspoon dried oregano

¼ teaspoon freshly ground black pepper

½ teaspoon salt (optional)

NUTRITIONAL FACTS (PER SERVING)

Calories: 223 Carbohydrates: 19 g Cholesterol: 75 mg Fat: 2.5 g Fiber: 3.5 g Protein: 31.5 g Sodium: 160 mg

PARSLEY-BROILED SCALLOPS

TIME: 25 minutes   YIELD: 4 servings

MAIN INGREDIENTS

1 tablespoon chopped fresh
  parsley

1 teaspoon grated fresh
  lemon rind

1¼ pounds sea scallops

1 lemon, cut into wedges

STAPLES

¼ cup flavored bread crumbs

1 teaspoon olive oil

This nearly effortless dish is simple and delicious.

1. Preheat an oven broiler.

2. Place the bread crumbs, parsley, and lemon rind in a large bowl, and stir to mix well. Stir in the oil.

3. Add the scallops to the bread crumb mixture, and toss until well coated. Coat a large nonstick baking sheet with cooking spray, and arrange the scallops in a single layer on the sheet.

4. Place the baking sheet under the broiler, about 4 inches below the heat source. Broil for 6 to 8 minutes, or until the coating is browned and the scallops are no longer translucent when cut with a knife.

5. Divide among 4 individual plates, garnishing each serving with lemon wedges.

NUTRITIONAL FACTS (PER SERVING)

Calories: 163 Carbohydrates: 9 g Cholesterol: 47 mg Fat: 2.5 g Fiber: 0.5 g Protein: 25 g Sodium: 428 mg

SCALLOPS WITH MUSHROOMS AND SUNDRIED TOMATOES

TIME: 25 minutes

YIELD: 4 servings

Presliced mushrooms and scallops—which cook in less than 5 minutes—help you make this deliciously saucy dish in no time flat.

1. Bring a 4-quart pot of water to a rolling boil. Add the pasta, and cook according to package directions.

2. While the water is heating up, place the dried tomatoes in a small heatproof dish. Pour the boiling water over the tomatoes, and set aside for 10 minutes.

3. Drain the tomatoes, reserving the liquid. Cut the tomatoes into thin strips and set aside.

4. Coat a 12-inch nonstick skillet or large wok with cooking spray, and preheat over medium-high heat. Add the garlic and mushrooms, and cook, stirring constantly, for 2 minutes. Add the scallops and tomato strips, and continue to cook and stir for about 3 minutes, or just until the scallops are opaque.

5. Place the lemon juice in a small dish, and stir in the cornstarch until well mixed. Add the cornstarch mixture, reserved tomato liquid, scallions, parsley, and oregano to the skillet or wok, and stir to mix well. Continue to cook until hot and bubbly; then cook for an additional minute.

6. Drain the cooked pasta well, and arrange it over a serving platter. Pour the scallop mixture over the pasta, and serve immediately.

COMPLETE MEAL

MAIN INGREDIENTS

8 ounces fettuccine pasta

6 sundried tomatoes

8 ounces packaged, presliced mushrooms (about 2½ cups)

1 pound bay scallops

3 scallions, sliced

STAPLES

⅓ cup boiling water

4 cloves garlic, minced

2 tablespoons lemon juice

2 teaspoons cornstarch

2 teaspoons dried parsley

⅛ teaspoon dried oregano

NUTRITIONAL FACTS (PER SERVING)

Calories: 365 Carbohydrates: 56.5 g Cholesterol: 37.5 mg Fat: 2.5 g Fiber: 6 g Protein: 29 g Sodium: 194 mg

SIMPLE SEAFOOD PAELLA

TIME: 30 minutes   **YIELD:** 4 servings

COMPLETE MEAL

MAIN INGREDIENTS

10 ounces peeled and deveined medium shrimp

10 ounces bay scallops

1½ cups long grain white rice

1 small red bell pepper, thinly sliced

½ cup chopped fresh parsley

STAPLES

1 teaspoon paprika

½ teaspoon turmeric

¼ teaspoon freshly ground black pepper

½ teaspoon salt (optional)

3½ cups reduced-sodium, fat-free chicken broth

1 medium onion, cut into wedges

1 tablespoon plus 1 teaspoon minced garlic

Succulent shrimp and tender scallops are featured in this flavorful one-pot rice dish.

1. Place the shrimp and scallops in a bowl. Sprinkle with the paprika, turmeric, black pepper, and salt, if desired, and stir to coat.

2. Place the broth in a 4-quart pot, and bring to a boil over high heat. Add the shrimp, scallops, onion, garlic, and rice, and stir to mix. Reduce the heat to low, cover, and simmer for 15 minutes.

3. Add the bell pepper and parsley to the rice mixture, stir once, and continue to simmer covered for 5 to 7 additional minutes, or until the liquid has been absorbed and the rice is tender. Serve immediately.

NUTRITIONAL FACTS (PER SERVING)

Calories: 447 Carbohydrates: 64.5 g Cholesterol: 131 mg Fat: 2.5 g Fiber: 2.5 g Protein: 38.5 g Sodium: 375 mg

SHRIMP PICCATA OVER RICE

TIME: 30 minutes   **YIELD:** 4 servings

Both easy to make and elegant, this entrée is perfect for weekday meals and festive dinners alike.

1. Place the water in a 1-quart saucepan, and bring to a boil over high heat. Stir in the rice, cover, and reduce the heat to medium-low. Cook for about 18 minutes, or until all of the water has been absorbed. Keep warm.

2. While the rice is cooking, place the wine, lemon juice, and capers in a small bowl, and stir to mix. Set aside.

3. Place the flour in a large, shallow bowl. Add the shrimp, and toss until well coated.

4. Coat a 12-inch nonstick skillet or large wok with cooking spray, and preheat over medium-high heat. Add the garlic, and cook, stirring constantly, for about 20 seconds. Add *half* the shrimp and cook, stirring or tossing frequently, for 3 minutes, or just until the shrimp have turned pink. Transfer the cooked shrimp to a bowl, and repeat with the remaining shrimp. Again, transfer the cooked shrimp to the bowl.

5. Stir the wine mixture, and add to the skillet. Cook a minute or 2 at a boil, stirring constantly, until slightly reduced. Add the shrimp and black pepper, stir to mix, and cook for 1 to 2 minutes, or until warmed through and well coated.

6. Divide the rice among individual serving plates, and top with the shrimp. Serve immediately.

MAIN INGREDIENTS

1 cup long grain white rice

2 teaspoons capers, drained

1 pound peeled and deveined medium shrimp

STAPLES

1½ cups water

⅓ cup dry white wine

2 tablespoons lemon juice

3 tablespoons all-purpose flour

3 large cloves garlic, thinly sliced

⅛ teaspoon freshly ground black pepper

NUTRITIONAL FACTS (PER SERVING)

Calories: 329 Carbohydrates: 44 g Cholesterol: 172.5 mg Fat: 2.5 g Fiber: 1 g Protein: 27.5 g Sodium: 224 mg

GARLIC SHRIMP FLORENTINE

TIME: 30 minutes   **YIELD:** 4 servings

COMPLETE MEAL

MAIN INGREDIENTS

2 packages (10 ounces each) frozen chopped spinach

1¼ pounds peeled and deveined medium shrimp

¼ cup chopped Canadian bacon

STAPLES

¼ teaspoon garlic powder

⅛ teaspoon freshly ground black pepper

¼ teaspoon salt (optional)

4 large cloves garlic, thinly sliced

¼ teaspoon Tabasco sauce

⅛ teaspoon crushed red pepper

A bed of lightly seasoned spinach perfectly complements these savory, easy-to-make shrimp.

1. Cook the spinach according to package directions. Drain well, season with the garlic powder, black pepper, and salt, if desired, and cover to keep warm.

2. While the spinach is cooking, coat a 12-inch nonstick skillet or wok with cooking spray, and preheat over medium-high heat. Add the garlic, and cook, stirring constantly, for about 2 minutes, or just until the garlic begins to turn golden. Do not allow it to turn brown.

3. Add the shrimp and Canadian bacon, and cook, tossing or stirring often, for 2 to 4 minutes, or just until the shrimp turn pink. Do not overcook the shrimp. Stir in the Tabasco sauce and crushed red pepper.

4. Arrange the spinach over a serving platter. Spoon the shrimp mixture over the spinach, and serve immediately.

NUTRITIONAL FACTS (PER SERVING)

Calories: 201 Carbohydrates: 8 g Cholesterol: 220.5 mg Fat: 3.5 g Fiber: 4.5 g Protein: 35 g Sodium: 394 mg

Top Left and Bottom: Crab-Stuffed Flounder Roll-Ups (page 150)

Top Right: Savory Crab Cakes (page 151)

Center: Chili-Lime Tabbouleh (page 60)

Top Left: Spicy Shrimp Stew (page 159)
Top Right: Swordfish Kabobs (page 149)
Bottom: Super Salmon Burgers (page 148)

Top and Center Right: Asparagus-Onion Frittata (page 162)
Center Left: Ratatouille Over Sweet Pepper Couscous (page 179)
Bottom: Southwestern Tortilla Pizzas (page 175)

Top Left: Zucchini, Onion, and Tomato Sauté (page 198)

Top Right: Curried Couscous with Raisins and Almonds (page 185)

Bottom: Green Beans with Caramelized Onions (page 186)

SPICY SHRIMP STEW

TIME: 45 minutes   YIELD: 4 servings

This festive-looking dish is delightfully spicy. For more or less heat, adjust the amount of cayenne pepper.

1. Place the water in a 1-quart saucepan, and bring to a boil over high heat. Stir in the rice, cover, and reduce the heat to medium-low. Cook for about 18 minutes, or until all of the water has been absorbed. Keep warm.

2. While the rice is cooking, coat a 12-inch nonstick skillet with cooking spray, and preheat over medium heat. Add the bell pepper, onion, garlic, and cumin, and cook, stirring often, for about 5 minutes, or until the onion is soft.

3. Stir the tomato paste into the bell pepper mixture, and cook for about 1 minute.

4. Stir the wine and bay leaf into the bell pepper mixture. Increase the heat to high, and bring the mixture to a boil. Reduce the heat to medium-low, just to the point of a simmer, and cook uncovered for 5 minutes.

5. Add the shrimp, and stir to mix. Cover and cook, stirring occasionally, for about 5 minutes, or just until the shrimp are done.

6. Remove and discard the bay leaf, and stir in the cayenne pepper. Spread the hot rice over a serving platter, and spoon the shrimp and sauce over the rice. Sprinkle with the cilantro, and serve.

COMPLETE MEAL

MAIN INGREDIENTS

1 cup long grain white rice

1 cup diced red bell pepper

¼ cup plus 2 tablespoons no-salt-added tomato paste

1 pound peeled and deveined medium shrimp

3 tablespoons chopped fresh cilantro

STAPLES

1½ cups water

1 cup diced onion

3 large cloves garlic, minced

¾ teaspoon ground cumin

1 cup plus 2 tablespoons dry white wine

1 bay leaf

⅛ teaspoon cayenne pepper

NUTRITIONAL FACTS (PER SERVING)

Calories: 384 Carbohydrates: 50 g Cholesterol: 172.5 mg Fat: 2.5 g Fiber: 3 g Protein: 28.5 g Sodium: 198 mg

9. VEGETARIAN DELIGHTS

The many benefits and pleasures of vegetarian meals cannot be disputed. By eliminating meat, you eliminate the fat found in even the leanest cuts. And by focusing on grains, legumes, and vegetables, you boost healthful nutrients like fiber, vitamins, and minerals. Perhaps best of all, these dishes give star status to ingredients usually cast in supporting roles, allowing you to fully savor the sweet chewiness of grains, the heartiness of beans, and the rich colors and flavors of vegetables.

But along with these rewards comes one drawback: When traditionally prepared, vegetarian meals often require lengthy preparation times. The cooking of dried beans alone takes hours, not to mention the time required to clean, chop, and cook vegetables. Fortunately, it now is possible for even the kitchen-quickies cook to prepare satisfying meatless meals. How? When creating the following recipes, we began with a number of high-quality products like quick-cooking rice, frozen vegetables, and salsa. To this base, we added garden-fresh vegetables, herbs, spices, and low-fat cheeses. The results are healthy, satisfying dishes that can be made in little time, without any sacrifice of flavor.

The following pages present a range of tantalizing meatless meals. If you love the velvety texture of black beans, be sure to try our Sassy Black Beans and Rice, a spicy dish that can be prepared in only thirty-five minutes. If even this is just too much time, prepare Fast Black Beans and Rice. Jarred salsa allows you to make this streamlined version in just *fifteen* minutes. Prefer a savory vegetable stir-fry? With frozen stir-fry vegetables and a few other handy ingredients, you can enjoy gingery Stir-Fried Vegetable Rice in a little over half an hour. Other possibilities include crisp Southwestern Tortilla Pizzas, and Hearty Lentil Stew.

So whenever you want a change of pace from the usual meat, chicken, and fish entrées, treat yourself to a dish like White Bean and Salsa Quesadillas or savory Asparagus-Onion Frittata. You need only a few minutes and even fewer ingredients to enjoy the incomparable rewards of vegetarian cuisine.

ASPARAGUS-ONION FRITTATA

TIME: 30 minutes   YIELD: 4 servings

COMPLETE MEAL

MAIN INGREDIENTS

9-ounce package frozen asparagus

2 cups fat-free egg substitute

2 tablespoons grated Parmesan cheese, divided

4 plum tomatoes, thinly sliced

STAPLES

2 teaspoons olive oil

1 large onion, coarsely chopped

1 teaspoon salt (optional)

½ teaspoon freshly ground black pepper

Serve this frittata along with a fresh green salad for a light lunch or dinner.

1. Preheat the oven broiler.

2. Set the frozen asparagus in a bowl of hot water for 4 to 5 minutes, or until thawed. Remove the asparagus, and gently squeeze to remove the excess water. Place on paper towels and pat dry. Cut the asparagus into ½-inch pieces, and set aside.

3. While the asparagus are thawing, coat a 12-inch non-stick ovenproof skillet with cooking spray, add the oil, and preheat over medium-low heat. Add the onion, and cook, stirring often, for 4 to 5 minutes, or until soft and beginning to brown.

4. Place the egg substitute in a medium-sized bowl. Add 1 tablespoon of the cheese, the salt, if desired, and the black pepper, and stir to mix well. Stir in the asparagus.

5. Pour the egg mixture over the sautéed onion. Allow the eggs to cook over medium-low heat for 5 to 6 minutes, or until the bottom is brown and set. Place the pan under the broiler, about 4 inches below the heat source, and cook for 3 to 4 minutes, or until the top of the frittata is cooked and light brown.

6. Slide the frittata onto a large platter, top with the tomato slices, and sprinkle with the remaining tablespoon of cheese. Cut into wedges, and serve immediately.

NUTRITIONAL FACTS (PER SERVING)

Calories: 175 Carbohydrates: 8 g Cholesterol: 3.5 mg Fat: 7.5 g Fiber: 2 g Protein: 20.5 g Sodium: 288 mg

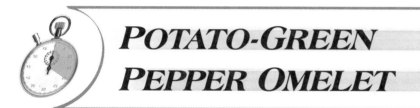

POTATO-GREEN PEPPER OMELET

TIME: 20 minutes   **YIELD:** 4 servings

Enjoy this omelet as is or in a sandwich between slices of fresh Italian bread.

1. Place the potato in a microwave-safe bowl. Spray with cooking spray, and toss to coat. Cover with plastic wrap or waxed paper and microwave on high power for 4 to 5 minutes, or until tender when pierced with a fork. Set aside.

2. Place the onion and green pepper in another microwave-safe bowl, and toss to mix. Add 1 or 2 tablespoons of water, cover, and microwave on high power for 2 to 3 minutes, or until the pepper and onion are soft.

3. Coat a 12-inch nonstick skillet with cooking spray, add the oil, and preheat over medium heat. Add the onion and green pepper, and cook just until the onion begins to brown. Add the potato and cook for another minute.

4. Place the egg substitute in a medium-sized bowl, and stir in the salt, if desired, and the black pepper. Pour the egg mixture over the ingredients in the skillet. As the egg begins to set, run a spatula around the perimeter of the omelet, lifting it up to allow the uncooked egg to run underneath. Continue lifting until the egg is completely cooked.* Cut into wedges and serve immediately.

* If you prefer, you can let the omelet cook for 3 to 4 minutes, or until the bottom is browned. Then carefully flip the omelet over, and cook the other side for 3 to 4 minutes, or until the egg is cooked.

COMPLETE MEAL

MAIN INGREDIENTS

1 medium potato, peeled and diced

1 small green bell pepper, thinly sliced

2 cups fat-free egg substitute

STAPLES

Cooking spray

1 medium onion, coarsely chopped

2 teaspoons canola oil

1 teaspoon salt (optional)

½ teaspoon freshly ground black pepper

NUTRITIONAL FACTS (PER SERVING)

Calories: 170 Carbohydrates: 11 g Cholesterol: 1.5 mg Fat: 6.5 g Fiber: 1.5 g Protein: 17.5 g Sodium: 225 mg

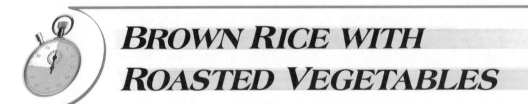

BROWN RICE WITH ROASTED VEGETABLES

TIME: 45 minutes   **YIELD:** 4 servings

COMPLETE MEAL

MAIN INGREDIENTS

1 medium green or red bell
  pepper (about 6 ounces),
  cut into bite-sized pieces

1 medium zucchini (about
  8 ounces), scrubbed well
  and cut into ½-inch rounds

1 small eggplant (about
  12 ounces), cut into
  bite-sized pieces

2 cups instant brown rice

STAPLES

1 cup reduced-sodium,
  fat-free vegetable broth

3 tablespoons light soy sauce

1 tablespoon Mrs. Dash
  original seasoning blend

½ teaspoon garlic powder

1 medium onion (about
  8 ounces), cut into wedges

2 cups water

Oven-roasted vegetables top steaming brown rice in this vegetarian delight.

1. Preheat the oven to 450°F. Coat a 9-x-13-inch baking dish with cooking spray, and set aside.

2. Place the broth, soy sauce, Mrs. Dash seasoning, and garlic powder in a small bowl, and stir to mix. Set aside.

3. Arrange the onion, bell pepper, zucchini, and eggplant in the baking dish. Pour the broth-soy sauce mixture on top. Cover with aluminum foil, and bake for 25 to 30 minutes, or just until the vegetables are tender, but not mushy.

4. While the vegetables are cooking, place the water in a 2-quart saucepan, and bring to a boil over high heat. Stir in the rice, cover, and reduce the heat to medium-low. Cook for 10 minutes, or until all the water has been absorbed.

5. Spoon the cooked rice onto a serving platter. Top with the roasted vegetables and their cooking juices, and serve immediately.

NUTRITIONAL FACTS (PER SERVING)

Calories: 352 Carbohydrates: 74.5 g Cholesterol: 0 mg Fat: 3 g Fiber: 10.5 g Protein: 10 g Sodium: 721 mg

The Greatness of Grains

We can't say enough in praise of grains. Nutritious, flavorful, and delightfully chewy, grains are deeply satisfying. They're versatile, too. In our recipes, we use them as a bed for stews and sautés, as a base for salads and side dishes, and as a hearty addition to soups. Sometimes we enhance our grains with herbs and spices, chopped vegetables, or broths. When unflavored, grains serve as "neutral" backdrops for well-seasoned entrées. Of course, in vegetarian dishes, grains do more than satisfy the appetite and tantalize the taste buds. Paired with beans or other legumes, with seeds and nuts, or with leafy greens, they form a complete protein, which is so important when you've eliminated meat from your meal.

As you may be aware, when cooking time is limited, your grain choices are a bit limited, too, as some whole grains do require long cooking times. Fortunately, even when time is in short supply, many grains are well within your reach. Following are just a few of the common, easily available grains that you may wish to try. If you find that you want to experiment further, pay a visit to your local health food or specialty store. They're sure to have additional grain choices.

Barley. Although most often thought of as a soup ingredient, with its light nutty flavor, barley makes a nice change from rice when cooking pilafs. Hulled barley takes nearly an hour to prepare. Instead, use a quick-cooking product, which can be prepared in ten to fifteen minutes.

Basmati Rice. This aromatic rice, which has gained popularity in the last few years, is prized for its nutty flavor and exotic fragrance. Although whole basmati rice requires a long cooking time, the white version cooks up in about twenty minutes. If you can't find basmati rice in your grocery store, check your health food or specialty store.

Brown Rice. With its firm texture and earthy flavor, brown rice is a great all-purpose grain. And because the bran layer has been left intact, it's far more nutritious than its white counterpart. Although regular brown rice takes forty minutes or more to cook, many quick-cooking brands are now available. Arrowhead Mills brand takes only about twenty minutes. When there's really no time to cook, try a brand like Uncle Ben's, which is ready in ten minutes.

Bulgur Wheat. Bulgur is whole grain wheat that has been steamed, dried, and cracked. It's a snap to prepare; all you do is pour boiling water over the bulgur and allow it to sit for about twenty-five minutes. Most commonly, this hearty grain is enjoyed as the main ingredient in tabbouleh, a cold salad. But it can also be served hot; after steeping the grain, just cover it tightly with plastic wrap and microwave for about four minutes.

Couscous. Although it looks like and is served as a grain, couscous is actually a mild-flavored miniature pasta. Traditional couscous requires a long cooking time. Most of the commonly available couscous, though, has been precooked and dried, so that you can prepare it in only five minutes. (Like bulgur, it's steeped in boiling water rather than being cooked over heat.) Be sure to check the cooking time on the package to ensure that the couscous you buy has been precooked.

White Rice. Most of us grew up with white rice, and love its smooth texture, as well as its ability to soak up the flavors of cooking broths and seasonings. Although instant varieties are available, we greatly prefer regular white rice, which cooks in only about twenty minutes.

COUSCOUS CONFETTI

TIME: 30 minutes   YIELD: 4 servings

COMPLETE MEAL

MAIN INGREDIENTS

*2 small plum tomatoes,
coarsely chopped*

*4½ cups (loosely packed)
chopped packaged,
prewashed spinach*

*2½ cups canned chickpeas,
rinsed and drained*

*1 cup frozen green peas,
thawed*

1 cup couscous

STAPLES

2 teaspoons olive oil

*1 medium onion, finely
chopped*

*1½ cups reduced-sodium,
fat-free vegetable broth,
divided*

*2 teaspoons Mrs. Dash
original seasoning blend*

*Easy to prepare, fast, and filling! For tips on quick thawing,
see page 10.*

1. Coat a 4-quart pot with cooking spray, add the oil, and preheat over medium heat. Toss in the onion and tomatoes, and cook, stirring often, for about 5 minutes, or until the onion begins to brown.

2. Add the spinach, chickpeas, and 1 or 2 tablespoons of the broth, and stir to mix. Continue to cook, stirring occasionally, for 2 to 3 minutes, or until the spinach begins to wilt.

3. Add the remaining broth, Mrs. Dash seasoning, and peas to the vegetable mixture, and stir to mix. Increase the heat to high, and bring to a boil. Stir in the couscous, cover the pot, and remove from the heat.

4. Let the ingredients sit for 10 minutes, or until the couscous is tender and the broth has been absorbed. Serve immediately.

NUTRITIONAL FACTS (PER SERVING)

Calories: 400 Carbohydrates: 72.5 g Cholesterol: 0 mg Fat: 6 g Fiber: 15 g Protein: 15.5 g Sodium: 317 mg

SASSY BLACK BEANS AND RICE

TIME: 35 minutes

YIELD: 4 servings

Spicy, saucy, and satisfying. Colorful, too! What more can you ask from a hot and hearty entrée?

1. Coat a 12-inch nonstick skillet with cooking spray, and preheat over medium-high heat. Add the onions, garlic, and green pepper, and cook, stirring frequently, for about 5 minutes, or until the onions are soft.

2. Stir the tomatoes into the onion mixture, and cook for 3 additional minutes, or until the tomatoes are soft.

3. While the vegetables are cooking, place the water in a small saucepan, and bring to a boil over high heat. Stir in the rice, cover, and reduce the heat to medium-low. Cook for 10 minutes, or until all the water has been absorbed.

4. Add all of the remaining ingredients, except for the sour cream, to the vegetable mixture, and stir to mix. Reduce the heat to medium, and cook, stirring occasionally, for about 5 minutes, or until the mixture is heated through and the liquid is slightly reduced.

5. Divide the rice among individual serving plates, and top with the beans. Serve immediately, as is or topped with a dollop of light sour cream.

COMPLETE MEAL

MAIN INGREDIENTS

1 large green bell pepper, chopped

2 large tomatoes, diced

2 cups instant brown rice

2 cans (1 pound each) black beans, rinsed and drained

½ cup no-salt-added tomato sauce

Light sour cream (optional)

STAPLES

2 medium onions, chopped

4 large cloves garlic, minced

2 cups water

2 tablespoons red wine vinegar

1½ teaspoons ground cumin

½ teaspoon freshly ground black pepper

⅛ teaspoon cayenne pepper

NUTRITIONAL FACTS (PER SERVING)

Calories: 413 Carbohydrates: 79 g Cholesterol: 0 mg Fat: 4 g Fiber: 17.5 g Protein: 19 g Sodium: 446 mg

FAST BLACK BEANS AND RICE

TIME: 15 minutes

YIELD: 4 servings

COMPLETE MEAL

MAIN INGREDIENTS

2 cups instant brown rice

2 cans (1 pound each) organic
black beans, drained

2 cups low-sodium salsa,
undrained*

Light sour cream (optional)

STAPLES

2 cups water

1 teaspoon dried oregano

* Green Mountain Gringo Salsa
is a good brand.

Although Sassy Black Beans and Rice (page 167) is delicious and doesn't take long to make, sometimes you want to get dinner on the table in just 15 minutes. By using commercial salsa as a ready-made sauce, this recipe allows you to do just that.

1. Place the water in a 2-quart saucepan, and bring to a boil over high heat. Stir in the rice, cover, and reduce the heat to medium-low. Cook for 10 minutes, or until the rice is tender and all of the water has been absorbed.

2. While the rice is cooking, place all of the remaining ingredients, except for the sour cream, in a 2-quart pot, and bring to a boil over high heat, stirring occasionally. Reduce the heat to medium-low, just to the point of a simmer. Cook, stirring occasionally, for about 5 minutes, or until the flavors are blended.

3. Divide the rice among individual serving plates, and top with the beans. Serve immediately, as is or topped with a dollop of light sour cream.

NUTRITIONAL FACTS (PER SERVING)

Calories: 333 Carbohydrates: 72 g Cholesterol: 0 mg Fat: 2.5 g Fiber: 12.5 g Protein: 16.5 g Sodium: 376 mg

HEARTY LENTIL STEW

TIME: 40 minutes   YIELD: 4 servings

Be sure to serve this hearty stew with crusty whole grain bread to soak up all of the delicious juices.

1. Place all of the ingredients, except for the Parmesan cheese, in a 4-quart pot, and stir to mix. Cover and bring to a boil over high heat.

2. Reduce the heat to medium-low, and simmer for 20 to 25 minutes, or just until the lentils are tender.

3. Spoon the stew into individual serving bowls and serve immediately, as is or topped with a sprinkling of Parmesan cheese.

COMPLETE MEAL

MAIN INGREDIENTS

1 cup dried lentils, rinsed and drained

1 medium carrot, peeled and thinly sliced

1 medium celery stalk, thinly sliced

1 large potato, peeled and diced

Grated Parmesan cheese (optional)

STAPLES

3 cups water

2 teaspoons minced garlic

1 teaspoon dried parsley

½ teaspoon salt

¼ teaspoon freshly ground black pepper

NUTRITIONAL FACTS (PER SERVING)

Calories: 208 Carbohydrates: 39.5 g Cholesterol: 0 mg Fat: 0.5 g Fiber: 13.5 g Protein: 13 g Sodium: 312 mg

MUSHROOM STROGANOFF

TIME: 40 minutes   YIELD: 4 servings

COMPLETE MEAL

MAIN INGREDIENTS

1½ pounds small whole white mushrooms

8 ounces "no-yolk" noodles

⅔ cup light sour cream

Whole mushrooms, blanketed in a well-seasoned sour cream sauce, make a savory topping for noodles in this meatless version of a classic Stroganoff.

1. Quickly rinse and dry the mushrooms, and trim off the ends of the stems. Cut any large mushrooms in half.

2. Bring a 4-quart pot of water to a rolling boil. Add the noodles, and cook according to package directions.

3. While the water is heating up, coat a 12-inch nonstick skillet or large wok with cooking spray, and preheat over medium-high heat. Add the onion and garlic, and cook, stirring frequently, for about 4 minutes, or until soft. Transfer the mixture to a bowl and set aside.

4. Again coat the skillet with cooking spray, and add the mushrooms. Cook over medium-high heat, stirring or tossing often, for about 5 minutes, or until the mushrooms are lightly browned and tender.

5. Stir the onion mixture, broth, Worcestershire sauce, and black pepper into the mushrooms, and bring to a boil. Continue to cook at a boil for about 2 minutes, or until the broth is slightly reduced.

6. Reduce the heat under the skillet to low, and wait until the mixture is no longer boiling. Stir the flour into the sour cream until smooth; then slowly stir the sour cream into the skillet mixture. Heat, stirring often, for about 5 minutes, or until the mixture has thickened.

7. Drain the noodles well, and divide among individual serving plates. Top with the Stroganoff and serve.

STAPLES

1 medium onion, chopped

4 cloves garlic, chopped

1½ cups reduced-sodium, fat-free vegetable broth

2 teaspoons Worcestershire sauce

¼ teaspoon freshly ground black pepper

2 tablespoons all-purpose flour

NUTRITIONAL FACTS (PER SERVING)

Calories: 348 Carbohydrates: 59 g Cholesterol: 13.5 mg Fat: 5.5 g Fiber: 4.5 g Protein: 16 g Sodium: 458 mg

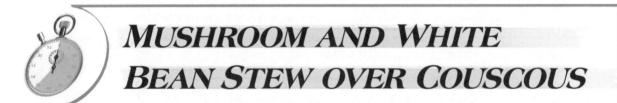

MUSHROOM AND WHITE BEAN STEW OVER COUSCOUS

TIME: 35 minutes   YIELD: 4 servings

COMPLETE MEAL

MAIN INGREDIENTS

1½ pounds small whole white
  mushrooms

1½ cups couscous

1-pound can stewed tomatoes

1-pound can cannellini beans
  (white kidney beans),
  rinsed and drained

¼ cup chopped fresh parsley

Grated Parmesan cheese
  (optional)

STAPLES

1 cup diced onions

4 cloves garlic, chopped

1½ teaspoons dried Italian
  seasoning

2 cups water

2 pinches cayenne pepper

Mushrooms lend a meaty taste and texture to this satisfying entrée.

1. Quickly rinse and dry the mushrooms, and trim off the ends of the stems. Cut any large mushrooms in half.

2. Coat a large nonstick wok or 12-inch skillet with olive-oil cooking spray and preheat over medium to medium-high heat. Add the mushrooms, onions, garlic, and Italian seasoning, and cook, stirring often, for 8 to 10 minutes, or until the mushrooms are tender.

3. While the mushrooms are cooking, place the water in a 1-quart saucepan, and bring to a boil over high heat. Stir in the couscous and cover. Remove from the heat, and allow to sit for 5 minutes, or until all of the water has been absorbed.

4. Using a knife, slightly cut up the tomatoes in the can. Add the tomatoes, beans, and cayenne pepper to the mushroom mixture. Stir to mix, and cook for about 3 minutes, or until heated through.

5. Stir the parsley into the couscous. Divide the couscous among individual serving plates, and top with the stew. Serve immediately, as is or topped with a sprinkling of Parmesan cheese.

NUTRITIONAL FACTS (PER SERVING)

Calories: 424 Carbohydrates: 86 g Cholesterol: 0 mg Fat: 2 g Fiber: 12.5 g Protein: 18 g Sodium: 447 mg

RATATOUILLE ITALIAN BREAD PIZZA

TIME: 45 minutes   YIELD: 4 servings

You'll love this pizza's crunchy crust and savory topping. For added zing, sprinkle with crushed red pepper flakes before serving.

1. Preheat the oven to 425°F.

2. Coat a large nonstick wok or 12-inch skillet with cooking spray, and preheat over medium-high heat. Add the eggplant, onion, and garlic, and cook, stirring frequently, for about 10 minutes, or until the eggplant is soft and lightly browned.

3. While the eggplant mixture is cooking, cut the bread in half lengthwise. Then cut each half in half to make 4 quarters.

4. Place the bread on a baking pan, crust side up, and bake for about 5 minutes, or until the crusts are lightly browned. Turn cut side up, and bake for another 3 minutes, or until lightly browned. Remove from the oven.

5. Add the tomato and Italian seasoning to the eggplant mixture, and cook for a minute or 2, or until the tomato is slightly soft.

6. Spread about ¾ cup of the eggplant mixture over each crust. Sprinkle each with a tablespoon of cheese, and return to the oven for 8 to 10 minutes, or until the cheese is melted and lightly browned. Serve immediately.

COMPLETE MEAL

MAIN INGREDIENTS

1 pound Japanese eggplant, unpeeled and cut into ½-inch cubes

8-ounce loaf Italian bread

1 pound tomatoes, seeded and diced

4 tablespoons grated Parmesan cheese

STAPLES

2 medium onions, thinly sliced

6 cloves garlic, thinly sliced

1 teaspoon dried Italian seasoning

NUTRITIONAL FACTS (PER SERVING)

Calories: 264 Carbohydrates: 47 g Cholesterol: 5 mg Fat: 4.5 g Fiber: 7 g Protein: 10.5 g Sodium: 464 mg

Tomato Tips

Packed with vitamins, vibrant in color, and bursting with a unique sweet-yet-acidic flavor, tomatoes are an essential ingredient in many of the recipes in this book, from sandwiches to salads to side dishes. Canned tomatoes, of course, are very handy. But many dishes need the special flavor and pleasing firmness of fresh produce. When using fresh tomatoes in your dishes, the following tips will help you get the best results.

❐ Whenever possible, use locally grown tomatoes that are allowed to ripen on the vine. These tomatoes have a garden-fresh flavor and wonderful texture not found in most commercial tomatoes, which are generally picked green.

❐ Whenever possible, allow tomatoes to ripen in a bowl, stem side up, at room temperature. Do not ripen them in the refrigerator, as this will both slow ripening and affect the flavor of the tomatoes.

❐ Whenever you want to hasten ripening, place the tomatoes in a closed paper bag and allow them to sit at room temperature overnight. The ethylene gas given off by the tomatoes will be trapped in the bag, helping them to ripen more quickly.

❐ When you need ripe tomatoes right away, and you have none on hand, take advantage of the small, ripe tomatoes-on-the-vine now available in most grocery stores. Although sizes vary, generally, two of these are equivalent to one medium tomato.

❐ When a recipe calls for seeded tomatoes, first cut each tomato in half crosswise. Then hold each half over a bowl, cut side down, and gently squeeze out the seeds. You can also use your fingers to remove the seeds from the tomato halves.

❐ When a recipe directs you to skin the tomatoes, first plunge the tomatoes into boiling water for 1 minute. Then immediately immerse them in cold water, drain, and peel.

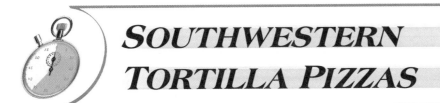

SOUTHWESTERN TORTILLA PIZZAS

TIME: 35 minutes

YIELD: 4 servings (2 pizzas each)

With their crisp tortilla crusts and a filling made spicy with salsa, these pizzas have a distinctive Southwestern flair. If you prefer a tamer pie, use a milder salsa.

1. Preheat the oven to 450°F.

2. Coat a 12-inch nonstick skillet with cooking spray, and preheat over medium-high heat. Add the mushrooms and onion, and cook, stirring frequently, for about 5 minutes, or until the vegetables are soft and the mushrooms are lightly browned.

3. Add the salsa, corn, chili powder, and cumin to the mushroom mixture, and stir to mix. Cook for another minute or 2, or until heated through. Reduce the heat to low to keep the mushrooms warm.

4. Arrange the tortillas on 1 or 2 large ungreased nonstick baking sheets, and place in the oven. Bake for 3 minutes, turn, and bake for 2 to 3 additional minutes, or just until crisp. Remove from the oven.

5. Spread about ½ cup of the mushroom mixture over each tortilla. Sprinkle with 2 tablespoons of the cheese, and return to the oven for 3 or 4 minutes, or just until the cheese is melted. Serve immediately.

COMPLETE MEAL

MAIN INGREDIENTS

1 pound packaged, presliced mushrooms (about 5 cups)

1½ cups hot low-sodium salsa, drained*

1 cup canned no-salt-added whole kernel corn, drained

8 corn tortillas (6-inch rounds)

1 cup shredded light Mexican cheese blend**

STAPLES

1 cup chopped onion

2 teaspoons chili powder

1 teaspoon ground cumin

* Green Mountain Gringo Salsa is a good brand.

** Sargento brand Light 4 Cheese Mexican Recipe Blend is a good choice.

NUTRITIONAL FACTS (PER SERVING)

Calories: 299 Carbohydrates: 44 g Cholesterol: 10 mg Fat: 8 g Fiber: 7 g Protein: 15 g Sodium: 554 mg

SPICY PINTO BEAN TACOS

TIME: 25 minutes   YIELD: 4 servings (2 tacos each)

MAIN INGREDIENTS

1-pound can pinto beans,
  rinsed and drained

½ cup no-salt-added tomato
  sauce

4-ounce can diced green chili
  peppers, drained

8 taco shells*

1 medium tomato, chopped

1½ cups shredded lettuce

½ cup shredded reduced-fat
  Cheddar cheese (optional)

STAPLES

1 teaspoon chili powder

¼ teaspoon dried oregano

¼ teaspoon ground cumin

4 dashes Tabasco sauce

* Look for a brand like Ortega Yellow
  Corn Taco Shells, which have less
  than 3 grams of fat per shell.

This filling is hot and spicy! If you want a milder dish, omit the Tabasco sauce.

1. Place the beans, tomato sauce, chili peppers, chili powder, oregano, cumin, and Tabasco sauce in a 1-quart saucepan, and stir to mix. Bring the mixture to a boil over high heat. Reduce the heat to medium-low, and simmer uncovered for about 5 minutes. Using a spoon or fork, slightly mash the beans against the side of the pot.

2. Heat the taco shells according to package directions. Place the tomato, the lettuce, and the cheese, if desired, in small serving bowls.

3. Spoon a small portion of the hot bean mixture into each taco shell. Top with tomato, lettuce, and cheese, and serve immediately.

NUTRITIONAL FACTS (PER SERVING)

Calories: 263 Carbohydrates: 41.5 g Cholesterol: 0 mg Fat: 8.5 g Fiber: 10 g Protein: 9.5 g Sodium: 547 mg

VEGETABLE CHILI

TIME: 30 minutes   YIELD: 4 servings

A blend of fresh and canned produce allows you to make this satisfying chili with a minimum of fuss. For a real treat, top each serving with a cooling dollop of light sour cream.

1. Coat a 4-quart pot with cooking spray, and preheat over medium-high heat. Add the onion and garlic, and cook, stirring frequently, for about 5 minutes, or until the onion is soft.

2. Add all of the remaining ingredients except for the sour cream to the pot, and stir to mix. Bring the mixture to a boil. Then reduce the heat to medium, cover, and cook for 5 minutes, or just until the zucchini is tender.

3. Uncover the pot and cook for 5 additional minutes, or just until the chili has thickened. Serve immediately, as is or topped with a dollop of light sour cream.

COMPLETE MEAL

MAIN INGREDIENTS

2 cans (14.5 ounces each) peeled diced tomatoes with green pepper and onion

2 cans (1 pound each) organic red kidney beans, drained

2 cans (8 ounces each) no-salt-added whole kernel corn, drained

1 medium zucchini, scrubbed, sliced lengthwise and thinly sliced crosswise

Light sour cream (optional)

STAPLES

1 large onion, coarsely chopped

4 large cloves garlic, chopped

2 tablespoons chili powder

1 tablespoon plus 1 teaspoon ground cumin

1 tablespoon plus 1 teaspoon dried oregano

NUTRITIONAL FACTS (PER SERVING)

Calories: 311 Carbohydrates: 64.5 g Cholesterol: 0 mg Fat: 2.5 g Fiber: 18.5 g Protein: 19 g Sodium: 590 mg

WHITE BEAN AND SALSA QUESADILLAS

TIME: 30 minutes   **YIELD:** 4 quesadillas

MAIN INGREDIENTS

1½ cups canned cannellini beans (white kidney beans), rinsed and drained

8 fat-free flour tortillas (7-inch rounds)

¾ cup medium-hot low-sodium salsa, well drained*

1 cup shredded light Mexican cheese blend**

Light sour cream (optional)

STAPLES

1 teaspoon ground cumin

½ teaspoon garlic powder

⅛ teaspoon cayenne pepper

* Green Mountain Gringo Salsa is a good brand.

** Sargento brand Light 4 Cheese Mexican Recipe Blend is a good choice.

Salsa comes to the rescue again in this dish, in which the handy ready-made sauce flavors the filling of hot quesadillas.

1. Place the beans in a small bowl, and stir in the cumin, garlic powder, and cayenne pepper. Using a fork, mash the mixture just slightly. (Note that the mixture will reduce a bit in volume as it's mashed.)

2. Arrange half of the tortillas on a flat surface, and place about ⅓ cup of the bean mixture over each, spreading the mixture to within ½ inch of the edge of each tortilla. Spread 3 tablespoons of the drained salsa over the beans. Sprinkle ¼ cup of cheese over the salsa, and top each with one of the remaining tortillas.

3. Coat a 12-inch nonstick skillet with cooking spray, and preheat over medium heat. Place one quesadilla in the skillet and cook for 2 to 3 minutes, or until the bottom is golden brown. Turn the quesadilla over and cook for an additional 2 to 3 minutes, or until the second side is golden brown. Remove from the skillet and cover to keep hot. Repeat with the remaining quesadillas.

4. Place each quesadilla on an individual serving plate, and cut into 4 wedges. Serve immediately, as is or topped with a dollop of light sour cream.

NUTRITIONAL FACTS (PER QUESADILLA)

Calories: 385 Carbohydrates: 60 g Cholesterol: 10 mg Fat: 9 g Fiber: 6 g Protein: 18 g Sodium: 1,030 mg

RATATOUILLE OVER SWEET PEPPER COUSCOUS

TIME: 45 minutes   **YIELD:** 4 servings

Colorful and full of garden-fresh flavor, this makes a great entrée or hearty side dish.

1. Coat a 12-inch nonstick skillet or a large nonstick wok with cooking spray, and preheat over medium-high heat. Add the eggplant, zucchini, onion, and garlic, and cook, stirring often, for 6 to 8 minutes, or until the eggplant is lightly browned and the vegetables are slightly soft.

2. Stir the tomatoes, wine, bay leaf, oregano, and black pepper into the eggplant mixture, and bring to a boil. Reduce the heat to medium-low, cover, and cook for 15 minutes, stirring occasionally.

3. While the ratatouille is cooking, place the water in a 1-quart saucepan, and bring to a boil over high heat. Stir in the couscous and green pepper, and cover. Remove from the heat and allow to sit for 5 minutes, or until all of the water has been absorbed.

4. Remove the cover from the ratatouille. Increase the heat to medium-high, and cook for about 3 minutes, or until the liquid is slightly reduced. Remove the bay leaf.

5. Divide the couscous among individual serving plates, and top with the ratatouille. Serve immediately, as is or topped with a sprinkling of Parmesan cheese.

COMPLETE MEAL

MAIN INGREDIENTS

1 pound Japanese eggplant, unpeeled and cut into ½-inch cubes

2 medium zucchini, scrubbed, halved lengthwise and cut into ½-inch slices

2 cans (14.5 ounces each) peeled diced tomatoes, undrained

1½ cups couscous

1 cup finely chopped green bell pepper

Grated Parmesan cheese (optional)

STAPLES

1 large onion, chopped

4 large cloves garlic, chopped

½ cup dry white wine

1 bay leaf

1 teaspoon oregano

½ teaspoon black pepper

2 cups water

NUTRITIONAL FACTS (PER SERVING)

Calories: 381 Carbohydrates: 76 g Cholesterol: 0 mg Fat: 1 g Fiber: 10.5 g Protein: 13.5 g Sodium: 368 mg

STIR-FRIED VEGETABLE RICE

TIME: 35 minutes

YIELD: 4 servings

COMPLETE MEAL

MAIN INGREDIENTS

3 cups instant brown rice

½ cup fat-free egg substitute, divided

2 tablespoons minced fresh ginger

8 cups frozen stir-fry vegetables*

1⅓ cups thinly sliced scallions (about 12)

* Bird's Eye Broccoli Stir-Fry—which contains broccoli, carrots, onions, red pepper, and other vegetables— is a good choice.

For ease of preparation, use a wok, if possible, to make this deliciously gingery dish.

1. Place the water in a 2-quart saucepan, and bring to a boil over high heat. Stir in the rice, cover, and reduce the heat to medium-low. Cook for 10 minutes, or until all of the water has been absorbed. Transfer the rice to a medium-sized bowl, and chill until ready to use.

2. While the rice is chilling, coat a large nonstick wok or 12-inch nonstick skillet with cooking spray, and preheat over medium-high heat. Pour in ¼ cup of the egg substitute, and tilt the pan to form a thin 8-inch omelet. Cook for a minute or 2, or until the bottom is browned. Turn and cook for another minute, or until the second side is

browned. Transfer the omelet to a cutting board, and cut into 2-x-$\frac{1}{2}$-inch strips. Repeat the process with the remaining egg substitute. Set the egg strips aside.

3. Coat the wok or skillet again with cooking spray, and add the ginger and frozen vegetables. Cook over medium-high heat, stirring frequently, for 4 or 5 minutes, or until the vegetables are just tender.

4. Add the scallions to the vegetable mixture, stir to mix, and cook for 1 minute.

5. Reduce the heat to medium, add the rice and soy sauce, and stir to mix. Cook, stirring often, for about 3 minutes, or until heated through.

6. Add the egg strips and black pepper to the rice mixture, and stir to mix. Serve immediately with additional soy sauce on the side.

STAPLES

3 cups water

2 tablespoons light soy sauce

$\frac{1}{2}$ teaspoon freshly ground black pepper

NUTRITIONAL FACTS (PER SERVING)

Calories: 396 Carbohydrates: 71.5 g Cholesterol: 0.5 mg Fat: 4.5 g Fiber: 10.5 g Protein: 16.5 g Sodium: 631 mg

10. VENERABLE VEGETABLES AND GRAINS

Creamy mashed potatoes aromatic with garlic. Spicy Szechuan-style green beans. Whole mushrooms sparked with fresh garlic and a splash of Marsala wine. These are not mere accompaniments to the main event. They are glorious dishes in their own right—dishes that can pull a ho-hum entrée out of the doldrums, or can complement an already special main dish to create a truly memorable meal.

In this chapter, we present a variety of tasty side dishes, from the simple to the sophisticated. All are low in fat, and because they make good use of both high-quality convenience products like frozen vegetables *and* quick cooking methods like microwaving, you'll find that you can prepare both your entrée and your side dish in under an hour—without a juggling act that leaves you too tired to enjoy your own dinner.

Our selection begins with a range of delectable vegetable dishes. If you love potatoes—and who doesn't?—choose from among recipes like Pan-Fried Potatoes with Onions, and Garlic and Herb Mashed Potatoes. Either one will please

true potato lovers. Want to add more green veggies to your diet? Stir-Fried Spinach with Garlic, made with packaged prewashed spinach, takes only minutes to prepare. Or choose Green Beans with Caramelized Onions—fresh green beans quick-cooked in the microwave, then sweetened with browned bits of onion.

Healthful grains like brown rice and couscous also are wonderful side dish ingredients, and several of the following recipes make use of these foods with great results. If you are looking for a super-fast, super-simple side dish, try Rice with Mushrooms and Onions, a deceptively rich-tasting dish that can be yours in only fifteen minutes. Is company coming? With its golden color and alluring aroma, Curried Couscous with Raisins and Almonds will make any meal special.

So the next time you want to round out a meal, choose one of our venerable vegetables or grains. Simple to prepare, yet simply delicious, these are side dishes that will do your table proud.

CORN SKILLET SCRAMBLE

TIME: 30 minutes   **YIELD:** 4 servings

MAIN INGREDIENTS

4 ounces lean Canadian bacon, diced (about 1 cup)

1 cup minced green bell pepper

2 packages (10 ounces each) frozen whole kernel corn, thawed

¼ cup plus 2 tablespoons minced pimiento

STAPLES

2 large onions, coarsely chopped

½ teaspoon freshly ground black pepper

Canadian bacon imparts a delectable flavor to this colorful skillet dish. For tips on quick thawing, see page 10.

1. Coat a 12-inch nonstick skillet with cooking spray, and preheat over medium-high heat. Add the Canadian bacon, onions, and green pepper, and cook, stirring often, for about 5 minutes, or until the onions are soft.

2. Stir in the corn and black pepper, and reduce the heat to medium-low. Cover and cook for about 4 minutes, or just until the corn is done and heated through.

3. Stir in the pimiento, and serve immediately.

NUTRITIONAL FACTS (PER SERVING)

Calories: 210   Carbohydrates: 40 g   Cholesterol: 16.5 mg   Fat: 3 g   Fiber: 6.5 g   Protein: 12 g   Sodium: 266 mg

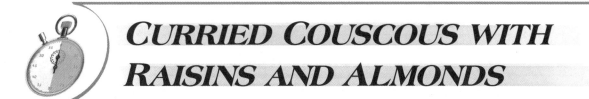

CURRIED COUSCOUS WITH RAISINS AND ALMONDS

TIME: 30 minutes

YIELD: 4 servings

With its golden color and exotic flavor, this fragrant dish will add drama to any meal.

1. Preheat the oven to 350°F.

2. Coat a 2-quart pot with cooking spray, and preheat over medium-high heat. Add the onion, and cook, stirring frequently, for about 4 minutes, or until soft.

3. Add the broth, raisins or currants, curry powder, bay leaf, and black pepper, and stir to mix. Increase the heat to high, and bring the mixture to a boil.

4. Stir the couscous into the boiling broth, cover the pot, and remove from the heat. Allow to sit for 5 minutes, or until all of the broth has been absorbed.

5. While the couscous is cooking, spread the almonds on a baking sheet, and place in the oven for 5 minutes, or until lightly toasted. Watch carefully to prevent burning.

6. Remove the bay leaf from the couscous. Stir in the almonds, and serve immediately.

MAIN INGREDIENTS

⅓ cup dark raisins or currants

1½ cups couscous (10-ounce package)

¼ cup sliced almonds

STAPLES

¾ cup finely chopped onion

2 cups reduced-sodium, fat-free chicken broth

1½ teaspoons curry powder

1 bay leaf

¼ teaspoon freshly ground black pepper

NUTRITIONAL FACTS (PER SERVING)

Calories: 348 Carbohydrates: 64 g Cholesterol: 0 mg Fat: 4 g Fiber: 5 g Protein: 14 g Sodium: 95 mg

GREEN BEANS WITH CARAMELIZED ONIONS

TIME: 30 minutes   **YIELD:** 4 servings

MAIN INGREDIENTS

1 pound fresh green beans, trimmed

STAPLES

2 tablespoons water

1 tablespoon olive oil

2 cups finely chopped onion

½ teaspoon salt

¼ teaspoon freshly ground black pepper

Browned bits of caramelized onion add the perfect touch of sweetness to fresh green beans in this super side dish.

1. Rinse the beans and place them in a large microwave-safe bowl. Add the water, and cover the bowl loosely with waxed paper.

2. Microwave the beans on high power for 8 to 10 minutes, or just until tender-crisp, occasionally removing from the oven and stirring to mix. Remove and set aside.

3. While the beans are cooking, coat a 12-inch nonstick skillet or large wok with cooking spray, add the oil, and preheat over medium-high heat. Toss in the onion, and stir-fry for about 8 minutes, or until the onion begins to brown.

4. Add the beans to the skillet, and sprinkle with the salt and black pepper. Reduce the heat to low, and toss the ingredients together well. Cook another minute, or until heated through, and serve immediately.

NUTRITIONAL FACTS (PER SERVING)

Calories: 96 Carbohydrates: 16 g Cholesterol: 0 mg Fat: 3.5 g Fiber: 5 g Protein: 4 g Sodium: 300 mg

SZECHUAN GREEN BEANS

TIME: 25 minutes   **YIELD:** 4 servings

This dish is not for the timid! Enjoy its spicy flavor and vivid color with broiled or grilled meat or poultry.

1. Place the ginger, scallions, garlic, oil, and crushed red pepper in a 2½-quart microwave-safe bowl, and microwave uncovered on high power for 3 minutes.

2. Add the green beans, soy sauce, and vinegar to the bowl, and toss to mix. Microwave uncovered on high power for about 12 minutes, or until the beans are crisp-tender, occasionally removing the beans from the oven and tossing to mix.

3. Serve immediately, or chill and serve cold.

MAIN INGREDIENTS

2 quarter-sized pieces fresh ginger, peeled and finely chopped

2 medium scallions, chopped

1 pound fresh green beans, trimmed

STAPLES

6 cloves garlic, finely chopped

1 tablespoon canola oil

1 teaspoon crushed red pepper

1 tablespoon light soy sauce

2 teaspoons red wine vinegar

NUTRITIONAL FACTS (PER SERVING)

Calories: 79 Carbohydrates: 11 g Cholesterol: 0 mg Fat: 4 g Fiber: 4 g Protein: 2.5 g Sodium: 231 mg

MARSALA MUSHROOMS

TIME: 20 minutes   YIELD: 4 servings

MAIN INGREDIENTS

2 pounds small whole white
mushrooms

STAPLES

2 teaspoons olive oil

4 cloves garlic, chopped

1/4 cup plus 2 tablespoons
Marsala wine

2 pinches salt

2 pinches freshly ground
black pepper

An elegant accompaniment to almost any entrée.

1. Quickly rinse and dry the mushrooms, and cut off the stems. Cut any large mushrooms in half.

2. Coat a 12-inch nonstick skillet with olive-oil cooking spray, add the olive oil, and preheat over medium-high heat. Add the garlic and mushrooms, and cook, stirring or tossing often, for about 8 minutes, or until done to taste.

3. Add the Marsala, salt, and black pepper to the skillet, and cook, stirring, for an additional minute. Serve immediately.

NUTRITIONAL FACTS (PER SERVING)

Calories: 115 Carbohydrates: 14 g Cholesterol: 0 mg Fat: 3 g Fiber: 3 g Protein: 5 g Sodium: 87 mg

ORANGE AND GINGER GLAZED CARROTS

TIME: 15 minutes   YIELD: 4 servings

Enjoy these lightly glazed, sweet and spicy carrots with poultry or pork.

1. Cook the carrots according to package directions. Cover to keep warm, and set aside.

2. Place the brown sugar, cornstarch, and ginger in a 2-quart saucepan, and stir to mix well. Slowly stir in the orange juice.

3. Place the saucepan over medium heat, and cook, stirring constantly, until the mixture reaches a boil. Continue to cook, stirring constantly, for about 1 minute, or until the mixture has thickened.

4. Add the carrots to the glaze, and stir to mix. Cook, stirring occasionally, for a minute or 2, or until the carrots are hot and well coated. Serve immediately.

MAIN INGREDIENTS

2 packages (10 ounces each) frozen baby carrots

½ cup orange juice

STAPLES

¼ cup brown sugar

2 teaspoons cornstarch

½ teaspoon ground ginger

NUTRITIONAL FACTS (PER SERVING)

Calories: 113 Carbohydrates: 27 g Cholesterol: 0 mg Fat: 0.5 g Fiber: 2.5 g Protein: 1 g Sodium: 119 mg

RICE WITH MUSHROOMS AND ONIONS

TIME: 15 minutes   YIELD: 4 servings

MAIN INGREDIENTS

2 cups instant brown rice

¾ cup frozen chopped onion

6-ounce can sliced mushrooms, undrained

STAPLES

2 cups minus 2 tablespoons reduced-sodium, fat-free beef broth

¼ teaspoon freshly ground black pepper

This richly flavored dish will enliven virtually any meal.

1. Place the broth in a 2-quart saucepan, and bring to a boil over high heat. Stir in the rice. Cover, reduce the heat to medium-low, and simmer for 10 minutes, or until all of the broth has been absorbed and the rice is tender.

2. While the rice is cooking, coat an 8-inch nonstick skillet with cooking spray, and preheat over medium heat. Add the onion and cook, stirring frequently, for about 3 minutes, or until soft and translucent.

3. Drain the mushrooms, reserving the liquid. Add the mushrooms to the onions, and cook for about 2 minutes, or until heated through.

4. Add the mushroom mixture and the black pepper to the rice, and stir to mix. If the mixture is too dry, add some of the reserved mushroom liquid. Serve hot.

NUTRITIONAL FACTS (PER SERVING)

Calories: 208 Carbohydrates: 39 g Cholesterol: 0 mg Fat: 2.5 g Fiber: 3.5 g Protein: 7 g Sodium: 199 mg

SPANISH RICE

TIME: 35 minutes

YIELD: 4 servings

This tomato-flavored rice classic can be enjoyed as a tasty side dish or as a meal by itself. For tips on quick thawing, see page 10.

1. Coat a 12-inch nonstick skillet or large wok with cooking spray, add the oil, and preheat over medium heat. Add the rice, and stir constantly for 5 minutes, or until the grains begin to brown.

2. Add the onion to the skillet, reduce the heat to low, and continue to cook, stirring frequently, until the onion is soft.

3. Stir in the tomatoes and broth, increase the heat to high, and bring to a boil. Reduce the heat to low, stir in the peas and salt, and cover. Simmer for 15 to 20 minutes, or until the liquid has been absorbed and the rice is tender. Serve immediately.

MAIN INGREDIENTS

1½ cups long grain white rice

2 cups crushed tomatoes in purée

1 cup frozen green peas, thawed

STAPLES

2 teaspoons canola oil

½ cup finely chopped onion

1½ cups reduced-sodium, fat-free chicken broth

¼ teaspoon salt

NUTRITIONAL FACTS (PER SERVING)

Calories: 360 Carbohydrates: 70 g Cholesterol: 0 mg Fat: 3 g Fiber: 5 g Protein: 11.5 g Sodium: 443 mg

SPINACH AND RICE

TIME: 20 minutes

YIELD: 4 servings

MAIN INGREDIENTS

1½ cups instant brown rice

10-ounce package frozen
chopped spinach

3 tablespoons grated
Parmesan cheese

STAPLES

1 cup fresh or frozen chopped
onion

1½ cups water

¼ teaspoon ground nutmeg

⅛ teaspoon salt

⅛ teaspoon freshly ground
black pepper

This savory, easy-to-make dish is perfect with poultry.

1. Coat a 2-quart pot with cooking spray, and preheat over high heat. Add the onion and cook, stirring often, for about 2 minutes, or until slightly soft.

2. Add the rice, water, and spinach to the pot, and bring to a boil. Reduce the heat to medium-low, cover, and simmer, without stirring, for about 15 minutes, or until the rice is tender and the spinach is thawed. (Note that the spinach will remain in a block even when it's thawed.) If any water remains, drain it off.

3. Break the spinach up with a fork, and stir it into the rice. Add the Parmesan, nutmeg, salt, and black pepper, and stir to mix. Serve immediately.

NUTRITIONAL FACTS (PER SERVING)

Calories: 182 Carbohydrates: 32 g Cholesterol: 3.5 mg Fat: 3 g Fiber: 4.5 g Protein: 7.5 g Sodium: 224 mg

GARLIC AND HERB MASHED POTATOES

TIME: 35 minutes

YIELD: 4 servings

Creamy and delightfully seasoned, these potatoes are sure to make any meal special.

1. Place the potatoes in a 2-quart saucepan, and add just enough water to cover. Bring to a boil over high heat; then reduce the heat to medium-low. Cover and boil for 10 to 12 minutes, or until the potatoes are tender when pierced with a fork.

2. Drain the water from the pot, and place the potatoes over low heat, shaking often, for a minute or 2, or until any moisture has evaporated. Mash the potatoes with a potato masher or electric mixer.

3. Stir in the cheese until melted. Add the milk and black pepper, and stir until well mixed. If a creamier consistency is desired, stir in an additional tablespoon or 2 of milk. Stir gently over low heat just until heated through, and serve immediately.

MAIN INGREDIENTS

4 medium baking potatoes (about 1½ pounds), peeled and cut into 1-inch cubes

¼ cup plus 2 tablespoons light garlic-and-herb flavored spreadable cheese*

STAPLES

¼ cup 2% reduced-fat milk

⅛ teaspoon freshly ground black pepper

* Alouette Light Garlic & Herb cheese is a good choice.

NUTRITIONAL FACTS (PER SERVING)

Calories: 160 Carbohydrates: 28.5 g Cholesterol: 15.5 mg Fat: 3.5 g Fiber: 3 g Protein: 4.5 g Sodium: 105 mg

PAN-FRIED POTATOES WITH ONIONS

TIME: 25 minutes

YIELD: 4 servings

MAIN INGREDIENT

4 medium potatoes (about
  1½ pounds), scrubbed and
  sliced ¼ inch thick

Chopped fresh parsley
  (optional)

STAPLES

Cooking spray

1½ cups slivered onions

¼ teaspoon freshly ground
  black pepper

¼ teaspoon salt

A slimmed-down version of an old favorite, these potatoes are wonderful with meat, poultry, eggs—just about anything!

1. Layer the potato slices in a medium-sized microwave-safe bowl, lightly spraying each layer with cooking spray to prevent the slices from sticking to one another as they cook. Cover the bowl tightly with microwave-safe plastic wrap, and microwave on high power for 5 to 6 minutes, or just until the potatoes are tender when pierced with a fork.

2. Coat a 12-inch nonstick skillet or large wok with cooking spray, and preheat over medium-high heat. Add the potatoes and onions, and cook, tossing often, for about 10 minutes, or until browned.

3. Sprinkle the black pepper and salt over the potato mixture, and toss to mix. Serve immediately, garnishing with parsley, if desired.

NUTRITIONAL FACTS (PER SERVING)

Calories: 121 Carbohydrates: 27.5 g Cholesterol: 0 mg Fat: 0 g Fiber: 3 g Protein: 3 g Sodium: 155 mg

Baked Potato Toppers

The simple baked potato goes with just about any entrée. Topped with the right ingredients and accompanied by a fresh green salad, it can even serve as a light meal. The problem is that the average-sized potato takes an hour or more to bake in the oven. The solution? Use a microwave oven to cook that same potato in only 5 to 7 minutes. Of course, microwaved potatoes do lack the crisp outer skin that comes with conventional oven baking. But by popping the microwaved potatoes into a preheated 425°F conventional oven for about 10 minutes, you will produce that delightfully crisp outer shell—all in less than 20 minutes!

Filled with vitamins B and C, protein, fiber, and a number of minerals, the potato is a nutritional arsenal—but watch out for those high-fat toppings! Instead of the traditional butter, margarine, and sour cream, choose one of the following low-fat or fat-free toppings to add the perfect crowning touch to your baked potato.

❐ Fat-free sour cream, ricotta, or cottage cheese flavored with snipped fresh chives or finely chopped scallions.

❐ Plain nonfat yogurt mixed with a sprinkling of dried dill weed.

❐ Your favorite salsa (try the Green Chili Salsa on page 63).

❐ Piping hot tomato sauce and a sprinkling of grated Parmesan cheese.

❐ Shredded low-fat or nonfat Cheddar cheese or cheese blend.

❐ A simple dash or two of salt and pepper. If you prefer a no-sodium topping, try a little Mrs. Dash original seasoning blend.

❐ Leftover chili (try the Chili con Carne on page 128 or the Vegetable Chili on page 177).

❐ Steamed broccoli or spinach topped with shredded low-fat or nonfat Cheddar cheese.

❐ Leftover Turkey Sloppy Joes (page 124).

❐ Your favorite low-fat or fat-free creamy salad dressings (try any of the creamy dressings found in the inset beginning on page 61).

STEAMED POTATOES WITH SWEET ONIONS

TIME: 20 minutes   YIELD: 4 servings

MAIN INGREDIENTS

4 medium red potatoes,
  peeled and cut into
  bite-sized pieces

STAPLES

2 medium onions

2 cloves garlic, minced

¼ teaspoon freshly ground
  black pepper

2 teaspoons olive oil

¼ teaspoon paprika

A microwave oven makes it a snap to prepare this super side dish. If you want to brown the cooked potatoes, place them in a preheated 450°F oven for 10 to 15 minutes.

1. Place the potatoes in a large microwave-safe bowl. Cut the onions in half lengthwise; then cut each half into thirds, and add to the bowl.

2. Sprinkle the garlic and black pepper over the potato mixture, and drizzle with the olive oil. Toss to mix well.

3. Cover the bowl with microwave-safe plastic wrap, and microwave on high power for 4 minutes. Stir the ingredients, and cook for 3 to 4 additional minutes, or until the potatoes and onions are tender. Sprinkle with the paprika, and serve immediately.

NUTRITIONAL FACTS (PER SERVING)

Calories: 160 Carbohydrates: 32.5 g Cholesterol: 0 mg Fat: 2.5 g Fiber: 3.5 g Protein: 3 g Sodium: 9 mg

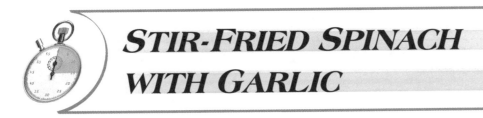

STIR-FRIED SPINACH WITH GARLIC

TIME: 15 minutes

YIELD: 4 servings

This is such an easy way to cook spinach that once you try it, you'll never cook spinach in water again. And just a few simple seasonings make this dish truly special.

1. Remove the stems from the spinach, and tear the leaves into bite-sized pieces. Set aside.

2. Coat a 12-inch nonstick skillet or large wok with cooking spray, and preheat over medium-high heat. Add the garlic, and cook, stirring constantly, for about 2 minutes, or just until the garlic begins to brown. Add the spinach, and cook, tossing constantly, for 2 to 3 minutes, or until the spinach is wilted and hot.

3. Add the soy sauce and black pepper to the spinach, and stir to mix well. Serve immediately.

MAIN INGREDIENTS

2 packages (10 ounces each) prewashed spinach

STAPLES

6 large cloves garlic, thinly sliced

1 tablespoon light soy sauce

¼–½ teaspoon freshly ground black pepper

NUTRITIONAL FACTS (PER SERVING)

Calories: 36 Carbohydrates: 6.5 g Cholesterol: 0 mg Fat: 0.5 g Fiber: 3.5 g Protein: 4 g Sodium: 330 mg

ZESTY SWEET POTATOES

TIME: 35 minutes   **YIELD:** 4 servings

MAIN INGREDIENTS

*4 medium sweet potatoes
(about 1½ pounds), scrubbed
and sliced ½ inch thick*

STAPLES

Cooking spray

Cayenne pepper

Cayenne pepper gives these baked sweet potato slices just the right spark. If substituting white potatoes for the sweet, add a sprinkling of salt to each slice before baking.

1. Preheat the oven to 350ºF.

2. Spray a large baking sheet with cooking spray, and arrange the potato rounds in a single layer. Lightly spray the top of each slice with cooking spray, and sprinkle with a little cayenne pepper.

3. Bake uncovered for 20 to 25 minutes, or until the potatoes are tender. Serve hot or warm.

NUTRITIONAL FACTS (PER SERVING)

Calories: 178 Carbohydrates: 41 g Cholesterol: 0 mg Fat: 0.5 g Fiber: 5 g Protein: 3 g Sodium: 22 mg

ZUCCHINI, ONION, AND TOMATO SAUTÉ

TIME: 25 minutes   YIELD: 4 servings

This piquant side dish is bursting with garden-fresh flavor.

1. Coat a 12-inch nonstick skillet with cooking spray, and preheat over medium-high heat. Add the onion, and cook, stirring constantly, for about 3 minutes, or until slightly soft.

2. Add the garlic to the skillet, and cook, stirring often, for about 2 minutes.

3. Add the zucchini to the skillet, and stir to mix. Reduce the heat to medium, cover, and cook, stirring occasionally, for about 5 minutes, or until the zucchini is crisp-tender.

4. Stir in the tomato, and cook uncovered for about 1 minute.

5. Stir in the lemon juice and seasonings, and serve immediately.

MAIN INGREDIENTS

1½ pounds zucchini (about 5 small), peeled and sliced ¼ inch thick

1 medium tomato, diced

STAPLES

1 large onion, diced

3 medium cloves garlic, chopped

¼ cup lemon juice

⅛ teaspoon salt

⅛ teaspoon freshly ground black pepper

⅛ teaspoon dried basil

¼ teaspoon dried thyme

NUTRITIONAL FACTS (PER SERVING)

Calories: 54 Carbohydrates: 12 g Cholesterol: 0 mg Fat: 0.5 g Fiber: 3.5 g Protein: 3 g Sodium: 85 mg

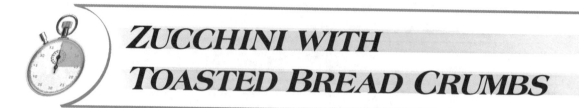

ZUCCHINI WITH TOASTED BREAD CRUMBS

TIME: 15 minutes   YIELD: 4 servings

MAIN INGREDIENTS

3 medium zucchini, scrubbed
(about 2½ pounds)

½ cup chopped fresh basil

2 tablespoons grated
Parmesan cheese

STAPLES

1 tablespoon olive oil

2 tablespoons minced garlic

½ cup flavored bread crumbs

Fresh basil is combined with toasted bread crumbs and Parmesan cheese to add wonderful flavor and aroma to this simple zucchini dish.

1. Cut the zucchini into 1-inch-thick circles; then cut each circle in half. Set aside.

2. Coat a 12-inch nonstick skillet with cooking spray, add the oil, and preheat over medium-low heat. Add the garlic, and cook, stirring often, until soft. Be careful not to burn.

3. Toss the zucchini and basil into the skillet, mixing well with the garlic. Reduce the heat to low, cover, and simmer, stirring occasionally, for 5 to 7 minutes, or until the zucchini is tender.

4. Add the bread crumbs to the skillet, and mix the ingredients well. Increase the heat to medium, and continue to cook, stirring often, for 5 minutes, or until the bread crumbs begin to brown.

5. Spoon the zucchini into a serving bowl, sprinkle with the Parmesan cheese, and serve immediately.

NUTRITIONAL FACTS (PER SERVING)

Calories: 105 Carbohydrates: 18 g Cholesterol: 3 mg Fat: 5 g Fiber: 2.5 g Protein: 6 g Sodium: 461 mg

11. DAZZLING DESSERTS

When we began creating the dishes for this book, we confess that neither of us knew how to make any quick-cooking desserts. So for inspiration, we turned to the many available fast-and-easy cookbooks. To our great disappointment, we found that the recipes in these books usually required little prep time, but *lots* of time for chilling or freezing. So while the cook needed only minutes to whip up that creamy pudding or fruit-filled pie, she couldn't actually serve it until, say, midnight.

Fortunately, through experimentation, we found that it is, indeed, possible to create sweetly tempting desserts that are ready in under forty-five minutes. In fact, this chapter presents well over a dozen delectable dishes, many of which can be prepared and on the table in twenty minutes or less.

Because sweet fruit is such a natural ingredient for fast desserts, many of our recipes begin with one or more fruits. Versatile and always available, bananas are a particular favorite of ours. You'll find them baked to perfection in Peachy Baked Bananas, kissed with a tart glaze in Orange-Glazed Bananas over Ice Cream, and whipped with vanilla yogurt and liqueur in Banana-Cacao Crème. Looking for a down-home delight? Fragrant with cinnamon, Homestyle Baked Apples are a delectable comfort food. And for an elegant conclusion to a special meal, try Classic Cherries Jubilee. Other deliciously fruity desserts include Baked Pears with Chocolate Fudge Sauce, Pineapples and Strawberries au Grand Marnier, and simple Raspberries and Cream.

But not all of our desserts begin with fruit. Double Chocolate Tarts are tiny pies filled with fudgy low-fat ice cream and crowned with a creamy topping. Candied Popcorn is another great choice, sweetened with brown sugar and studded with almonds. And for the cookie monster in your house, try making sweet-and-spicy Cinnamon Tortilla Crisps.

So the next time your sweet tooth demands satisfaction, but your schedule gives you little time, do not despair. A variety of dazzling desserts can be yours—quickly, easily, and above all, deliciously.

APPLE HAYSTACKS

TIME: 10 minutes

YIELD: 4 servings

MAIN INGREDIENTS

4 medium red Delicious apples, unpeeled

½ cup dark or golden raisins

1 cup vanilla nonfat yogurt

4 teaspoons sliced almonds

STAPLES

1 tablespoon plus 1 teaspoon lemon juice

1 tablespoon plus 1 teaspoon honey

Be sure to use crisp, cold apples for this light, refreshing dessert.

1. Core and coarsely grate the apples into a large bowl. Add the lemon juice and honey, and toss to coat.

2. Toss the raisins into the apple mixture. Then fold in the yogurt.

3. Divide the apple mixture among individual serving bowls, top with the almonds, and serve.

NUTRITIONAL FACTS (PER SERVING)

Calories: 226 Carbohydrates: 53 g Cholesterol: 1 mg Fat: 1.5 g Fiber: 4.5 g Protein: 4.5 g Sodium: 45 mg

BAKED HONEYED PEACHES

TIME: 40 minutes   YIELD: 4 servings

When ripe peaches are in season, be sure to try this light dessert.

1. Preheat the oven to 350°F.

2. Place the honey, lemon juice, and water in a small bowl, and stir to mix. Set aside.

3. Halve the peaches, remove the pits, and peel. Place the peach halves cut side up in an 8- or 9-inch-square casserole dish. Spoon the honey mixture over the peaches.

4. Cover the peaches with aluminum foil, and bake for 15 to 20 minutes, or until tender when pierced with a fork. Reserving the honey mixture, transfer the peaches to individual serving bowls, and allow to cool for about 10 minutes.

5. While the peaches are still warm, drizzle with the remaining honey mixture. Top each half with a tablespoon of whipped topping, and serve immediately.

MAIN INGREDIENTS

4 fresh ripe peaches*

½ cup light whipped topping

STAPLES

¼ cup honey

1 tablespoon plus 1 teaspoon lemon juice

½ cup water

* Freestone or cling-free peaches are the best.

NUTRITIONAL FACTS (PER SERVING)

Calories: 121 Carbohydrates: 29 g Cholesterol: 0 mg Fat: 1 g Fiber: 1.5 g Protein: 0.5 g Sodium: 1 mg

Fast and Easy Desserts

This chapter presents a variety of healthy desserts that can be easily made in forty-five minutes or less. But our selections are only a small sampling of the many sweet temptations that can be prepared quickly and with a minimum of fuss. Following are a few more ideas for super-fast desserts. Use your imagination, and you're sure to come up with your own kitchen-quickies creations.

❒ Purchase some ready-made fruit salad at your local deli, gourmet shop, or salad bar, and toss in a few teaspoons of your favorite fruit liqueur to add a greater depth of flavor. Apricot liqueur and Grand Marnier orange liqueur are always good choices. Pile the salad into a pretty serving bowl, and—to add eye appeal—top it with slices of star fruit. This is one bowl of fruit salad that will not go unnoticed!

❒ Place a wedge of angel food cake on each individual dessert plate. Available at both bakeries and grocery stores, angel food cake is fat-free, and has a wonderfully light consistency. Next to the cake, spoon some sliced fresh strawberries or store-bought fruit salad. For a final touch, add a scoop of low-fat ice cream or frozen yogurt.

❒ Arrange some fresh fruit on each individual dessert plate. Melon slices and whole strawberries are good choices, as are bunches of seedless grapes. Next to the fruit, arrange squares or wedges of your favorite low-fat cheese, such as Swiss or Cheddar. If desired, add a small dish of dipping sauce—low-fat vanilla yogurt sparked with a sprinkling of nutmeg, perhaps. This dessert is so satisfying that it also makes a great snack or light lunch.

❒ Start with a store-bought "dessert cup"—individual shells made of yellow cake. These cups, which can often be found in the produce section of grocery stores, usually contain only about 2 grams of fat per serving. Then fill each one with a scoop of low-fat ice cream or frozen yogurt, or with fresh ripe berries. If you have a bit more time, make a fast strawberry shortcake by lightly sugaring sliced strawberries, and allowing them to sit in the refrigerator until the juices develop. Spoon some of the fruit over the dessert cup, top with low-fat whipped topping, and dessert is ready!

❒ Use your imagination to create taste-tempting parfaits. Begin with your favorite flavor of low-fat ice cream, frozen yogurt, or ready-made low-fat pudding. Alternate this with layers of fresh or frozen (thawed) fruit, or with the canned fruit pie filling of your choice. For low-fat crunch, spoon some Grape-Nuts cereal over each layer. Finally, garnish with a dollop of low-fat whipped topping. To make your parfaits as pretty as they are yummy, serve them in see-through parfait glasses or in large wine goblets.

❒ Place a cup of low-fat vanilla yogurt in a small serving dish, and add a teaspoon of chocolate syrup. Stir just enough to create a swirl effect. Serve this dipping sauce with a bowl of whole ripe strawberries, leaving the stems on, if possible, so that it's easy to dip each strawberry into the vanilla-chocolate sauce.

❒ Scoop a serving of low-fat vanilla ice cream or frozen yogurt into an oversized brandy snifter. Add a splash of Kahlua coffee liqueur and a light sprinkling of cocoa powder, and serve. Simple and elegant!

BAKED PEARS WITH CHOCOLATE FUDGE SAUCE

TIME: 30 minutes   YIELD: 4 servings

Simple to make, and simply elegant.

1. Slice a thin piece from the bottom of each pear so it stands upright. Remove the core from the bottom, leaving the stem intact. Carefully peel the pears, and place them in a large microwave-safe baking dish.

2. Add the water to the baking dish, cover with micro-wave-safe plastic wrap, and microwave on high power for 4 to 5 minutes. Turn the dish, and cook for 4 to 5 additional minutes, or until the pears are tender when pierced with a fork.

3. Reserving the cooking liquid, carefully transfer the pears to individual serving bowls, and allow to cool for about 10 minutes.

4. Add the remaining ingredients to the reserved cooking liquid, and stir to mix well. Spoon over the warm pears, and serve immediately.

MAIN INGREDIENTS

4 medium pears

¼ cup plus 2 tablespoons jarred chocolate fudge topping*

2 teaspoons vanilla extract

STAPLES

2 tablespoons water

2 tablespoons lemon juice

2 teaspoons honey

½ teaspoon ground cinnamon

* Choose a brand like Smuckers, which has only 1.5 grams of fat per 2-tablespoon serving.

NUTRITIONAL FACTS (PER SERVING)

Calories: 215 Carbohydrates: 50 g Cholesterol: 0 mg Fat: 2 g Fiber: 5 g Protein: 0.5 g Sodium: 46 mg

BANANA-CACAO CRÈME

TIME: 45 minutes   YIELD: 4 servings

MAIN INGREDIENTS

4 medium ripe bananas,
   peeled

4 containers (8 ounces each)
   vanilla low-fat yogurt

2 tablespoons Crème de
   Cacao liqueur

½ cup fat-free whipped
   topping (optional)

8 banana slices (optional)

*How can you turn vanilla yogurt into something really special?
Add whipped fresh bananas and Crème de Cacao liqueur. The
result is a creamy, flavorful confection that is sure to please.*

1. Slice the bananas into a blender, and process for a few
seconds, or just until smooth.

2. Open the yogurt containers, and drain off any accumu-
lated liquid. Empty the yogurt into a large bowl, and add
the blended bananas and the liqueur. Gently fold the ingredients together until well mixed.

3. Divide the yogurt mixture among four 10-ounce dessert
bowls, and refrigerate for 30 minutes, or until well chilled.

4. If desired, top each dish of the chilled yogurt with a
2-tablespoon dollop of whipped topping. Garnish each
dollop with 2 banana slices, and serve immediately.

NUTRITIONAL FACTS (PER SERVING)

Calories: 343 Carbohydrates: 64.5 g Cholesterol: 12 mg Fat: 3.5 g Fiber: 2.5 g Protein: 14.5 g Sodium: 163 mg

Top: *Stir-Fried Vegetable Rice (page 180)*

Center Left: *Pork Stir-Fry Over Sesame Noodles (page 140)*

Center Right: *Crab-Scallion Foo Young (page 152)*

Top Left: Easy Grilled Chicken Fajitas (page 110) and Black Bean Salad with Corn and Peppers (page 56)

Top Right: Southwest Rice and Smoked Turkey Salad (page 76)

Bottom: Chile Con Carne (page 128)

Top Left: Candied Popcorn (page 207)

Top Center and Bottom Left:
Chocolate-Banana Parfaits (page 209)

Center Right and Bottom Right: Golden Cake
with Fresh Strawberry Sauce (page 213)

Center Left: Cinnamon Tortilla Crisps (page 210)

Top Right: Orange-Glazed Bananas Over Ice Cream (page 215)

Bottom: Raspberry Pears (page 218)

BANANA-CHOCOLATE SHAKES

TIME: 10 minutes   **YIELD:** 4 shakes

These frosty delights are flavorful, filling, and so thick you'll be tempted to eat them with a spoon. For an added touch, top each with a plump fresh strawberry.

1. Place the bananas and ice cubes in a blender, and blend until the banana is puréed and the ice is coarsely crushed.

2. Add the milk, chocolate syrup, and vanilla extract. Blend until smooth.

3. Divide the mixture among four 10-ounce glasses and enjoy immediately.

MAIN INGREDIENTS

4 medium-sized ripe bananas, slightly mashed (about 3 cups)

½ cup chocolate syrup

1 teaspoon vanilla extract

STAPLES

3 cups ice cubes

2 cups cold low-fat milk

NUTRITIONAL FACTS (PER SHAKE)

Calories: 280 Carbohydrates: 67.5 g Cholesterol: 2.5 mg Fat: 1 g Fiber: 5 g Protein: 6.5 g Sodium: 100 mg

CANDIED POPCORN

TIME: 45 minutes   YIELD: 12 cups

MAIN INGREDIENTS

12 cups air-popped popcorn
  (½ cup unpopped)

½ cup sliced almonds
  (optional)

½ cup corn syrup

STAPLES

¼ cup brown sugar

Enjoy a big bowl of this sweet, crunchy confection any time.

1. Preheat the oven to 350°F.

2. Lightly coat a nonstick baking sheet with cooking spray, and set aside. Place the popcorn and, if desired, the almonds in a large bowl, stir to mix, and set aside.

3. Place the corn syrup and brown sugar in a 1-quart pot, and cook over medium-low heat, stirring constantly, until the sugar is dissolved. Slowly pour the sugar mixture over the popcorn, and stir well to coat.

4. Empty the bowl onto the baking sheet, and spread out with a spatula or wooden spoon that has been sprayed with cooking spray. Bake for about 20 minutes, or until the popcorn starts to dry.

5. Remove the sheet from the oven, and cool for 10 to 15 minutes. (Although the popcorn will be sticky when removed from the oven, it will dry as it cools.) Break apart and serve immediately, or store in an airtight container.

NUTRITIONAL FACTS (PER 3-CUP SERVING)

Calories: 259 Carbohydrates: 63.5 g Cholesterol: 0 mg Fat: 1 g Fiber: 3.5 g Protein: 3 g Sodium: 56 mg

CLASSIC CHERRIES JUBILEE

TIME: 15 minutes

YIELD: 4 servings

No dessert is more impressive than flaming cherries served over creamy vanilla ice cream.

1. Scoop ½ cup of the ice cream into each individual serving bowl, and set aside.

2. Drain the cherries, reserving the juice (about ½ cup).

3. Place the sugar and cornstarch in a small bowl. Slowly add the reserved cherry juice, stirring until the sugar is dissolved. Transfer the mixture to an 8-inch skillet, and place over medium-low heat. Stir constantly for about 3 minutes, or until the juice thickens. Add the cherries to the skillet, and mix with the sauce.

4. Pour the brandy over the cherries, and carefully ignite with a match. Using a long serving spoon, spoon the flaming cherries and their flavorful sauce over the ice cream, and serve immediately.

MAIN INGREDIENTS

1 pint low-fat vanilla ice cream*

1-pound can pitted black cherries

¼ cup kirsch or other brandy

STAPLES

1 tablespoon sugar

1 tablespoon cornstarch

* Choose a brand like Healthy Choice, which has only 2 grams of fat per ½-cup serving.

NUTRITIONAL FACTS (PER SERVING)

Calories: 232 Carbohydrates: 46 g Cholesterol: 5 mg Fat: 2 g Fiber: 2.5 g Protein: 3.5 g Sodium: 55 mg

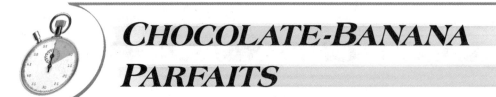

CHOCOLATE-BANANA PARFAITS

TIME: 10 minutes   YIELD: 4 parfaits

MAIN INGREDIENTS

4 small ripe bananas, peeled

*8 containers (3.5 ounces each)
fat-free chocolate pudding*

2 cups light whipped topping

4 ripe strawberries, hulled

Layers of rich chocolate pudding, fresh banana slices, and creamy whipped topping are crowned with ripe, juicy strawberries in this luscious parfait. We use 12-ounce parfait glasses or oversized brandy snifters.

1. Thinly slice the bananas. Divide half the slices among 4 individual parfait glasses. Top the slices in each glass with the contents of one pudding container; then add $\frac{1}{4}$ cup of the whipped topping. Repeat the layers.

2. Crown each parfait with a strawberry and serve immediately, or chill until ready to serve.

NUTRITIONAL FACTS (PER PARFAIT)

Calories: 347 Carbohydrates: 67.5 g Cholesterol: 0 mg Fat: 6.5 g Fiber: 2.5 g Protein: 6 g Sodium: 187 mg

CINNAMON TORTILLA CRISPS

TIME: 25 minutes   **YIELD:** 16 crisps

Enjoy these light, delicate cookie crisps with a cup of tea, a scoop of your favorite ice cream or frozen yogurt, or all by themselves.

1. Preheat the oven to 325°F.

2. Place the sugar and cinnamon in a small bowl, and stir to mix.

3. Arrange the tortillas on a flat surface, and lightly spray the tops with the cooking spray. Sprinkle with half the cinnamon-sugar mixture. Turn the tortillas over, and cut each into quarters. Lightly spray with the cooking spray, and sprinkle with the remaining cinnamon-sugar mixture.

4. Arrange the tortilla quarters on a large ungreased baking sheet, and bake for 8 minutes, or until the tortillas begin to curl. Turn and bake for 5 additional minutes, or until light brown and crisp. Be careful not to burn.

5. Remove the crisps from the oven, and allow to cool for several minutes before serving.

MAIN INGREDIENTS

Four 98% fat-free flour tortillas (6-inch rounds)

STAPLES

¼ cup sugar

2 teaspoons ground cinnamon

Cooking spray

NUTRITIONAL FACTS (PER 4 CRISPS)

Calories: 131 Carbohydrates: 30.5 g Cholesterol: 0 mg Fat: 0.5 g Fiber: 2.5 g Protein: 3 g Sodium: 220 mg

CREAMY STRAWBERRY SOUP

TIME: 20 minutes   YIELD: 4 servings

MAIN INGREDIENTS

4 cups sliced ripe strawberries

1 banana, peeled and sliced

1 cup pineapple juice, chilled

1 cup light or nonfat sour
cream, chilled

2 tablespoons raspberry liqueur,
such as Chambord

STAPLES

1 tablespoon plus 1 teaspoon
honey

Use the sweetest, ripest strawberries you can find to whip up this delightfully fruity soup. Cool, creamy, and a snap to make, this is perfect summertime fare.

1. Place all of the ingredients in a blender, and process for several seconds, or until smooth. Taste, adding another teaspoon or 2 of honey if additional sweetness is desired.

2. Serve immediately, or cover and chill until ready to serve.

NUTRITIONAL FACTS (PER SERVING)

Calories: 267 Carbohydrates: 59 g Cholesterol: 0 mg Fat: 1 g Fiber: 4.5 g Protein: 5 g Sodium: 48 mg

DOUBLE CHOCOLATE TARTS

TIME: 45 minutes
YIELD: 4 tarts

Fill the individual pie shells before sitting down to dinner, and pop the tarts into the freezer. Dessert will be ready by dinner's end!

1. Place the ice cream in a bowl, and use a fork to *slightly* soften. The ice cream should be spreadable but not runny.

2. Place ⅓ cup of ice cream in each crust, and spread the ice cream into the shell, smoothing the top. Wrap each shell in plastic wrap, and place in the freezer for 30 minutes, or until the ice cream is once again firm.

3. Remove the plastic wrap, and top each tart with 3 tablespoons of whipped topping, swirling the topping over the ice cream. If desired, garnish each tart with a few chocolate shavings. Serve immediately.

MAIN INGREDIENTS

1⅓ cups Healthy Choice Chocolate Chocolate Chunk Low-Fat Ice Cream

4 packaged individual graham cracker tart crusts*

¾ cup fat-free whipped topping

Chocolate shavings (optional)

* Keebler brand Single Serve Graham Cracker Ready Crust is a good choice.

NUTRITIONAL FACTS (PER TART)

Calories: 229 Carbohydrates: 36 g Cholesterol: 3 mg Fat: 7.5 g Fiber: 2 g Protein: 3 g Sodium: 197 mg

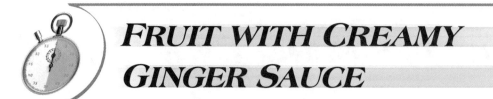

FRUIT WITH CREAMY GINGER SAUCE

TIME: 30 minutes   **YIELD:** 4 servings

MAIN INGREDIENTS

1 cup vanilla low-fat yogurt

2 tablespoons finely chopped crystallized ginger

4 small navel oranges, peeled

8 ripe strawberries, hulled

2 medium bananas, peeled

In this unusual dessert, oranges, bananas, and strawberries are arranged over an easy-to-make sauce. This coats each forkful of fruit with the creamy, flavorful mixture.

1. Place the yogurt in a small bowl. Add the ginger, and stir briskly for about 1 minute, or until the yogurt has a saucelike consistency. Set aside.

2. Cut each orange crosswise into 5 slices. Cut each strawberry lengthwise into 4 slices. Cut each banana crosswise into 14 slices.

3. Spoon ¼ cup of the ginger sauce onto each of 4 individual 8-inch plates, and spread the sauce over the plate. Arrange 5 orange slices around half the plate, overlapping the slices. Arrange 8 of the strawberry slices around the second half of the plate. Pile 7 banana slices in the center of each plate, and serve.

NUTRITIONAL FACTS (PER SERVING)

Calories: 181 Carbohydrates: 41 g Cholesterol: 3 mg Fat: 1.5 g Fiber: 4 g Protein: 5 g Sodium: 45 mg

GOLDEN CAKE WITH FRESH STRAWBERRY SAUCE

TIME: 15 minutes   YIELD: 4 servings

An easy-to-make strawberry sauce gives this super-fast dessert its fresh taste and brilliant color. Use this same sauce to dress up a dish of your favorite ice cream.

1. Cut each strawberry into several pieces, and place the pieces in a bowl. Use a potato masher or the back of a fork to mash the strawberries into a slightly chunky sauce. (Be careful, as the strawberries may squirt you with juice as they are mashed!) Stir the sugar into the sauce.

2. Place a slice of cake on each individual dessert plate. Top each with ¼ cup of sauce, and, if desired, a sprig of mint. Serve immediately.

MAIN INGREDIENTS

2 cups (1-pint box) ripe strawberries, hulled

4 slices (1 inch thick) packaged fat-free golden loaf or pound cake*

4 sprigs fresh mint (optional)

STAPLES

1 tablespoon sugar

* Entenmann's brand is a good choice.

NUTRITIONAL FACTS (PER SERVING)

Calories: 154 Carbohydrates: 36 g Cholesterol: 0 mg Fat: 0.5 g Fiber: 2 g Protein: 2.5 g Sodium: 161 mg

HOMESTYLE BAKED APPLES

TIME: 35 minutes   YIELD: 4 baked apples

MAIN INGREDIENTS

¼ cup dark or golden raisins

4 teaspoons sliced almonds

4 large Rome apples

STAPLES

½ cup dark brown sugar,
  packed

2 teaspoons ground cinnamon

These baked apples are a snap to make and perfect every time. For an even speedier version, cover the filled apples with waxed paper and microwave on high power for 4 to 5 minutes.

1. Preheat the oven to 350°F.

2. Place the brown sugar, cinnamon, raisins, and almonds in a small bowl, and stir to mix well. Set aside.

3. Core each apple to within ½ inch of the bottom. Fill with a quarter of the sugar mixture, packing it slightly.

4. Place the apples in a small baking dish, adding just enough water to cover the bottom. Basting occasionally with the pan liquid, bake uncovered for 25 to 30 minutes, or just until the apples are tender but not mushy when pierced with a fork.

5. Remove from the oven, baste with the pan juices, and serve hot, warm, or chilled.

NUTRITIONAL FACTS (PER APPLE)

Calories: 270 Carbohydrates: 67.5 g Cholesterol: 0 mg Fat: 2 g Fiber: 7 g Protein: 1 g Sodium: 12 mg

ORANGE-GLAZED BANANAS OVER ICE CREAM

TIME: 20 minutes

YIELD: 4 servings

Sweet bananas in a slightly tart glaze are the perfect complement to creamy coffee ice cream.

1. Place the brown sugar and cornstarch in a 1-quart saucepan, and stir to mix well. Slowly stir in the orange juice.

2. Place the saucepan over medium heat, and cook, stirring constantly, until the mixture reaches a boil. Continue to cook, stirring constantly, for about 1 minute, or until the mixture has thickened.

3. Add the bananas to the glaze, and cook, turning gently, for 1 to 2 minutes, or until the bananas are warmed through.

4. Scoop ½ cup of ice cream into each individual dessert dish. Spoon some of the bananas and sauce over the ice cream, and serve immediately.

MAIN INGREDIENTS

¾ cup orange juice

3 medium bananas, peeled and sliced

1 pint low-fat coffee ice cream or frozen yogurt

STAPLES

3 tablespoons brown sugar

1 tablespoon cornstarch

NUTRITIONAL FACTS (PER SERVING)

Calories: 246 Carbohydrates: 54.5 g Cholesterol: 5 mg Fat: 2.5 g Fiber: 3 g Protein: 3.5 g Sodium: 56 mg

SIMPLY PEACHES

TIME: 25 minutes   **YIELD:** 4 servings

MAIN INGREDIENTS

4 medium-large ripe peaches*

1 cup vanilla nonfat yogurt

4 teaspoons grated orange rind

Orange peel curls (optional)

STAPLES

¼ cup honey

1 tablespoon plus 1 teaspoon
   lemon juice

* Freestone or cling-free
   peaches are best.

Fresh peaches take center stage in this quick and easy dessert.

1. Halve the peaches, remove the pits, and thinly slice. Place in a medium-sized bowl, and set aside.

2. Place the honey and lemon juice in a small bowl, and stir to mix. Add to the peaches, and toss to coat.

3. Place the yogurt and orange rind in a small bowl, and stir to mix. Add to the peaches, and gently fold to mix. Cover and chill for at least 15 minutes.

4. Divide the peaches among individual dessert bowls or oversized brandy snifters. Garnish with orange curls, if desired, and serve.

NUTRITIONAL FACTS (PER SERVING)

Calories: 159 Carbohydrates: 38 g Cholesterol: 1 mg Fat: 0 g Fiber: 2 g Protein: 4 g Sodium: 43 mg

PINEAPPLES AND STRAWBERRIES AU GRAND MARNIER

TIME: 15 minutes   YIELD: 4 servings

Start with sweet, juicy pineapple rings and strawberries purchased at your local salad bar. Then add a spoonful of liqueur! Nothing could be easier or more delicious.

1. Arrange 2 pineapple rings on each of 4 dinner-sized plates, overlapping the rings. Arrange the strawberries around the pineapples.

2. Pour 1 tablespoon of liqueur over each plateful of fruit. Allow the fruit to sit for 10 minutes, and serve.

MAIN INGREDIENTS

8 ripe pineapple rings

24 whole ripe strawberries

¼ cup Grand Marnier liquer

Variations

Feel free to adjust this versatile recipe to suit your own preferences, as well as the availability of ingredients. If you don't like Grand Marnier, or you have none on hand, try substituting Kirschwasser cherry brandy or apricot liqueur. Sliced bananas would make a wonderful addition to this fruit plate, as would fresh cherries. For an exotic touch, add chunks or slices of fresh mango.

NUTRITIONAL FACTS (PER SERVING)

Calories: 162 Carbohydrates: 34 g Cholesterol: 0 mg Fat: 1 g Fiber: 3.5 g Protein: 1 g Sodium: 4 mg

RASPBERRY PEARS

TIME: 40 minutes

YIELD: 4 pears

MAIN INGREDIENTS

4 medium pears

2 teaspoons vanilla extract

4 tablespoons jarred
  raspberry syrup

STAPLES

2 tablespoons lemon juice

½ teaspoon ground cinnamon

Simple baked pears are coated with a lemony cinnamon mixture and drizzled with sweet raspberry sauce in this special dessert.

1. Preheat the oven to 375°F.

2. Slice a thin piece from the bottom of each pear so it stands upright. Remove the core from the bottom, leaving the stem intact. Carefully peel the pears, and place them in a large baking dish. Add ½ inch of water to the bottom of the dish.

3. Place the lemon juice, vanilla extract, and cinnamon in a small bowl, and stir to mix. Using a pastry brush, coat the pears with this mixture.

4. Cover the baking dish with aluminum foil, and bake for 30 minutes, or until the pears are tender when pierced with a knife.

5. Remove the pears from the oven, and carefully transfer each to an individual dessert plate. Drizzle each with a tablespoon of raspberry syrup, and serve immediately.

NUTRITIONAL FACTS (PER PEAR)

Calories: 137 Carbohydrates: 33.5 g Cholesterol: 0 mg Fat: 0.5 g Fiber: 4.5 g Protein: 0.5 g Sodium: 3 mg

RASPBERRIES AND CREAM

TIME: 20 minutes

YIELD: 4 servings

This recipe works well with a variety of fresh fruits. Try it with plump blueberries or sliced ripe strawberries.

1. Place the sour cream and brown sugar in a medium-sized bowl, and stir until the sugar is dissolved. Toss in the raspberries, and fold gently to mix. Cover and chill for at least 15 minutes.

2. Divide the raspberries among 4 individual serving bowls. Top with an additional dollop of sour cream, if desired, and serve.

MAIN INGREDIENTS

1 cup light sour cream

1 quart fresh raspberries

STAPLES

½ cup light brown sugar, firmly packed

NUTRITIONAL FACTS (PER SERVING)

Calories: 254 Carbohydrates: 45 g Cholesterol: 30 mg Fat: 7.5 g Fiber: 8.5 g Protein: 3 g Sodium: 51 mg

PEACHY BAKED BANANAS

TIME: 25 minutes

YIELD: 4 servings

MAIN INGREDIENTS

1-pound can peaches in
light syrup

¼ cup apricot liqueur
(optional)

4 medium bananas, peeled

STAPLES

Ground cinnamon

Baking bananas in a peach purée gives them a delectable puddinglike texture and a wonderful aroma. Although the liqueur is optional, it does add a sophisticated flavor to the dessert.

1. Preheat the oven to 400°F.

2. Drain the peaches, reserving the liquid. Place all of the peaches in a blender along with 2 tablespoons of the reserved liquid and, if desired, the apricot liqueur.

3. Process the peaches for several seconds, just until they form a smooth purée.

4. For each banana, tear off 1 square of aluminum foil large enough to enclose the banana. Place each banana in the center of a square, and bend up the sides to form a cup around the banana. Pour about ⅓ cup of the purée over each banana, and seal the packet by crimping the edges together. Seal carefully to prevent leaking.

5. Place the packets seam side up in a baking pan, and bake for about 15 minutes. When done, the bananas should be soft throughout when pierced with a toothpick, but should still hold their shape.

6. To serve, open each packet and lightly sprinkle each banana with cinnamon. Serve in the foil.

NUTRITIONAL FACTS (PER SERVING)

Calories: 166 Carbohydrates: 43 g Cholesterol: 0 mg Fat: 0.5 g Fiber: 4 g Protein: 1.5 g Sodium: 7 mg

METRIC CONVERSION TABLES

Common Liquid Conversions

Measurement	=	Milliliters
¼ teaspoon	=	1.25 milliliters
½ teaspoon	=	2.50 milliliters
¾ teaspoon	=	3.75 milliliters
1 teaspoon	=	5.00 milliliters
1¼ teaspoons	=	6.25 milliliters
1½ teaspoons	=	7.50 milliliters
1¾ teaspoons	=	8.75 milliliters
2 teaspoons	=	10.0 milliliters
1 tablespoon	=	15.0 milliliters
2 tablespoons	=	30.0 milliliters

Measurement	=	Liters
¼ cup	=	0.06 liters
½ cup	=	0.12 liters
¾ cup	=	0.18 liters
1 cup	=	0.24 liters
1¼ cups	=	0.30 liters
1½ cups	=	0.36 liters
2 cups	=	0.48 liters
2½ cups	=	0.60 liters
3 cups	=	0.72 liters
3½ cups	=	0.84 liters
4 cups	=	0.96 liters
4½ cups	=	1.08 liters
5 cups	=	1.20 liters
5½ cups	=	1.32 liters

Converting Fahrenheit to Celsius

Fahrenheit	=	Celsius
200–205	=	95
220–225	=	105
245–250	=	120
275	=	135
300–305	=	150
325–330	=	165
345–350	=	175
370–375	=	190
400–405	=	205
425–430	=	220
445–450	=	230
470–475	=	245
500	=	260

Conversion Formulas

LIQUID When You Know	Multiply By	To Determine
teaspoons	5.0	milliliters
tablespoons	15.0	milliliters
fluid ounces	30.0	milliliters
cups	0.24	liters
pints	0.47	liters
quarts	0.95	liters

WEIGHT When You Know	Multiply By	To Determine
ounces	28.0	grams
pounds	0.45	kilograms

INDEX